# How Real Is Race?

## *A Sourcebook on Race, Culture, and Biology*

Carol C. Mukhopadhyay
Rosemary Henze
Yolanda T. Moses

Rowman & Littlefield Education
Lanham, Maryland • Toronto • Plymouth, UK
2007

Published in the United States of America
by Rowman & Littlefield Education
A Division of Rowman & Littlefield Publishers, Inc.
A wholly owned subsidiary of The Rowman & Littlefield Publishing Group, Inc.
4501 Forbes Boulevard, Suite 200, Lanham, Maryland 20706
www.rowmaneducation.com

Estover Road
Plymouth PL6 7PY
United Kingdom

British Library Cataloguing in Publication Information Available

**Library of Congress Cataloging-in-Publication Data**

Mukhopadhyay, Carol Chapnick.
  How real is race? : a sourcebook on race, culture, and biology / Carol C.
Mukhopadhyay, Rosemary Henze, Yolanda T. Moses.
    p.  cm.
  Includes bibliographical references and index.
  ISBN-13: 978-1-57886-560-4 (hardcover : alk. paper)
  ISBN-10: 1-57886-560-3 (hardcover : alk. paper)
  ISBN-13: 978-1-57886-561-1 (pbk. : alk. paper)
  ISBN-10: 1-57886-561-1 (pbk. : alk. paper)
  1. Race.  2. Race relations.  3. Culture.  4. Sociobiology.  5. Nature and
nurture.  6. Education.  I. Henze, Rosemary C.  II. Moses, Yolanda T.  III. Title.
HT1521.M785  2007
305.8–dc22                                                                    2006027399

# Contents

# List of Tables and Figures

# Acknowledgments

This book draws upon experiences and ideas we have accumulated throughout our careers as educators. Over the years, we have drawn inspiration and ideas from numerous sources, including colleagues at several institutions, precollege educators with whom we have worked and taught, our own professors, and perhaps most of all, our students, to whom we dedicate this book.

More immediately, we wish to thank the many individuals who have contributed time, energy, ideas, manuscript reviews, editing suggestions, and general enthusiasm and support for the book. They are too many to list. But special thanks go to Dorothy Allen, Gilberto Arriaza, Nick Bridger, Kathleen Densmore, Helen Finks, Lorie Hammond, Judith Lessow-Hurley, Piper McNulty, Sandy Miller, Elizabeth Morrison, Oscar Penaranda, Mica Pollock, Siv Kristin Spain, Athena Waite, and Elizabeth Weiss. We appreciate UC Riverside anthropology graduate student Scott Smith's diligent efforts at ferreting out useful resources and his review of part 1.

Tom Koerner, our editor at Rowman and Littlefield Education, first suggested the book. Without his encouragement, we probably would not have taken on this enormous task! A fine support staff at R&L Education eased the production process.

The book has benefited from its connection to the RACE Project of the American Anthropological Association (AAA). A traveling museum exhibit scheduled to open in 2007, the RACE AAA Project has provided a significant forum for intellectual exchange and collective brainstorming on how to effectively engage with the public. We believe the AAA RACE Project and our book project are mutually reinforcing.

Finally, we thank our spouses, families, and friends for putting up with late nights, long conference calls, endless progress reports, and way too many "working" weekends and holidays.

# Foreword

James A. Banks

This significant, informative, and engaging book is being published at a critical time in the history of U.S. public education. Racial, cultural, religious, and language diversity in U.S. public schools is greater than at any time since the early 1900s, when thousands of immigrants from Central, Southern, and Eastern Europe came to America in search of their dreams (Graham, 2005). The percentage of students of color in U.S. schools almost doubled in the thirty years between 1973 and 2004, increasing from 22 to 43 percent (Dillon, 2006). Students of color in U.S. public schools will equal or exceed the percentage of White students within one or two decades if current growth rates continue. In 2000, 18 percent of the total U.S. population aged five and over spoke a language other than English at home (Shin & Bruno, 2003). English-language learners are the fastest-growing population in U.S. public schools. The general U.S. population is also becoming more racially, culturally, religiously, and linguistically diverse. The U.S. Census projects that people of color will make up about half of the population by 2050 (cited in El Nasser, 2004). Cultural, racial, ethnic, and religious diversity is also increasing in other nations around the world (Banks, 2004).

The rich diversity in the United States and in nations around the world presents opportunities as well as challenges to teachers and other educators. Yet one frequent response by the students in my courses for future and practicing teachers is that they are colorblind and do not "see" the racial, ethnic, and cultural differences among their students. There is often a wide racial, cultural, and language gap between U.S. teachers, most of whom are white and female, and students. This gap may be one factor that makes teachers reluctant to teach about race and to have open conversations about it in their classrooms (Lewis, 2004; Pollock, 2004; Schofield, 2007).

This incisive, well conceptualized, and informative book by three perceptive anthropologists who care deeply about and understand schools contains a plethora of essential concepts and principles about race and diversity that will help teachers at all levels to re-envision and transform their curriculum and pedagogy. One of the most salient and important lessons is that race is a social construction that has no basis in biological science. As the authors insightfully point out, "races are not biologically real but are cultural and social inventions created in specific cultural, historical, and political contexts" (Introduction, Part 1, this volume).

A significant body of social science theory and research supports the authors' keen insights and analyses about race and its meanings. Jacobson (1998) calls races "invented categories" (p. 4). Omi and Winant (1994) state that the "determination of racial categories is an intensely political process" (p. 3). Montagu (1997) calls race "man's most dangerous myth." In his classic book with this title—first published in 1942—Montagu documents extensively and in poignant details the human tragedies that have been justified and facilitated by race and racism. These painful and unconscionable historical events include chattel slavery in the United States in which people of African descent were treated as non-humans and many perished in brutal ways (Davis, 2006; Fredrickson, 2002). They also include the massive destruction and deaths perpetuated by the Nazis in Europe during the 1930s and 1940s, in which 12 million people were killed—six million Jews and six million other members of stigmatized groups, including people with disabilities and people who were gay. The pain, suffering, and discrimination that are justified by theories of race and by racism continue today.

As the authors of the book explicate, teaching about race as a social construction is an essential component of teacher education. I have incorporated this idea into my multicultural teacher education courses. In lectures, I present ideas about the construction of race by the theorists mentioned previously. My lectures are supplemented by readings and videotapes that powerfully depict the ways in which various racial and ethnic groups—including White ethnic groups, such as Italians

(Guglielmo & Salerno, 2003), the Irish (Ignatiev, 1995), and Jews (Brodkin, 1998)—have been victimized by racism and discrimination. The videotapes include *The Shadow of Hate: A History of Intolerance in America* (Guggenheim, 1995).

One of the most trenchant and powerful examples in the videotape is the description of the way Leo Frank, a Jewish northerner living in Atlanta, became a victim of anti-Semitism and racial hostility when he was accused of murdering a White girl who worked in a pencil factory he co-owned. The Leo Frank case provides students an opportunity to understand the ways in which race is a social construction, is contextual, and how the meaning of race has changed historically and continues to change today. The pain, suffering, and discrimination that are justified by theories of race and by racism continue today.

This rich sourcebook will help teachers and teacher educators to implement the kinds of teaching strategies that will enable their students to understand how race is socially constructed. I have found in my teaching that this is a difficult concept for college and university students to grasp. Elementary and high school students will also find the notion perplexing. A significant strength of this book is that it combines biological and cultural anthropological approaches to race and helps readers to understand the complex ways that culture shapes the ways in which we construct and interpret the biological aspects of race.

This theoretically strong, useful, and practical book is being published at a time when it is greatly needed. It contains well-conceptualized and engaging teaching activities and strategies that teachers at all levels will welcome. I hope this book will receive the warm reception that it deserves. If used wisely and seriously engaged, it will help educational practitioners to create schools and classrooms that are just and democratic, and that foster equality for all students in the nation's schools.

## REFERENCES

Banks, J. A. (Ed.). (2004). *Diversity and citizenship education: Global perspectives.* San Francisco: Jossey-Bass.

Brodkin, K. (1998). *How the Jews became white folks and what that says about race in America.* New Brunswick, NJ: Rutgers University Press.

Davis, D. B. (2006). *Inhuman bondage: The rise and fall of slavery in the new world.* New York: Oxford University Press.

Dillon, S. (2006, August 27). In schools across U.S., the melting pot overflows. *The New York Times,* vol. CLV [155] (no. 53,684), pp. A7 & 16.

El Nasser, H. (2004, March 18). Census projects growing diversity: By 2050: Population burst, societal shifts. *USA Today,* p. 1A.

Fredrickson, G. M. (2002). *Racism: A short history.* Princeton, NJ: Princeton University Press.

Graham, P. A. (2005). *Schooling America: How the public schools meet the nation's changing needs.* New York: Oxford University Press.

Guggenheim, C. (1995). *The shadow of hate: A history of intolerance in America* [Videotape]. Available from: Teaching Tolerance, 400 Washington Avenue, Montgomery, AL 36104.

Guglielmo, J. & Salerno, S. (Eds.). (2003). *Are Italians White? How race is made in America.* New York: Routledge.

Ignatiev, N. (1995). *How the Irish became White.* New York: Routledge.

Jacobson, M. F. (1998). *Whiteness of a different color: European immigrants and the alchemy of race.* Cambridge, MA: Harvard University Press.

Lewis, A. E. (2004). *Race in the schoolyard: Negotiating the color line in classrooms and communities.* New Brunswick, NJ: Rutgers University Press.

Montagu, A. (1997). *Man's most dangerous myth: The fallacy of race* (6th ed.). Walnut Creek, CA: Altamira Press.

Omi, M., & Winant, H. (1994). *Racial formation in the United States: From the 1960s to the 1990s* (2nd ed.). New York: Routledge and Kegan Paul.

Pollock, M. (2004). *Colormute: Race talk dilemmas in an American school.* Princeton: Princeton University Press.

Schofield, J. W. (2007). The colorblind perspective in school: Causes and consequences. In J. A. Banks & C. A. M. Banks (Eds.), *Multicultural education: Issues and perspectives* (6th ed., pp. 271–295). Hoboken, NJ: Wiley.

Shin, H. B., with Bruno, R. (2003). *Language use and English-speaking ability: 2000.* Washington, DC: U.S. Census Bureau. Retrieved August 16, 2006 from http://www.census.gov/prod/2003pubs/c2kbr-29.pdf

**James A. Banks** is Kerry and Linda Killinger Professor in Diversity Studies and director of the Center for Multicultural Education at the University of Washington, Seattle. His books include *Educating Citizens in a Multicultural Society; Cultural Diversity and Education: Foundations, Curriculum and Teaching; Diversity and Citizenship Education: Global Perspectives*; and *Race, Culture, and Education: The Selected Works of James A. Banks.* Professor Banks is a past president of the American Educational Research Association (AERA) and the National Council for the Social Studies (NCSS). He is also a member of the National Academy of Education and holds honorary Doctorates of Humane Letters from five universities and the UCLA Medal, UCLA's highest honor. He was a Spencer Fellow at the Center for Advanced Study in the Behavioral Sciences at Stanford during the 2005–2006 academic year.

# Introduction

## WHY WE WROTE THIS BOOK

Everyone has heard the statement "There is only one race—the human race."[1] Yet we have also heard and seen contradictory evidence. There are certainly observable physical differences among people, including skin color, eye shape, hair texture, and so on. But is this race? The U.S. Census divides us into groups based on race—but we can select our own race, based on our cultural identity, regardless of how we look. In schools and colleges, the message of race as culture, rather than biology, is underscored when teachers are taught that children from diverse cultures have "different learning styles" and that students' cultural backgrounds are the cause of the racial achievement gap.

How can we make sense of these contradictory messages? How *real* is race? Or rather, in what sense is race real? What is biological fact and fiction? Where does culture enter? And what does it really mean to say that race is a "social construction"? If race is an invention, who invented it? Why? For what ends? And can we eliminate it if we wish to? Most of all, how can educators help students address these same questions in their everyday lives and in the school context? And why is it important that they do this? These are the key questions that frame this book.

Anthropologists have long argued that the concept of biological races, such as Black, White, Asian, and Native American, is not scientifically valid. In a biological sense, there are no such things as distinct human races. Contemporary humans are, and have always been, one variable species, with roots in Africa. There are no subspecies of humans!

Yet this idea seems to contradict the experiences of many people in the United States and other countries where racial classification is used daily, both by individuals and by institutions, and where racism is very much alive. How can race not be real when we experience its effects every day?

To make matters more complex, the U.S. cultural system of race *has* had biological consequences. For example, segregating people and restricting intermarriage has tended to preserve visible distinctions between racial groups.

The idea that race, races, and racism are cultural inventions—that is, created historically to legitimize social inequality between groups with different ancestries, national origins, and histories—helps explain this contradiction. Race is very much real and has real consequences.

Anthropologists such as Montagu have been writing about the "fallacy of race" as biology since the 1940s (Montagu, 1997, 1942). Yet little of this knowledge has reached the wider public, partly because it is difficult to "translate" into accessible language, and partly because anthropologists writing for teachers and the public did not do so in widely disseminated media. However, reaching a wider readership is critical, especially for secondary and postsecondary educators who are in a position to influence others. Why?

First, it is important because children should learn about major intellectual and scientific ideas and discoveries in school. Race plays an enormously important and visible role in contemporary social life—from how we group and perceive others and ourselves to the friendships we form, to politics, to whom we marry. It affects where we live and go to school, our economic status, and our encounters with the law and the medical profession. Yet, surprisingly, scientific knowledge about the biological fallacy and cultural reality of race plays little role in the curriculum for K–12 students, and in colleges it only surfaces if a student takes an anthropology course.

Race as biology is reinforced through racial terms (e.g., "Black," "White") which highlight physical differences. At the same time, many educators avoid any discussion of race and claim instead to be "color-blind." Either way, students do not gain access to current scientific knowledge on race and human biological diversity—nor are they exposed to new anthropological understandings of race as a cultural phenomenon.

If this were mathematics, astronomy, or any other area of inquiry, major discoveries would sooner or later find their way into textbooks or supplementary curricula. Yet the race concept, especially the relationship between race, human biological variation, culture, and social inequality, has remained shrouded in misinformation, fear, and ignorance. We think young people have a right to learn about "big ideas" in their education, and surely the concept of race not only deserves but requires attention in the curriculum.

Learning about race will increase the overall science literacy of our students at a time when there appear to be competing doctrines. Exposure to science grounded in the social reality of our students' lives can lead to a renewed interest in science by young people. Equally important, this more sophisticated understanding of race and human variation provides the kind of broader biocultural knowledge base students will need in order to become informed and engaged citizens in a culturally pluralistic democracy.

Finally, if race and racism are cultural inventions, then we (as individuals and as members of institutions such as schools) have the power to alter them. Discovering the cultural origins and uses of racial classifications can empower students and teachers to become agents of change.

Combining biological and cultural anthropological approaches to race in one book will stimulate educators and students to consider the complex issues surrounding the uses (and abuses) of racial categories. It will give them access to knowledge they can use, in their personal and public lives, to shape a world in which classifications of people reflect the categories they find most meaningful—rather than those foisted upon them through the legacy of racism that we find in North America.

## READERSHIP

This book is written primarily for middle and high school teachers, pre-service teachers, and teacher educators in the U.S. But the book will be useful to a broader readership as well. Few books integrate both biological and cultural perspectives on race. K–8 teachers can take the conceptual background material and develop more appropriate activity versions for younger students. Community college and undergraduate college teachers and students may find this a useful resource simply for the conceptual background material. But the book also contains teaching activities suitable at the postsecondary level.

In terms of content areas, the book is appropriate for those who teach science, health education, social studies, language arts, life skills, or other courses that address human biological or cultural diversity, human relations, and multicultural education. It lends itself particularly well to interdisciplinary teaching, such as a unit on inheritance, on the environment, or on dating and marriage. The themes addressed by this book include biological variation among humans; social inequality (e.g., including race, class, and gender); diversity; peace and conflict; marriage and mating; family and ancestry; human rights; language; environmental adaptations; and of course, race, ethnicity, and culture. It addresses many of the content standards in social studies, science, and language arts (see Alignment with Standards in part 4).

Other audiences include professional development staff in school districts, school board members, counselors, librarians, administrators, diversity consultants in education and business, parents and family members, and community groups. The book could be a catalyst for developing community-school dialogues about issues of race.

Finally, although the book is designed primarily for U.S. educators, the conceptual framework is anthropological and cross-cultural. Many of the chapters discuss human diversity in a global context. These cross-cultural comparisons may be useful to educators in other countries. Europeans, Canadians, and Australians might find it relevant as they come to terms with the growing presence of racially and ethnically diverse citizens who feel at odds with the schools they and their children attend. Educators in other countries, especially those heavily impacted by European colonial racial ideas, might find it a useful update and synthesis of contemporary anthropological ideas and approaches to teaching about race.

In order to make the book accessible, we have tried to avoid unnecessary educational and scientific jargon. However, the topics covered in this volume are complex and wide ranging, from biology to history to culture to contemporary school issues. In some cases, specialized terms are essential. Part 1, especially chapters 2 and 3, is a bit more technical and especially relevant to science teachers and those interested in current understandings of human biological variation.

## ORGANIZATION OF THE BOOK

The book has three substantive sections. Parts 1 and 2 address the key anthropological themes of the book: the myth of race as biology and the reality of race as a cultural invention. Part 3 extends the discussion to hot-button issues that arise in school settings. In each chapter we provide relevant links to previous and later material.

Each chapter begins with a conceptual background section that includes an overview of relevant anthropological and other scholarly approaches to the topic and a list of key conceptual points and terms. This is followed by descriptions of teaching activities. Part 1, The Fallacy of Race as Biology, explains misleading notions of race and provides teachers with accessible information and examples to help them understand the reasons why anthropologists have rejected race as a scientific or adequate description of human biological variation.

Part 2, Culture Creates Race, explores in detail the concept of race as culturally constructed, using concrete cultural and historical materials. It begins with the concept of culture and then provides an overview of how racial classifications were manipulated in the U.S. to justify and maintain a system of social inequality. Race is also examined from a cross-cultural perspective and from the perspective of social restrictions on mating and marriage.

Part 3, Race and Hot-Button Issues in Schools, takes the everyday realities of school and uses them as a starting point for uncovering the way racial ideologies work in schools and colleges, both from the perspectives of the students and the teachers/administrators. Students tend to be naturally curious about race, especially since it is rarely part of the standard curriculum; educators can use the material to develop inquiry-based lessons and units in which students examine their own school communities with race, culture, and biology as an analytical lens.

Part 4, Resources, provides comprehensive lists of references and websites cited, activities, and illustrations, including relevant Web sources. It also includes a table showing how the concepts in the book map onto national standards in science, language arts, and social studies.

Ideally, the book should be read as a whole since each part builds on and is related to prior sections. However, each part and chapter can also stand on its own. Within each chapter, we suggest links to other chapters and other parts of the book. For those who want to get a quick sense of the whole without reading every chapter in sequence, we suggest reading the introductions to each of the three parts.

To keep the price of the book affordable, we made a number of strategic decisions. First, we kept graphics to a minimum. Many beautiful color graphics that illustrate concepts in the book are available free on the Internet, and we have listed them throughout the book and in part 4. Secondly, rather than providing lengthy, detailed lesson plans for many teaching activities, we included three formats: short lesson plans (Activity Plans); brief descriptions of activities (Activity Ideas) that teachers can develop on their own or that have more detailed online instructions; and Web sources for relevant, well-developed, teaching activities. The websites we list are stable. A comprehensive list of all the teaching activities appears in part 4.

## WHAT'S SPECIAL ABOUT AN ANTHROPOLOGICAL PERSPECTIVE ON RACE?

Race and racism has been the subject of thousands of books written from a multitude of disciplinary perspectives. Practically every discipline and field has something to say about race. Educators may wonder why we need yet another book on teaching about race when there are so many excellent books on antiracist and multicultural education (e.g., Adams, Bell, & Griffin, 1997; Banks & Banks, 2007; Hernández, 2001; King, Hollins, & Hayman, 1997; Lee, 1998; Nieto, 2000; Sleeter, 1996; Tatum, 1997; Villegas & Lucas, 2002).

Anthropology offers a unique and essential perspective on race and human variability. First of all, anthropology is the only discipline that takes a biocultural approach to human variation—that is, one that includes both biological and cultural perspectives. No other discipline offers such a broad, integrated approach to the phenomenon of race.

This book brings together race-related research and scholarship on this topic from the three most significant subfields of anthropology—biological, cultural, and linguistic anthropology.

One major advantage of an anthropological perspective is its cross-cultural, comparative approach, that is, its use of the full array of world cultures in constructing its theories. For instance, in the United States we think of racial categories as universal, but cross-cultural evidence reveals this is not the case. In fact, many societies do not even have systems of inequality, let alone inequality based on race.

This book complements another major effort to communicate anthropological findings to the public, the American Anthropological Association's public education project, RACE. It consists of a traveling museum exhibit due to open in 2007, and a website and other educational materials for teachers and for the general public (see http://www.understandingrace.org). The content of this book is closely aligned with the content of the museum exhibit. Two authors (Moses and Mukhopadhyay) serve as key advisors on the project, and Moses chairs the advisory board. Henze is former chair of the Association's Anthropology Education Committee. Anyone who sees or plans to see the exhibit will find the concepts presented there reinforced and elaborated in this book.

It is often difficult to assert the importance of one perspective without implying that other perspectives are somehow less worthy. In the case of research on race and racism, we recognize the value of the research by scholars in other disciplines. Indeed, we are familiar with this literature and have gained many insights from it. At the same time, we feel adding our anthropological voice to the conversation about race can only enrich our collective understanding of this complex phenomenon. In particular, the integrated biological and cultural perspectives and the cross-cultural data we offer in this book are simply not found elsewhere in the educational literature. We think they are essential parts of the educator's toolkit on race.

## AUTHORS' ASSUMPTIONS AND VALUES

This book is not only about conveying scientific knowledge. We hope educators and students will apply this knowledge to look critically at how race is used in the world around them. We believe more young people should be engaged in learning about science and the scientific process, and then using this knowledge to consider actions they can take to erase racism and other forms of social injustice.

Our own diverse ethnic, racial, religious, and cultural identities—Western European and African American Christian and Eastern European Jewish—helped bring different perspectives to this book, as did our research in other countries and our teaching and research in the United States. And we are all immersed in cultural and racial diversity in our personal and professional lives, on our campuses, in our neighborhoods.

Our decision to write this book comes from our own experience as educators. We believe in the power of knowledge and the role of education in creating a more equitable society. Educators are preparing the next generation of teachers, adults, parents, and citizens, and we want this generation to be equipped with the most recent anthropological knowledge about race. Our experience as educators also guided our choices of teaching activities. We emphasize activities that use a constructivist approach. That is, we assume that students and teachers already possess valuable knowledge; the book builds upon this to construct new knowledge and skills relevant to their lives. Many activities engage students in small-scale inquiry projects. We believe that students acquire concepts more readily and become more engaged when they discover them through their own research. Some activities also explicitly promote student empowerment, student leadership, and students as change agents.

## ABOUT TERMINOLOGY

Given the subject matter of this book and evidence that language shapes people's perceptions of reality (Lakoff, 2004), choice of terminology was obviously a key issue for us (see Mukhopadhyay, in press).

When referring to the United States and its people, we used U.S. or U.S. Americans rather than the shortened forms "America" or "Americans" because these latter terms actually include North, Central, and South America. We have capitalized the names of major ethnic/racial groups (e.g., White) because they are formal social groupings and not descriptive adjectives (e.g., "white"). We prefer terms that reflect ancestral origins, such as African American rather than Black and European American or Euro-American rather than White. When possible, we differentiate people residing in the U.S. from those residing elsewhere (e.g., Asian Americans versus Asians). In general we avoided the term "people of color" because it implies a false binary distinction (color vs. no color) and overemphasizes biology. However, we recognize that it is an important term of solidarity among people with common experiences of racial discrimination (see chapter 13).

Pronouns in English are especially problematic. To avoid gender bias, we generally prefer plural pronouns (e.g., they) instead of constantly moving between he and she or the awkward he/she. We tried to restrict our use of the royal "we" such that in most cases it refers to "we the authors." If we used it more broadly, we tried to pinpoint who is included in the "we."

Although we sometimes used the term "teachers," we preferred to use "educators" because this connotes a broader group that includes parents, counselors, social service providers, professors, community leaders, and others.

The term "race" presents special problems. Some authors use "scare quotes" in every instance to hammer home the message that this word is problematic. We decided this would impede the flow of the book and instead generally use quotes only the first time the term appears in a chapter.

## FINDING A PLACE IN K–12 CURRICULUM FOR TEACHING ABOUT RACE

Teachers in K–12 schools are already struggling to keep up with all the mandates of the No Child Left Behind law, which places particular emphasis on math and reading. How, then, do we expect teachers to find time to teach the concepts in this book?

We offer several suggestions. First, readers should acquaint themselves with the standards alignment table we have provided in part 4, which maps the book's content onto the content standards provided by national professional organizations for social studies, science, and language arts.

It will come as no surprise that we would like to see the book's content become an integral part of all state and national curricular frameworks, but that will be a long-term process that will take many years. In the meantime, teachers and administrators will have to find creative ways to insert it.

In addition to linking the content to state or national standards, another strategy is to see if teaching the book's content can help accomplish one or more district and school goals. Teachers can appeal to school and district administrators, other teachers, and parents to form an advocacy group to make the case as to why these ideas are important for students in your school. The rationale provided at the beginning of this introduction can serve as a basis for your talking points.

Teachers might also apply for grants and other funding opportunities that would allow them to integrate the book's content in an after-school curriculum, summer program, or other type of co- or extra-curricular class. Programs to increase science awareness and curiosity are particularly appropriate, given the components on human biological variation, genetic ancestry, environmental adaptation, and mating patterns. The material also lends itself well to interdisciplinary science-social studies-language arts units and to use with small learning communities of teachers.

## THE SOCIAL CONTEXT FOR TEACHING ABOUT RACE: PREPARING FOR DIALOGUE ACROSS DIFFERENCES

Educators who want to be effective in teaching the content of this book have to be ready to engage in dialogue with people who have a wide range of perspectives on race and teaching about race. Some may find themselves in an environment where teaching about human biological variation, about issues of social justice, and especially unlearning racism is embraced. Others may find that teaching about race is contentious. And in the middle of this imaginary continuum are many schools where discussions of race, and even human biological variation, are consciously avoided.

How can a teacher address students and parents who see science, especially evolutionary theory, as "just another belief system, like religion"? In the educational literature on teaching controversial issues, authors suggest building on constructivist pedagogy by "using existing student beliefs as a kind of scaffolding to scientific exploration" (Loving, 1997, p. 438, citing Cobern, 1995) and teaching the relationship between science and religion (Reiss, 1992, cited in Loving, 1997). Loving proposes a model that balances respect for beliefs with an understanding of what counts as best evidence in scientific learning. She also suggests how teachers can justify to parents and students that scientific learning is for the common good. Understanding science can be a way to engage students in exploring their own values and learning.

Some educators and parents equate racial justice with being colorblind and not bringing up race and racial issues unless absolutely necessary. Although the intention may be good, this attitude can cause students to feel as if their racial or ethnic identity is something to be ashamed of. It deprives students of an understanding of the relationship between race, human biological variation, culture, and social inequality!

Children do not all arrive in school on a "level playing field." Pretending that differences do not exist will not make inequalities go away; it will only drive discussion of them underground. It is important for educators to talk with others openly about these beliefs and to acknowledge the good intentions of those who hold them.

Not all schools have a strong tradition of supporting student inquiry. When engaging students in the active inquiry projects suggested in this book, we strongly urge teachers to discuss the activity with school administrators and other teachers beforehand and seek their support, rather than keeping them out of the loop. In this way, the concepts in the book are made available to influential adults as well as to students.

As we noted earlier, we assume educators have a powerful capacity to act as change agents. In the classroom they prepare young people of all backgrounds to meet challenging standards and reach their fullest potential academically and socially. However, they can also be agents of change beyond the classroom. The ideas presented in this book about race and human biological variation are too important to remain hidden in the privacy of a few classrooms.

Our hope is that educators will make this content part of the broader change/reform agenda in their schools and colleges, including the science awareness components. They can have informal conversations or develop a support group of faculty who share an interest in making this content part of the regular curriculum. Teachers can ask to be put on the agenda for a faculty meeting or staff development day so that others can be informed of what they are teaching, how it relates to standards and to learning outcomes, and why they are teaching it.

Above all, teaching about race from the perspective presented here clearly supports rather than undermines student learning and student achievement. It creates critical thinkers. And it helps students become scientifically literate, historically and socially informed, and thoughtful citizens in a diverse society and globalized economy!

## ENDNOTES

1. Some segments of this introduction have been adapted from Mukhopadhyay and Henze (2003).

# THE FALLACY OF RACE AS BIOLOGY—INTRODUCTION

Anthropologists have for years struggled with how to communicate the idea that races are not biologically real but are cultural and social inventions created in specific cultural, historical, and political contexts. Our experience shows that even people with a fairly sophisticated understanding of human biological variation find it difficult to abandon the concept of race as biology. Long-time social justice and antiracism activists are often visibly upset when we inform them that "races are biological fiction, not fact." As for journalists, even the most jaded wake up during press conferences when we announce that "there is no such thing as race, biologically speaking."

## WHAT IS RACE?

Part of the confusion stems from the term *race*, itself! Historically it has referred to everything from one's nationality, religion, ancestry, regional identification, or class status to biological subcategories within a species.

Anthropologists and other scientists have also struggled with the multiple meanings of race. In the biological sciences and in physical anthropology, race was used to describe human biological variation and subdivisions of the human species.

Most scientists now reject the validity of biological races, yet the idea persists in the wider culture. Indeed, it seems obvious to many people that races *are* biologically real. People will say, just look around you, on a school playground or in the local diner or grocery store. One can *see, with one's own eyes,* that race is real!

How can race not be biologically real, fellow educators ask, when I can walk into an advanced calculus class and tell at a glance that the composition is mainly Whites and Asians with only a few Black and Latino students? Why, the forensic anthropologists ask, can I racially identify murder victims from their physical remains? How can race not be biological, our physician colleagues ask, when African American women are less likely to get osteoporosis than "Caucasian" women?

Part of the problem stems from misunderstanding what anthropologists mean when they say races aren't biologically real. Anthropologists aren't arguing that there is *no* biological component in U.S. racial categories. Biology *has* played a role in the cultural invention of what we call race, as we shall see in part 2. But most of what we believe or have been taught about race as biology, as valid subdivisions of the human species, and as an important part of human biological variation is a myth.

## THE FALLACY OF RACE AS BIOLOGY

Part 1 focuses on unraveling the myth of race as biology. We explore the reasons scientists have rejected the concept of race as a scientifically valid description of human biological variation. We also look at the reality of human biological variation and its relationship to the concept of race.

We address the question that students will surely ask: if biological race is not real, then what are we seeing? How are students to make sense of the human variation that they normally think of as race? Why are groups of people different from each other in observable ways? And what is the biological significance of skin color? Why do U.S. Americans with ancestors from Africa or South Asia or Central America tend to have darker skin then those with ancestors from England, Russia, or Korea? And what does this mean, biologically? Are these traits linked to other biological traits or capacities?

Each chapter in part 1 is designed to help educators effectively communicate one or more key concepts to their students. We first provide conceptual background on the topic followed by teaching activities.

Chapter 1—Why Contemporary Races Are Not Scientifically Valid—addresses the artificiality and arbitrariness of what we call race.

Chapter 1 demonstrates that there are no biological traits that allow us to consistently and reliably divide the human species into the same set of racial groupings.

Chapter 2—Human Biological Variation: What We Don't See— explores relatively invisible biological variation. We show that some of the most interesting and significant areas of human biological diversity consist of traits that cannot be seen. Unlike racial traits, these can have a major biological impact on peoples' lives.

If there is no such thing as biological race, then how do we explain skin color and other so-called racial traits? We tackle this in chapter 3—If Not Race, How Do We Explain Biological Differences? We show how geography and environment influence the genetic structures of human populations through the processes of natural selection. We discuss other evolutionary forces that affect populations. We note that cultural processes also shape human biology and genetics, whether through humans altering the environment or spreading their genes through trade, travel, and even warfare.

Finally, chapter 4—More Alike Than Different, More Different Than Alike—builds upon earlier ideas. We provide further evidence that there is more diversity within than between racial groups. We also show that most biological variability exists at the individual level. Race is rather meaningless when it comes to DNA and genes.

We conclude with the latest evidence on the "Out of Africa" theory. We now know that modern humans originated in Africa, as one species, and remained a single species, despite migrations to different parts of the world. Human history has always been the story of multiple populations of a single species moving, mixing, and settling, again and again.

Human biological variability is a fascinating ever-changing reality. Ultimately, however, it is rather insignificant compared to our shared biological inheritance as a species. It is culture, and the human capacity for creating meaning out of observable biological variability, that has made biology so significant historically. Part 2 will tell that story.

# Why Contemporary Races Are Not Scientifically Valid

This chapter challenges the popular myth that American racial categories represent scientifically valid biological divisions of the human species. The race concept has historically been associated with the idea that there are "natural" divisions of the human species, that there are clear-cut, discrete, homogenous, and easily distinguishable subgroups or "races," and that people can be easily categorized into these racial groups.

This idea originally came from early 18th-century European scientists' attempts to classify the natural world. The resulting systems of classification were called taxonomies, and plants and animals were organized into related divisions, subdivisions, sub-subdivisions, and so forth. Words like "order," "family," and "kingdom" described different levels or subdivisions.

Within this system, the concept of race referred to subspecies of humans. Among nonhuman species, like gorillas, subgroups are usually both physically and geographically distinct and subspecies can be easily identified. But, as we shall see shortly, this is not the case for humans.

This chapter focuses on the arbitrary, subjective, and artificial nature of any attempt to divide the human species into biological races. We show that races are not scientifically valid because there are no objective, reliable, meaningful criteria scientists can use to construct or identify racial groupings.

## CONCEPTUAL BACKGROUND

Despite decades of anthropological evidence to the contrary, many people continue to believe there are three to five basic and natural subcategories of the human species, called races. Until the 1970s, American racial groups were commonly described using terms like "Caucasian," "Negroid," and "Mongoloid." Yet these categories excluded vast populations and regions of the world, such as South Asia, Indonesia, and Brazil. In recent years, geography-oriented terms, like Asian or African or European American, have replaced old racial categories—but the notion that these represent natural, scientific, biological divisions persists.

What are the scientific grounds for rejecting the idea of biological races? One fundamental basis is that there are no reliable procedures for dividing humans into races!

Let us look at the common definition of a biological race popular in the 1950s: "We may define a human race as a population which differs significantly from other populations in regard to the frequency of one or more of the genes it possesses . . ." (Boyd, cited in Lieberman, 1997, p. 3). Sounds simple! But this definition does not specify which of nearly 30,000 genes or which genetically controlled traits are to be used. Perhaps that is why the number of races identified has fluctuated so widely. Estimates have ranged from three to three hundred or more (Staski & Marks, 1992, p. 342).

More recently, Relethford has defined a biological race this way: "A group of populations sharing certain biological traits that makes them distinct from other groups of populations" (2005, p. 133). This avoids the "single trait equals race" problem. He goes on, however, to state, "In practice, the biological concept of race has been difficult to apply to human populations" (p. 133). And like other biological anthropologists, he rejects the idea that American racial groups constitute biological races. Why?

## What Traits Shall We Use to Classify People Into Different Races?

Historically, in the United States, racial classification was based on a few visible traits.[1] Skin color was the most widely used, partially because it easily distinguished Northwestern Europeans from West Africans, who—along with indigenous peoples—were the most significant groups in colonial America. Skin color was also a central feature in the earliest scientific attempts at racial classifications (see chapter 6).

In addition, hair texture as well as eye, lip, and nose shapes figured in popular racial descriptions. This is apparent in 18th- and 19th-century American depictions of non-European populations.

But skin color, hair texture, and facial features are only a few of the many observable variations in the human species. If we are going to classify humans into races based on visible traits, what about the other ways in which humans differ?

*Cranial Shape and Body Type*

In the 19th century, the emerging "science" of racial classification began to explore other human biological variations. Scientists developed methods to measure the human face and skull, called craniofacial measures. A Swedish anatomist developed a measure of cranial shape (not size) called the **cephalic index**. The index was derived by dividing the maximum width by the maximum length of the skull and multiplying by 100. Individuals, and then entire populations, were classified and compared by head shape. For example, Northern Europeans tended to be narrow headed while Southern Europeans were broader headed (Jurmain, Kilgore, Trevathan, & Nelson, 2003, pp. 393–394).

Today we can measure the length and width of the face and the skull from different locations. Often scientists use the eyes, the lower jaw, and the cheekbones as base points. Measures are also taken of the height and width of the nose. There is a **nasal index** based on the width and height of the nasal opening, again multiplied by 100 (Relethford, 2005, pp. 131, 201).

Early racial science developed other measures of the body. Entire populations were classified into different body types based on total body size and shape, and on limb lengths (see chapter 3). These measures have been used to reconstruct past history and the relationships between human populations.

*Other Visible Features*

What about other traits that scientists could use to classify human groups into races? Let's take color . . . but not just skin color. Eyes come in an array of colors. So does human hair . . . from numerous shades of black, brown, and reddish to nearly colorless. Humans also differ in the number of concentrated spots of pigment that we call freckles.

If we extend our analysis of skin beyond color, we find that some groups experience significant skin wrinkling when they age while others do not. And there are variations in where wrinkles appear or where skin begins to sag.

Hairiness is another trait that varies among human populations. Humans differ not only in amount of hair but in hair location. Some people resemble the Buddha, with very hairy ears. Others are hairless. Human balding patterns also vary; in some populations, men lose most of their hair as they age; in others, they do not, even at an advanced age.

*Facial Features*

The face, and specifically the mouth, contains numerous features that could be used to "race" populations. Lips are quite variable in shape and size. Ears, too, come in an enormous array of shapes. Even earlobes vary—some lobes are attached while others are free-standing.

Then there is earwax. Scientists have found two basic kinds. One is gray, dry, and crumbly; the other is yellow, wet, and sticky. In European populations, about 90% of individuals have the wet and sticky kind. In Northern China, only about 4% of people have this type of earwax (Jurmain et al., 2003, p. 383).

Look inside the mouth and you find that some people can make the edges of their tongues curl—that is, the edges roll up and inward, creating a kind of trough. Others find it impossible to do this. Their tongue remains flat. This is not simply a skill or learned behavior. Tongue curling is another innate, biological difference among humans.

*Teeth*

Looking further into the mouth, scientists find that human teeth come in all sizes and shapes. Because teeth tend to preserve well, compared to soft tissue, archeologists and paleontologists are more likely to find teeth than other fossil skeletal remains, even at burial sites. For archeological reconstruction and to identify contemporary human remains, scientists have created a specific type of caliper to measure teeth. Populations can also be classified by tooth size.

Human teeth vary in shape. Some individuals have what are called shovel-shaped incisors, that is, ridges on the inside margins of their front teeth. Some populations—for example, East Asians and Native Americas—are more likely to have this variation than others.

*Hands*

Human hands are a wonderful indicator of how human genetics, through slight and generally meaningless mutations, can produce variant forms of what are functionally identical parts of the human body. Our fingers vary in shape, size, and nail pattern. Some of us have longer fingers. Some of us have a *hitchhiker's thumb*—that is, we can bend our thumb so that it is almost at a right angle. Some of us have double-jointed fingers. Some of us have flat nails; others have more rounded forms.

*Finger and Palm Prints*

Some scientists devote their lives to studying variations in finger and palm prints. While each individual has a unique set of fingerprints, certain features and patterns occur more often in some populations than others. For example, there are variations in the number of ridgelines on each finger if you take a count between specified points. And there are different kinds of prints, described as loops, arches, and whorls, for each finger. (For online illustrations, see www.pbs.org/race/000_About/002_02_a-godeeper.htm.) Palms, too, show different patterns and designs. This keeps palm readers quite busy!

*Height and Weight*

Why not use height as a basis for racial classification? This is certainly a trait that differentiates human groups. Mbuti and Aka ethnic groups in Central Africa average around 4 feet 7 inches. Scandinavians average around 6 feet, as do the Tutsi of Rwanda in East Africa. Of course, if we were to use height to describe races, it would force us to alter the historical racial groupings. In this case, African Tutsis and European Swedes would be in the same race. African Mbuti, Filipinos, Vietnamese, and some Eastern Europeans and Russians would end up in the same race. And while Africa contains the tallest and smallest people, Europe and Asia have a similar range of height variability.

Clearly there are numerous visible traits available for classifying humans into races. Our entire bodies vary—our faces, our limbs, our chest sizes, our necks, our buttocks, our ankles, fingers, toes—one could go on and on. And we're only talking about *visible* human biological traits.

So, which should we use? Is there any scientific basis for selecting some traits over others? Is there any scientific reason to choose skin color or hair form over other traits? The answer, in one word, is no! We could use any one or any combination of these to create groups that fit the definition of a biological race. But, as we shall see shortly, one's racial classification depends on which traits you choose. Change the trait—and your racial membership may change! This is not a very reliable system for dividing the species into biologically distinct subgroups.

### Fuzzy Boundaries: Most Visible Traits Are Not Discrete but Vary Continuously

Let's say we wanted to use just a few traits like skin color or height to create our racial groups. We'd immediately find it virtually impossible to use either trait to create clear-cut groups. The reason is that few visible traits are what scientists call *discrete traits*—with clear differences between alternative forms, like apples versus oranges. There are some exceptions. Take shovel-shaped incisors—you either have them or you don't. This makes it easy to "race" people. People with the trait would be in one racial category; those without it in the other. So using shovel-shaped incisors, we'd have two races. If we used a discrete trait with three different forms, we'd have three races.

But most visible (and many internal) genetic traits, like skin color or height, are what we call *continuous traits*. There are infinite gradations or forms of the trait. Consider color in the natural world or paint colors in a paint store. There is a continuum of colors. There are no clear breaks between green, blue, purple, brown. They shade imperceptibly into each other.

Skin color is like that. There are just shades . . . infinite variations along a continuum from very light to very dark. So even though we may talk about races as "black" and "white," there are no such clear visual boundaries. Blacks and Whites come in various shades, as do all humans.

To create a reliable racial division based on color, we'd have to figure out a way to divide the spectrum of color. In theory we could create a "dividing line." With a spectrometer, we could measure the color of skin of an individual. We'd want, of course, to select the same part of the body for our measurement. Most anthropologists use the inner part of the arm because it is less exposed to the sun and "tanning." Even if we did this, we'd still have to find a dividing line and it would be arbitrary. Individuals with nearly imperceptible differences in skin color could end up in different racial categories!

This problem affects virtually all traditional racial traits. And it applies to other external physical characteristics we've discussed: height, eye color, nose shape, lip shape, hairiness, face shape, teeth size. None have natural subdivisions. All are just infinite variations on a theme. Any division of the spectrum into separate categories is artificial and unreliable. And folks at the edges of categories would be more similar to each other than to people within their own category. It's the same dilemma as with grades. When percentages on an exam are translated into grades, a B student at the 80% cutoff point is as close or closer to many Cs (70–79%) than to other Bs (80–89%).

The only time traits with continuous gradations work for racial categories is when you don't sample the entire world population but select populations at extreme ends of the continuum. You could create races based on height in a region with two populations—one very tall and one very short. Or you could use skin color in a country like 18th-century United States, with two of the major populations (Northwestern Europeans and West Africans) from opposite poles of a continuum—very pale and very dark.

But that is hardly a scientific way to divide the entire human species into races! Any dividing line is purely arbitrary. When we have a continuum, the number of divisions or categories is also arbitrary. We could have 5, 10, 20—indeed, 50—races depending on where we put the dividing line. And that's just using skin color.

An additional complication is that many traits like skin color, height, or weight are influenced by environmental factors. To race people on skin color, for example, we'd have to find a part of the body not exposed to the sun since tanning is a universal human bodily response to sunlight (see chapter 3).

**Racial Traits Do Not Covary**

So how are we, as scientists, to divide people into races? We don't know which traits to use. And virtually all traits will be continuous, with no clear racial divisions. How many different races are we going to create, using any single trait? It's easy to see why there has been so much confusion and disagreement regarding the concept of race—and how many races there are!

What, however, if we simply return to the original traits used to classify humans—skin color, hair form and texture, nose shape, and eye shape. Let's forget that we've arbitrarily selected these visible traits rather than other ones we could have used. Let's forget that we'll have to arbitrarily create divisions within a spectrum of many different variant forms.

What happens when we examine the distribution of traits across the populations of the world? Biological anthropologists in the 1960s started mapping so-called racial traits, one at a time, tracing alternative forms of a trait among populations in different geographic regions. They found that most individual traits exhibit a *gradual* change in the frequency of alternative forms as you move from one population to another across geographic space. There are no abrupt divisions. This type of geographic distribution of a biological trait is called a *cline* (Jurmain et al., 2003, p. 397).

The Palomar College website provides several examples of clinal maps, including one for skin color (see http://anthro.palomar.edu/vary/vary_1.htm). The site also contrasts clinal and nonclinal distributions of hair color. One clinal map shows how the frequency of yellowish-brown hair among Australian Aborigines increases as you move farther from the coast. In contrast, the geographic distribution of red hair in Britain does not demonstrate a clinal pattern. Rather, the map shows there are simply pockets of red-haired populations.

In order to create biologically distinct groups, each racial trait must have approximately the same distribution. That is, populations with particular forms of one trait, such as darker skin, would also have straighter hair or noses.

C. Loring Brace created clinal maps of skin pigmentation, nasal index, body shape, and tooth size. Brace's maps dramatically illustrated the continuous nature of human population variation. The frequency of alternative forms of a trait (for example, nose length) gradually changes over geographic space. There are no sharp boundaries, just gradations.

More important, C. Loring Brace and his colleagues found that each trait showed a distinct geographic distribution. No two traits had the same distribution; none of the populations overlapped! The distribution of skin colors was not the same as that of nasal index, body shape, or tooth size. For other traits as well, each time one introduces a new trait, a new racial configuration appears.

These clinal approaches dramatically illustrate the artificial nature of U.S. and North American and European racial categories. Racial traits are what scientists call *discordant*, that is, they do not *covary*; they are not *concordant*. Virtually every genetic trait has a different geographic distribution. Each produces a different partitioning of the human species.

Simply put, this means that individuals in one racial group based on skin color would not necessarily be in the same racial group if we used a second trait, like hair form, or a third trait like nose shape. Adding more traits just increases the number of different, nonoverlapping, divisions of humanity! We would produce one set of racial categories based on skin color, another using hair form, another using eye shape, another based on nose shape. One's racial identity or category would depend on what trait was used and would constantly shift!

Visual illustrations of the geographic distribution of traits can be found online at the "Race: The Power of an Illusion" website. For maps showing variations in nose shape, head shape, and skin color, go

into the Physical Appearance module at this Web source, www.pbs
.org/race/004_HumanDiversity/004_01-explore.htm. For a Web-based
interactive example of how individuals change racial groups, depending on the trait, see the Sorting People sorting interactivity at www
.pbs.org/race/002_SortingPeople/002_01-sort.htm.

Clinal approaches, with their emphasis on the geographical distribution of racial traits, have stimulated scientists to ask new questions
about the origins of some human biological variation. Why, they ask,
should a particular trait (such as nose size or skin color) have a specific
geographical pattern? Why are certain forms closer or farther from the
equator? Is it possible that so-called racial traits are linked causally to
the environments in which their ancestral populations resided?

Chapters 2 and 3 explore these geographic patterns in more detail,
for both visible and invisible biological traits. And chapter 3 offers a
contemporary explanation for why racially marked traits like skin color
vary among different populations.

To summarize, races are unstable, unreliable, arbitrary, culturally
created divisions of humanity. This is why scientists and anthropology
as a discipline have concluded that race, as scientifically valid biological divisions of the human species, is fiction not fact.

**KEY CONCEPTUAL POINTS**

- There are no scientifically valid biological subdivisions of the
  human species (i.e., races).
- Contemporary U.S. racial categories arbitrarily utilize only a few
  of many visible biological traits that differentiate humans.
- Most so-called racial traits are continuous rather than discrete. The
  number and criteria for racial divisions are therefore arbitrary.
- Racial traits do not covary. They are nonoverlapping and discordant. Using different traits produces different racial classifications
  or divisions of the human species. Clinal approaches document
  this.
- There are no biological races—i.e., there are no visible biological
  traits that allow us to consistently and reliably subdivide the
  human species.

## KEY TERMS (ITALICIZED AND BOLDED IN TEXT)

cephalic index                          discordant (discontinuous) traits
cline                                   discrete traits
concordant (or covarying) traits        nasal index
continuous traits

## TEACHING ACTIVITIES

*Overall Objectives:* Each activity illustrates a major conceptual point in this chapter. There are many ways to vary these activities and they can be adapted to illustrate points made in other part 1 chapters.

*Other Information:* Appropriate for all grades, with modifications. For all of the following activities, it is useful to have visual illustrations of human variability that may not be found in your students. See previously mentioned websites for examples. Many pictures are downloadable or printable. Students can also bring in pictures from magazines and other sources.

### Activity Plan 1: How Many Ways Are There to Create "Races"?

*Objective:* Students will realize how many visible human differences could be used to create races.

*Procedure:*

Step 1. Optional (you may want to do this later). Ask students to define (individually or in small groups) the word "race." Then ask how you can tell someone's race. This should produce a list of racial traits. Save responses for later discussion. For a more detailed version, see the first activity in the teaching module at www.pbs.org/race/000_About/002_04-teachers-04.htm.

Step 2. Write on the board a scientific definition of a biological race, using one of the definitions in this chapter.

Step 3. See if students can apply the definition. Ask what biological traits they would use and list them on the board. They will likely produce conventional racial traits. Ask them why only those traits and not others? Then proceed to Step 4.

Step 4. Ask students (in pairs, small groups, or as a class) to look closely at their classmates (parts of their faces, body shapes, hair, hands and fingers, palms, feet, height, etc.). Then create a list of additional visible human differences. Students may be surprised at how much biological variability they discover once they go beyond conventional U.S. racial traits.

Step 5. Introduce and add traits missed by students (e.g., tongue curling, hairiness, hitchhiker's thumb, etc.). Save list for later activities in this and other chapters.

Step 6. Emphasize key point: Many visible traits can be used to create biological races. Questions for them to ponder:
- With so many traits, which should we use for creating racial groups?
- Why do U.S. racial categories emphasize some traits and ignore all the rest?

Step 7. Potential homework: Look at other people (in their family, community, on TV/videos) and identify additional visible human differences. Add to class list.

## Activity Plan 2: Where Is the Dividing Line for Racial Groups?

*Objective:* Students will understand, experientially, the concepts of discrete vs. continuous traits as applied to race.

*Procedure:*

Step 1. Teacher introduces concept of discrete vs. continuous here or at end of lesson.

Step 2. Select three to five traits from students' list of visible physical traits (in Activity Plan 1). Students will use these traits to create racial groups in the class. Make sure list includes racial markers (e.g., skin color) as well as both discrete traits (tongue curling, hitchhiker's thumb) and continuous traits (skin color, lip thickness, eye color, hair texture, height). In a math class, students could calculate nasal index, cephalic index, body ratios, or teeth size.

Step 3. Select one discrete trait (e.g., tongue curling) and use to separate the class physically into different racial groups. This should be easy because there are natural categories or divisions. You either have the trait or you don't have it. In preparation for Activity Plan 3, you could select another discrete trait as the basis for races (e.g., hitchhiker's thumb, nail shape, dimples). Many students will change races. Note this.

Step 4.    Select a continuous trait and follow above procedure. Start with a nonracial trait like height. Have a student divide the class after students align themselves from shortest to tallest (or use a measuring stick). Students will ask about the number of categories. Discuss how to decide. You may arbitrarily pick a number. Then decide where the divisions should be. Again, there are no objective criteria for deciding. Make the point about the arbitrariness of categories and category boundaries for continuous traits.

Step 5.    Select a racialized trait, such as skin color. Even in relatively ethnically homogeneous classes, there will be variability. Have students compare skin color on the inside of their arm because this is least altered by environmental factors like exposure to the sun (see discussion earlier in this chapter). Students can line up by shades. A continuum should appear. As before, students decide the number of categories and the dividing lines. They will usually have difficulty.

If students are of predominantly Northwestern European ancestry, slight skin color variations may be dismissed as meaningless given total human variation. To some degree, they are correct. But the variations are still real.

Step 6.    If necessary, use pictures to illustrate the human spectrum of skin colors. Avoid geographic "extremes," such as Sweden and Nigeria. Chose from the "mainstream," from densely populated nations like Indonesia, India, Bangladesh, the Circum-Mediterranean area (Italy, Greece, Morocco, Egypt), the "Middle East," Iran and Iraq.

Avoid "exotics," that is people from small-scale societies, in places like New Guinea. Most U.S. major urban areas offer equally diverse samples of human biological diversity. (For one array of 20 faces, see www.pbs.org/race/002_Sorting People/002_01-sort.htm.)

Alternatively, develop a slide or PowerPoint collage of observable human variability in body shape, heights, limb lengths, hairiness, and so forth. Students, especially in relatively homogeneous schools, can experience vicariously the concept of continuous variability. After viewing the collage, you can ask the students, "Based on what you have seen, how difficult or easy would it be for you to classify these people into 'racial' groups using any so-called racial traits?"

**Activity Plan 3: Racial Traits Do Not Covary**

*Objective:* Students will understand the concept of co-variance of traits and how most racial traits do not covary.
*Procedure:*
Step 1. Utilize previous list of visible traits. Students select several traits to create races. Be sure list includes at least skin color, hair form, or nose shape.
Step 2. Select one or two student "racial classifiers" or let students self-classify. You could link this to material in part 2 on the census.

Identify different parts of the room as "homelands" for each racial group. Select the first racial trait, let's say skin color. Decide how many racial categories to use, say three to five. Then have students go to their homelands based on their skin color. If students have difficulty "racing" themselves, remind them that boundaries are often arbitrary. Once students are in racial communities, list members of each racial group (on board, transparency, etc).
Step 3. Select a second, racially identified trait, such as hair form, eye color, or nose or lip shape. Select what works best for your class. Have members of each racial group classify themselves into one of three races based on this trait. Most traits will require arbitrary divisions. For hair you might suggest three categories: tightly curled, wavy, straight hair.

Ask students how much variability there is in their group. Is everyone in the same category based on curliness? Generally, the answer will be no, especially if your class is fairly diverse.

Next, reshuffle the students into new races, designating one area of the room curlies, one straights, and one wavies. Students will then switch racial locations. Record, for each new racial group, how many members were in the same "race" for the groups based on skin color.

Alternatively, create more races to cover the new combinations this second trait has created. List the new combinations on the board: darker skin-curly hair, darker-wavy, darker-straight, medium-curly, medium-wavy, medium-straight, lighter-curly, lighter-wavy, lighter-straight. You now have nine racial categories.

Step 4. Select a third trait, one that is variable within your own class (e.g., nasal index, eye or hair color, tongue curling). Repeat the "racial shuffle."

Step 5. Summarize results using a table like Table 1.1.

**Table 1.1.  Sample chart showing that many physical traits do not co-vary.**

| Student Name | Trait 1: Color | Trait 2: Hair | Trait 3: Body Shape |
|---|---|---|---|
| JS | Medium | Curly | Round |
| CM | Lighter | Wavy | Round |
| SD | Darker | Straight | Linear |
| AM | Darker | Wavy | Round |

Continue with additional traits until students understand the concept of *discordant* or noncovariance among visible traits.

**Activity Plan 4: What Racial Traits Shall We Choose?**

*Objective:* Students will understand that that while racial classification is biologically arbitrary, those in power deliberately select racial criteria that are in their own self-interest.

*Procedure:*

Step 1. Introduce activity. State that class will be divided into racial groups but they will not have equal power or status. Only one race will have the right to decide on the grades the rest of the class will receive for this activity. Race A will be the top-ranked group. Race B will be the lower-ranked group.

Step 2. Arbitrarily divide class into two groups. If class is too large, use three or four groups.

Step 3. Each group will select one visible racial trait to categorize people into races A and B (and perhaps C or D). People possessing one version of the trait will be in Race A; people with the other form of the trait will be in Race B.

Step 4. List the traits groups selected including which form is group A. See if class can agree on which trait should be used to divide the class into races.

Step 5. Discussion. Reflect on how students selected traits. Students will probably try to select a racial trait that will enable them to end up in Race A rather than Race B. Since the groups were arbitrarily divided initially, it may be difficult to find a common trait. But students are creative and will probably come up with one that works. This serves to make the point that racial categories are in part social inventions and those who invent them often are motivated by the desire for power. They select traits that will put their own group at an advantage.

Step 6. Tell students this will prepare them for part 2 on the social invention of race in the U.S.

**Additional Activity Ideas**

Explore these ideas further at the American Anthropological Association, Anthropology and Education Commission website, www.aaanet .org/committees/commissions/aec/, in the Teaching About Race section. See the downloadable teaching-oriented article, Races or Clines (Lieberman & Rice, 1996), which includes illustrative clinal maps.

**ENDNOTES**

1. For illustrations of some traits described in the following section, see Mukhopadhyay's website, www.sjsu.edu/faculty_and_staff/faculty_detail.jsp?id = 1472.

# CHAPTER 2

# Human Biological Variation: What We Don't See

Most long-time residents of the United States have been raised to see race, to notice physical characteristics such as skin color, hair texture, and nose and eye shape. This is not surprising, given the history of the United States. For nearly 200 years, U.S. religious, legal, political, and educational institutions promoted a belief that physical traits were markers of fundamental biological divisions of humanity (see part 2). And U.S. racial ideology, especially racial science, tried unsuccessfully to link visible traits, like skin color, to more profound biological differences in capacities, especially the capacity for civilization and intellectual achievement. This is called *biological determinism* (Jurmain et al., 2003, p. 394).

Yet biological race is truly "skin deep," as over a half century of scientific research has shown. Advances in modern evolutionary theory produced startling new discoveries. We now know that much of human biological variation is invisible to the human eye. Equally important, most significant genetic variation, with major biological and health consequences, is not visible.

Perhaps the most significant finding for our purposes is that virtually none of this invisible but biologically significant human variability is racial. That is, knowing one's U.S. racial category—knowing whether one's ancestors are from Africa, Asia, Europe, or the Americas—will tell you little about the kind of biological variability that can save——or cost you—your life!!

This chapter reviews human biological variability of the "invisible" type. For science-oriented or other interested readers, we begin with an accessible overview of some basics of human biological variability, genetics, and DNA. Although a bit technical, we feel it is useful background material. However, readers can skip these sections and still understand the remainder of the chapter. We have noted this within the text.

## CONCEPTUAL BACKGROUND

### Human Biological Variation: Some Basics

Human biological variation is all around us, as we saw in chapter 1. But the new forms of biological variation that we are discovering are those less visible to the human eye.

Historically, the study of human biological variation focused on external and visible physical traits. This is not surprising. We are a visually oriented species and, as we shall see in part 2, there is some evidence we are predisposed to notice body and facial features.

Some internal traits, like blood or saliva, can also be seen. However, these substances look pretty much the same to the human eye. It took the invention of the microscope, the emergence of modern genetics, and more recent technological advances in understanding DNA for us to fully comprehend the human biological variability that we cannot see.

We now know that visible traits, such as hair color or lip shape, are manifestations of more complex, invisible processes and substances. Scientists are beginning to *directly* identify exact sequences of DNA responsible for particular traits, whether a visible trait like skin color or something less visible, like the substances in our blood. And we are discovering enormous diversity in individual DNA, to the point that we can identify, with high likelihood, an individual based on a DNA sample. Ironically, most of this variability in human DNA has no biological impact. It is simply a marker, a remnant of our past, as we shall see in chapter 4.

But let's return to the story of invisible human biological variability. It exists, most fundamentally, at the level of our DNA. However, the significant DNA that is functional and that impacts our body lies in the portion of DNA that we call *genes*. So what is DNA, what are genes, and how are they linked to human variability and race?

## What Is DNA?

Scientists have identified *DNA* (deoxyribonucleic acid) as the fundamental "building block" of living organisms, and, specifically, of cells.[1] DNA is a large molecule that carries the genetic information that cells need to replicate and to produce proteins. This is why it is described as a "recipe" for making a protein, and proteins are the major constituents of all body tissues. They are also responsible for the functioning of cells, tissues, organs. In short, they are our body!

The structure of DNA is often described as a ladder, or more accurately, a twisted ladder. The "rungs" on the ladder consist of four different chemicals (A, T, G, C) which occur in specific pairs (AT, GC). So AT is one rung; GC is another rung.

This ladder is enormously long with millions of base pairs or rungs. Human DNA is estimated to contain approximately 3 billion base pairs![2] It is the particular sequences or segments of the ladder, the particular arrangements of base pairs, rather than individual base pairs, that are significant and that are the source of human biological traits— and human biological variation.

With so many base pairs, many combinations are possible. It's like language. Every language consists of a rather small set of basic sounds. By repeating and combining these sounds into different sequences of varying length, we can produce a nearly infinite number of words, phrases, conversational streams. Using writing, we can produce sentences, paragraphs, chapters—indeed, entire books! All out of fewer than 25 basic sounds. DNA works similarly, generating different combinations and permutations, segments of the ladder called DNA sequences.

Just as a word is a sequence of sounds, DNA sequences can form larger and more meaningful units. These are known as *genes*. And just as words are meaningful sequences of sounds, so are genes biologically meaningful sequences of base pairs. These units have functions in the body, just as words do in human language.

### DNA: The Substance of Heredity

The ability of DNA to replicate itself makes it responsible for the transmission of genetic information to the next generation. We inherit our

DNA from each of our parents through the DNA contained in the sex cells (the egg and the sperm).

Every cell contains DNA. Virtually all DNA lies within the nucleus of the cell. A tiny portion is outside, in the cytoplasm of the cell. This so-called *mitochondrial DNA (mtDNA)* has become famous because of its use in tracing the ancestry of our species (see chapter 4). Only females can transmit mtDNA to the next generation. By the time of fertilization, only the nucleus of the sperm cell remains. So the father transmits only its nuclear DNA to the fertilized egg. The female egg cell, however, retains both nuclear and mtDNA, so all the mtDNA in the fertilized egg comes from the mother (Jurmain et al., 2003, p. 87).

### Genes: The DNA That Counts

Most DNA (about 98–99%) has no recognized biological function. Scientists were initially surprised at this discovery and for a time called it "junk" DNA. Efforts are underway to identify roles for some of this DNA.

But it is the remaining 1–1.5% of our DNA that seems to be crucial. This is what we think of as our genetic material, our genes. Most of us have heard of genes and understand that some variable physical traits, like eye shape, come from genetic variability. Actually, our culture tends to attribute to biology a lot of things that aren't genetically rooted, as in comments like "It's all in our genes."

In the past, we talked about genes as though they were a unitary thing. Given new understandings of DNA, genes are really a sequence of DNA that has a "coding" function; that is, DNA contains the information for making proteins (see Relethford, 2005, p. 37). A single gene is a specific segment of DNA, at a particular location on a *chromosome*. The location or site of that gene is called a *locus*. Some traits are controlled by one gene, others by many genes.

There are about 30,000 genes in the DNA of a human. A few (about 40) are found outside the nucleus of the cell, in the mtDNA, mentioned earlier. Most genes are located on the chromosomes in the nucleus of the cell.

There are 23 pairs of chromosomes, for a total of 46 chromosomes. They are referred to as pairs because each chromosome in the pair is exactly the same. That is, they contain the genetic material that governs the same biological functions.

There is one exception, only for males. This is the 23rd pair, the sex-determining chromosomes. Females have a matched pair, the so-called XX pair. Males, however, have an X and a Y. There is virtually no genetic material on the Y chromosome. The 23rd chromosome's genetic material lies mainly on the X chromosome.

Most cells carry all 23 pairs of chromosomes—a total of 46 chromosomes. However, our sex cells (that is, the sperm or egg cells) have only one set of each of the 23 pairs of chromosomes. When the sperm and egg cells fuse during conception or fertilization, the fertilized egg or conceptus[3] will receive one set (23) of chromosomes from each parent's sex cell, and hence end up with the full 23 *pairs* of chromosomes. It is the fusion of these two different sex cells, one from the mother and one from the father, that produces the "fertilized egg" or conceptus that eventually becomes a human baby.

It is important to emphasize that we inherit two different "sets" of these 23 chromosomes, one from each parent. Since chromosomes carry our genes, we will have two versions of virtually every gene, one from our father, one from our mother. There are two exceptions. The first is the genetic material in the mtDNA that comes only from our mother. The second is the bit of genetic material on the Y chromosome that we inherit from our father, and then only if we are a male.

**DNA, Genes, and Human Variation**

So . . . where does human variation come into all of this? There are different kinds of variation. There is variation at the individual level, at the level of a person's DNA. As noted earlier, we inherit DNA from both our parents, yielding new combinations or arrangements of DNA. Other processes produce additional variability. As a result, every individual, except for identical twins, is somewhat unique. However, most of this DNA variation is nongenetic, that is, it has no apparent biological significance.

But there is also human biological variation at the genetic level, the type that manifests itself in the human body, producing traits that have some function. This is responsible for visible as well as invisible differences between individuals and sometimes, between different populations.

The main source of genetic variability comes from slightly different forms of genes. Most genes (about 75%) are exactly the same in all humans. But some genes come in one, two, or several slightly different versions. These alternative versions of a gene are called *alleles*. In more technical terms, alleles represent very slight differences in the sequence of DNA base pairs that constitute a gene.

**The Genes We Have versus the Traits We See**

Genes that have alternative versions are called *polymorphisms*, literally many forms (of a trait). Since we inherit genes from both parents, we could end up with two different versions of a trait. An example is hitchhiker's thumb, mentioned in chapter 1. Perhaps only one parent has the gene version for this thumb variation. The other has the "normal" version.

What happens when we inherit two versions of a trait partially depends on other factors. Not all forms (alleles) express themselves the same way. They can be **dominant, recessive,** or **codominant.** Dominant versions always have an impact, even if paired with a different form. Their presence masks or suppresses the alternative form. So if hitchhiker's thumb is a dominant trait, you will have it even if you inherited that form only from your mother.[4]

Recessive alleles usually express themselves only if they are paired with another recessive allele. If hitchhiker's thumb is recessive, both of your parents must have it for you to have the trait. Codominance occurs when each of two different alleles in a pair partially expresses itself in the trait. You could end up with a version of hitchhiker's thumb—it can bend slightly.

The existence of dominant and recessive forms of genes means that much of human genetic variability never expresses itself. It exists in the human cells, is part of our DNA, our genes, our genetic inheritance, and can be transmitted to our offspring. It constitutes what is called our *genotype*, our total genetic endowment, all the genetic material we have as individuals.

What gets expressed, that is in the form of detectable biological traits, both visible and invisible, represents a smaller portion of our genotype. Scientists call this our *phenotype*.[5]

But . . . all of our genetic material will remain in our cells and can be transmitted to our offspring. A recessive genetic form could be passed on to several generations before it actually expresses itself. Eventually, however, both parents may carry the recessive version. This is why some traits, like albinism, the inability to produce the pigment that colors all human skin, may show up suddenly in the offspring of families whose parents, grandparents, and even great-grandparents were normal.

Eye color is another example. Eye color is more complex than we used to think. It is influenced by at least two to three genes and brown eyes are not automatically dominant to blue eyes. However, for each of the controlling genes, blue eyes appears to be recessive to other shades, such as green or brown (Jurmain et al., 2003, p. 78). If an ancestor, even generations ago, had blue eyes, the genetic material could be transmitted to subsequent generations. Eventually, a blue-eyed child could appear if both parents happened to carry this same recessive gene. This has happened in African American families whose ancestors, especially during slavery, may have included some Northwestern Europeans (see chapter 9).

**Mutation and Other Sources of Genetic Variability**

How did different gene forms or alleles come about? Something caused a change in the DNA base pairs at a particular location or locus. This is technically called a *mutation*. Contrary to popular usage, mutations can be positive, negative, or neutral (see chapter 3). In fact, mutations are the only source of totally new variability in the human gene pool. Mutation rates for any trait, however, are quite low; most mutations have no genetic impact, and those that do usually take thousands of years to show up.

Other processes, some during cell development and fertilization, alter or reshuffle the DNA in our genes. Over time, these and other processes discussed in chapter 3 have produced the biological variability we see in the human species.

## Genetic Variation at the Population Level

The biological variability we have been describing occurs primarily at the individual level. Nevertheless, human biological variability *can* be examined at the population level. We can ask whether some forms of a *genetic trait* occur more often in some populations than others. Of course, this is not a new idea. The U.S. concept of race drew upon and manipulated a few visible population differences (see part 2). But, as we saw in chapter 1, there are many other variable traits to explore!

More important, some of the most significant genetic differences between populations occur at the invisible level. New approaches, especially statistics, allow us to more precisely describe these differences. For example, every population is genetically variable. But we can calculate the frequency of alternative forms of a genetic trait within each population. We can then compare different populations.[6] This produces intriguing results, as we'll see when we look at blood groups.

## Invisible Genetic Traits: Neutral and Not

Visible genetic traits represent only the tip of the human iceberg. Once we go more than "skin deep," we find an enormous number of genetically variable traits. They range from some that are virtually neutral to others that can have severe health consequences.

Many genetic variations are perfectly viable alternatives. There is no particular advantage of having one form or another. For example, some genes control our ability to taste certain substances. One chemical, PTC, is controlled by a single gene with two different forms, a taster and a nontaster form. The taster form is dominant—so if you inherit it from just one parent you will be able to taste PTC. But being a taster or nontaster has virtually no impact on your life.

### Lactase: The Gene for Tolerating Cow's Milk

Another relatively neutral variation is the gene that affects your ability to tolerate milk. All infant mammals have the ability to digest lactose (a complex sugar in milk). They produce an enzyme, *lactase*, which helps break down lactose into a more digestible form. However, as humans grow older, they stop producing lactase and lose their ability to digest milk. In most populations, this occurs before adolescence and as early as five years of age. People who are lactose intolerant may experience diarrhea and severe intestinal cramps if they drink milk, although they may be able to tolerate other milk products, such as cheese. Some people, however, apparently possess an alternative form (one dominant allele), which enables them to produce lactase throughout their life. Even as adults, they can digest milk without experiencing any problems.

Lactose intolerance does not present a problem except if you are in a culture with a heavy emphasis on milk products, such as the United States. As we shall see shortly, this genetic trait varies among geographic populations.

*Genetic Defects*

At the opposite extreme of relatively neutral variations are genetic defects. As scientists find out more about our genes, they are focusing on genetic sources of diseases that have severe consequences. One example is Tay-Sachs, a disease that can cause blindness, mental retardation, and destruction of the central nervous system. Children with it rarely live more than a few years. Cystic fibrosis is another example along with hemophilia, a disorder that interferes with the blood's normal ability to clot.

Even when genetic forms have potentially harmful impacts, they may emerge only in particular environments. Hypertension and diabetes are partially linked to variant forms of several genes. However, both diseases have a significant environmental component.

*Blood: A Major Site of Invisible Genetic Variability*

Blood is essential to human life. Without blood we simply cannot survive. We can, literally, bleed to death. Although human blood looks pretty much the same across the human landscape, it exemplifies human biological variability.

Our red blood cells are particularly rich sources of human genetic variation. On their surfaces are numerous molecules, each controlled by a different genetic system. Many of the genes involved have alternative forms (or alleles). There are at least 10 different blood systems that show significant variations among humans. Interestingly, some of this variability is linked to particular populations and geographic regions. Yet none of these blood group variations correlate with conventional racial groupings. There are no racial blood types. Rather, blood types cross-cut races.

Most of us are familiar with the ABO system, especially if we have ever donated (or received) blood. But in addition, there is the Duffy system, the MN system, the Diego system, the Rh system, the Kell system, and several variant forms of hemoglobin, the proteins in red blood cells. Human blood varies in other ways. G-6-PD is an enzyme in red blood cells and it has different forms.

Our white blood cells also vary in the substances that are found on their surfaces. The HLA system (human leukocyte antigen) is particularly important because it plays a role in the body's autoimmune response (or how it responds to foreign substances). A person's HLA type can affect the success of an organ transplant! Like most complex biological traits, the HLA system is controlled by several linked genes rather than by only one gene. And each gene has between 8 and 40 different forms (Relethford, 2005, p. 127).

*The ABO Blood System*

The ABO blood system is an excellent example of invisible but significant human genetic variation. ABO blood type is inherited and remains throughout a person's lifetime. It is not influenced by environmental factors. The ABO system is governed by a single gene that has three forms or alleles—A, B, and O. These forms produce different antigens, substances found on the surface of blood cells. If only antigen A is present, the blood type is A. If only B is present, the blood type is B; if both are present the blood type is AB, and when neither antigen is present, the blood type is O.[7]

Normally, it makes no difference whether one is blood type A, B, O, or AB. Problems only arise when blood types mix, as in a blood transfusion. The most common reaction is the clumping of blood cells. This happens when a "foreign" antigen stimulates the production of antibodies that attack the antigen. For blood type O (no antigen), any blood type containing A or B antigens will cause problems. Those with A antigen will have problems with B antigen and vice versa.

This potential clash of blood types is not a trivial issue. Many of us contribute our blood to relatives or friends or to blood banks. And we may some day need someone else's blood. Blood type becomes significant in these circumstances. Those with blood type O are universal donors—they carry no antigen. But only type AB can receive all blood types (A, B, O, AB). Otherwise, you must receive blood compatible with your own blood type. This is why many people carry a card showing their blood type. It could save their life!

In this example of human variation, like so many others, one's blood type has a greater *biological* impact than one's skin color. And finding someone with the same blood type when you need a blood transfusion is far more important than finding someone with the same racial classification. It is ironic that for many years some Euro-Americans refused to accept blood transfusions from African Americans. Yet race does not predict blood type. This is an example of the power of folk beliefs and ignorance to trump science.

*Rh Blood Group*

Another potentially problematic variation, especially for pregnant women, is the Rh or Rhesus Blood Group system. This is a system of three linked genes (linked means they are inherited together). One gene has two different forms, one dominant and one recessive. Individuals with at least one dominant form are called Rh positive; those with both recessive forms are called Rh negative.

Problems arise when the alternative forms come into contact. During pregnancy, if the mother has Rh negative blood, the mother's antibodies can harm or even destroy her conceptus if it is Rh positive (Relethford, 2005, p. 83). If you are thinking of having a child, knowing your partner's Rh status is far more important, healthwise, than knowing your partner's racial classification. And knowing your partner's race will not tell you anything about your partner's Rh type.

*Harmful Alternative Forms, but Relatively High Frequencies*
*in Some Populations*

Some of the biggest puzzles in human biological variation are harmful alleles that occur in high frequency among some populations and in some environmental contexts. One form of the gene is definitely the normal form while the other has harmful effects. The so-called sickle-cell gene is one such example.

Hemoglobin is one of the proteins in red blood cells. Its function is to carry oxygen to body tissues. The most famous hemoglobin is hemoglobin B ( referring to a *beta* chain), which is controlled by one gene. The normal form of this gene is A. But there are several other forms, including S, C, and E.

The S form (Hb$^S$) is known as the "sickle cell allele." This form alters the blood cells making them less round and more "sickled," thereby reducing their oxygen carrying capacity. This can cause severe anemia and death. In the United States, the sickle-cell gene is more common among African Americans than other populations—but it is not an "African" gene. It occurs among some populations in India and the Mediterranean region. And it is found in only some areas of Africa. Anthropologists have puzzled over how such a harmful genetic form survived over time in human populations.

*CCR5*

Another recently discovered but potentially important invisible human biological variation is the CCR5 gene. Some scientists suggest one form of this gene may be linked to resistance to the HIV virus. Other forms of the CCR5 gene do not prevent infection but do seem to retard the severity of the disease and how quickly it progresses (Relethford, 2005).

**Population-Level Variations**

Several variations on the theme of human genetics are distributed differently among ethnic groups or geographic or regional populations around the world. The CCR5 gene, just described, may be linked to particular geographic populations, the result of mutations that arose centuries ago. The HIV-resistant form has so far been found only in Northeastern Europeans. Other forms, however, have been found in both Northeastern European and African American populations, although it is unclear whether the HIV impact is the same in different populations (Bamshad & Olson, 2003).

One of the most interesting examples of population variability is blood-related genetic substances. Years ago, anthropologists and geneticists began tracking the frequency of ABO blood types in different human populations. We now have good cross-cultural data on the distribution of ABO blood types. When we plot these data on a world map, we find that the frequencies of the blood forms, A, B, and O, vary enormously among human populations.

Maps showing the geographical distributions of A, B, and O blood types in different regions of the world are available at the Palomar College website, http://anthro.palomar.edu/vary/vary_3.htm. These maps graphically illustrate how much variability there is within populations and within each large geographic land mass. Most populations have people with each blood type.

There are some exceptions. Native South and North American populations have high frequencies of type O blood, usually at least 80% (Jurmain et al., 2003, p. 377). You might start to think type O blood is a racial trait. Yet we find the same high frequencies of O among Native Australians in the northern and some coastal regions. Clearly race and blood type are not the same thing.

Type O is relatively infrequent among Eastern Europeans and Central Asians. People are more likely to be Type A or B. Actually, B is the rarest blood form. But at least 20% of the population in Central Asia, Western Siberia, and Central Mongolia has it and nearly 30% in the Himalayan area. It also occurs among North American Inuit, but it is virtually absent from other American Indian populations.

Type A also displays interesting patterns. It is most common among Blackfoot Indians and neighboring groups in North America, with frequencies greater than 50% (Jurmain et al., 2003, p. 379). Clearly, the Blackfoot "bloodline" is different from other Native American groups! Type A high frequencies also occur in Australian native groups . . . except for those living in Northern Australia.

Scientists are intrigued by and trying to explain these data. They note that persons with Type A blood are more likely to get stomach cancer and anemia; Type O individuals are more likely to have gastric and duodenal ulcers. Some suggest infectious diseases, such as malaria, smallpox, tuberculosis, syphilis, bubonic plague, cholera, or leprosy, may have played a role in the emergence of particular blood types (see chapter 3).

At this point, however, little is known about the origins of these patterns. What is clear is that this significant area of human biological variability is not correlated with race. Indeed, there is variability within continents and even among smaller populations.

Other blood substances have intriguing geographic distributions, such as the HLA system on the white blood cells, mentioned earlier. Within Europe, some groups like the Lapps, Sardinians, and Basques are different from other European populations. Many areas of Australia and New Guinea show high frequencies of divergent forms.

The sickle-cell form of hemoglobin B, mentioned earlier, is particularly well-known and well-studied. As noted earlier, it is an example of a potentially very harmful genetic variation that for some reason managed to persist in certain populations. As we shall see in chapter 3, scientists have found that these distributions reflect environmental factors and the workings of natural selection on genetic variability.

Milk intolerance (lactase deficiency) also varies among populations in different regions of the world. For some actual figures, see http://anthro.palomar.edu/adapt/adapt_5.htm. Tay-Sachs is more frequent among European (Ashkenazi) Jews than among other populations. And the data on CCR5, described earlier, suggests some links to particular populations.

Population differences in these invisible traits interest anthropologists and geneticists. Exploring their roots provides us with insights into the mechanisms through which human variation emerges. We will treat these mechanisms in chapter 3.

Clearly, genetic variability is all around us, affecting our lives, impacting our health, and in some cases, threatening our lives. And human populations do differ genetically, in ways that can have health and other impacts. But these populations are not traditional racial groupings. They are much smaller units, for one thing. And different populations show different patterns depending on the trait examined—that is, there is no covariation among traits. Most important, there is no evidence that the genetic variability described here is linked to other visible, external racial markers, such as skin color or eye shape.

To summarize, much of human genetic diversity is invisible. If we wanted to classify people by genetic traits, it would probably make more sense to form races based on ABO blood type or lactose intolerance than to base them on skin color or nose shape. Knowing someone's blood type is more biologically significant than knowing their skin color! And knowing your lactase-enzyme status could be useful if you lived in a culture that promoted milk drinking throughout adulthood!

## KEY CONCEPTUAL POINTS

- U.S. race emphasizes a few external, visible biological traits, whereas much of human genetic variation is invisible and often more significant medically.
- Populations differ genetically but these populations do not correspond to major racial groupings.
- Most human genetic variability is at the individual level; much of it is not expressed, but is part of one's total genetic makeup (genotype) and can be transmitted to offspring.
- Additional variability exists at the human *genome* level, that is, all of an individual's DNA. However, most of this DNA has no apparent function, even though it is inherited. It is what makes us unique, however.

## KEY TERMS (ITALICIZED AND BOLDED IN TEXT)

For more detailed definitions, see the glossaries linked to the Palomar College website Biological Anthropology tutorials.

| | |
|---|---|
| allele | lactase |
| biological determinism | locus |
| chromosomes | mitochondrial DNA (mtDNA) |

codominant alleles
DNA
dominant allele
genes
genome
genotype

mutation
phenotype
polymorphism
recessive allele
trait (genetic trait)

## TEACHING ACTIVITIES

*General Overview:* These activities link to other chapters in part 1. They are appropriate for secondary school social studies, science, and health classes and for introductory college level courses in the social sciences, biology, and health education.

*Objective:* Students will understand that significant invisible genetic variation, such as in the ABO blood system and intolerance for milk, does not covary with race.

*Additional Information:* Students will need to find out their ABO blood type and, if possible, their tolerance for milk and their Rh status (from family members, health providers, blood bank, etc.). Milk intolerance may have to be inferred. Similar information about other family members is also useful.

Illustrative ABO blood type maps and lactose tolerance data are available online (see earlier text references).

### Activity Plan 1: Sorting by Blood Type and Race

*Procedure:*

Step 1. Students find out their own blood type (A, B, AB, O). Class can calculate frequencies of each blood type for the class.

Step 2. Designate sections of the room by blood type: A, B, AB, O. Students go to the section of the room for their blood type.

Step 3. Each blood type group records the "races" of group members, using self-identification and the 2000 Census categories. Multiracial students can select more than one racial category. (See Table 2.1 for a list of U.S. Census classifications.)

Step 4. Summarize results in matrix or table (see Table 2.1). Is there any pattern? Can you predict blood group from knowing race?

**Table 2.1.    Sample matrix of blood type by race**

| Blood Type by Race | Euro-American | African American | Asian American | Native American | Hawaiian or Pacific Islander | Latino or Hispanic | Other |
|---|---|---|---|---|---|---|---|
| A | | | | | | | |
| B | | | | | | | |
| AB | | | | | | | |
| O | | | | | | | |
| Total | | | | | | | |

Adapted from 2000 Census categories; see http://www.census.gov

Step 5. Optional. Students compare their geographic ancestry (even if many generations ago) to maps showing geographic distribution of blood types. Discuss findings. Brainstorm what factors (historical, environmental) might be linked to geographic variations in blood types. See chapters 3 and 4 for follow-up discussions.

**Activity Plan 2: Lactose-Intolerance and Race**

Follow the same procedures as for ABO blood groups but have students divide themselves based on their difficulty digesting milk. Students can discuss how they might infer whether they are lactose tolerant or intolerant. A third category ("not sure") can be created for students in between or unsure.

**Activity Plan 3: Rh Factor**

Repeat the same procedures if enough students can identify their Rh status.

**Additional Activity Ideas**

1. Explore human blood in more depth at http://anthro.palomar.edu/blood/default.htm Also see www.nobel.se/medicine/educational/landsteiner/index.html and "Play the Blood Typing Game."

For chart showing percentages of ABO blood types in the U.S., and donor and receiver blood types, see www.pbs.org/race/ 000_About/002_02_b-godeeper.htm. All these sites provide additional Web links.

2. Explore the Human Genome Project website at www.ornl.gov/ sci/techresources/Human_Genome/home.shtml.

3. Explore genetics and human heredity in more depth through the excellent tutorials at the Palomar College website at http://anthro-.palomar.edu/tutorials/physical.htm.

4. Exploring My Ancestry. Students collect ABO blood type and milk tolerance data on family members (immediate, more distant) as part of a broader exploration of their ancestral roots (see part 2 and the Mukhopadhyay website in references). Be as precise as possible about ancestral roots, for example, India (West Bengal state), Italy (Sicily), China (Shanghai area), West Africa (Northern Nigeria). Do blood type and milk tolerance of relatives match worldwide geographic regional patterns? If not, why not? (e.g., see migration patterns of ancestors, variability within regions and populations, adoption).

## ENDNOTES

1. Readers who wish to omit these more detailed sections can go directly to the section titled "Invisible Genetic Traits: Neutral and Not."

2. "If you were to read the sequence aloud (A,T, T, etc.) at the rate of one base per second, it would take you close to 100 years to finish, assuming you never slept or did anything else" (Relethford, 2005, p. 40).

3. "Conceptus" is the human organism from fertilized egg to birth (Hyde & DeLamater, 2006).

4. Apparently recessive alleles often have a minor impact not detectable in the phenotype but at the biochemical level (Jurmain et al., 2003, p. 78)

5. Phenotype, though often defined as "observable" traits, includes invisible traits like blood type, in short, all "detectable" traits. It also includes environmentally influenced traits, like height and skin color.

6. Technically, a gene is defined as polymorphic only when the alternative form (allele) reaches a certain frequency in some population. Polymorphic genes, then, are always relative to a population.

7. Dominant and recessive genes are clearly shown in the ABO system. The O allele is recessive to both A and B. Therefore, anyone with type O blood must have two copies of the O allele! Since both A and B are dominant to O, an individual with blood type A can have either of two genotypes: AA or AO. The same is true of B: BB and BO. However, blood type AB represents an example of codominance.

# CHAPTER 3

# If Not Race, How Do We Explain Biological Differences?

Scientists may have abandoned the concept of biological races, but human biological variation is real and can have life-threatening impacts. Differences in skin color, facial traits, and body form—which our culture has taught us to notice—are real even though biological race isn't. So . . . how are we to explain group differences, especially ones that we have historically associated with race?

## CONCEPTUAL BACKGROUND

This chapter introduces new and more useful scientific approaches to human biological variation. In the past, the scientific emphasis was on classification, on trying to divide the human species into subgroups, into static, homogeneous types or categories, usually called races. Today, scientists focus on describing and understanding specific traits, one at a time, whether the ABO blood system, hitchhiker's thumb, or skin color. And they utilize modern genetic and evolutionary theory.

### Genetics, Evolutionary Theory, and Human Biological Variation

We can talk about human biological variation at the level of the individual, at the population level, and at the species level. We saw in chapter 2 that there is individual biological variation—we are all somewhat unique, except for identical twins—although most of it has no biological impact.

At the species level, compared to other species, we are genetically homogeneous. Only a small percentage of human genes have variant forms and these are relatively insignificant. *Macroevolution*, that is, major genetic changes in our species, occurred thousands of years ago and we have long been one species, with one basic gene pool.

It is population-level differences, the small and relatively minor biological group characteristics, such as skin color, that have historically preoccupied North Americans. This chapter focuses on populations, especially on new ways of understanding differences between groups whose ancestral populations have inhabited different geographic regions of the world.[1]

## Evolutionary Forces in the Emergence of Visible Human Variation

Today, biological anthropologists and geneticists approach human population variability from a modern evolutionary perspective. This combines Charles Darwin's idea of natural selection with current understandings of genetics. From this perspective, *evolution* is defined as changes in allele frequencies in a population over time (Kottak, 2006). More simply put, it is genetic change over time, such as in the proportions of A, B, AB, or O blood type in a population.

The modern evolutionary synthesis explains evolutionary change, whether macro or micro,[2] in terms of four basic processes: mutation, gene flow, genetic drift, and natural selection. These are sometimes called the *four forces of evolution*. Mutation is the only source of new genetic variability in a species. But at the population level, genetic variation can occur through two other processes: gene flow or genetic drift.

Briefly stated, *gene flow* involves the exchange of genes between two populations through intermating. This has been a constant feature of human populations and is the reason we are still one species. *Genetic drift*, another evolutionary force, alters the genetics of small populations, purely by chance—that is, not through natural selection.

*Natural selection* is the fourth evolutionary force and one of the most powerful sources of human variation. Natural selection, acting on mutations, is now viewed as the source of many visible traits that have figured so prominently in U.S. racial theories.

*Mutation*

In chapter 2, we introduced the concept of a genetic *mutation*. In popular culture, especially science fiction, mutation evokes an image of a monster or a freak of nature. The truth is that most human characteristics have been shaped over time through trial and error and mutation.

Occasionally mutations have a positive or negative impact, but most are neutral. The important point is that mutation is the only way that *new* genetic forms are introduced into the human species, and mutations can be transmitted to the next generation through our sex cells. Genetic variability within a species therefore depends heavily on mutations.

Mutations are introduced into a population at the individual level, but evolution occurs at the population level. Every individual mutation transmitted to the next generation will cause a minor shift in the gene pool or genetic structure of that population. Mutation rates, however, are usually quite low and normally take many, many generations to have a discernible impact on a population.

Scientists do not even define a trait as polymorphic, that is having alternative forms, unless the occurrence is fairly high, usually at least .01 or 1:100 people in the population (Relethford, 2005, p. G-8). But when levels are this high, scientists assume that something other than mutation is occurring, that other evolutionary forces are at work.

Mutations by themselves, then, do not cause most evolutionary change. Contemporary population genetic variability, whether in skin color or body size, cannot simply be explained by mutation. We must look at other processes that affect mutations. The most important of these is natural selection.

*What Is Natural Selection?*

Most mutations are neutral and would take thousands of generations to accumulate in high numbers in human populations. Natural selection, however, works on existing genetic variation, selecting for genetic forms that contribute to the reproductive success of individuals with that particular version of a trait.

What do we mean by "selecting for"? Mutations, or variable forms of a trait, aren't really selected for in any conscious way. Rather, some mutations enable carriers to survive or reproduce at higher rates than others. As a result, some individuals are more likely to transmit their genetic version of a trait to the next generation. These genetic forms will be passed on to the next generation at higher rates than other forms. Over time, these changes will alter the population. So natural selection describes this process of differential reproduction.

For example, if a new mutation of the ABO blood system causes an individual to die before the age of 10, then that mutation will be quickly eliminated (or selected against)! If another form enables carriers to resist major killer diseases, they will be more likely to have descendents who carry the same gene. Over time, these transmission differences accumulate and alter the genetic structure of the population. In short, the frequencies of alternative forms of the trait change over time—and the population becomes somewhat genetically distinct from other populations.

What causes some genetic mutations, some alternative forms of a trait, to do "better" than others? More technically, what makes some versions of a trait more adaptive than others? And some individuals more *reproductively fit* than others? The concepts of **adaptation** and **fitness** are always relative to a particular environment. What makes a skin color, nose shape, or blood type adaptive depends on the context. As we shall see, some blood traits, like the sickle-cell gene, might confer a selective advantage in some environments.

Natural selection, then, is a mechanism through which, over time, genetic forms better adapted to a particular environment predominate over less-adaptive alternatives. More technically, "Natural selection operates to change allele frequencies through variations in the survival and reproduction opportunities of individuals with different genotypes" (Relethford, 2005, p. 171). This is what we mean when we say that evolution has resulted from natural selection. Adaptation, reproductive fitness, different survival rates of alternative forms, natural selection, and evolution are linked concepts and processes.

Individuals with reproductively advantageous genetically transmitted traits are by definition more **reproductively fit**. But survival of the fittest, contrary to popular usage, says nothing about what kinds of genetic traits will be more or less fit. "Fit" at one point in time or in one environment may become "unfit" in another time and place. Fitness simply measures the reproductive impact of a specific trait or, put simply, the relative number of viable offspring different genetic forms produce.

## Natural Selection and Human Variation: Skin Color, Nose Shape, and Body Type

Natural selection provides a framework for understanding some human biological population differences that we have historically called racial. In the 1960s, biological anthropologists and geneticists started using the *clinal approach* to describe and explain human biological variation. As you will recall from chapter 1, this approach looks at single traits, one at a time, and maps their distribution across geographic space.

Frank Livingstone, C. Loring Brace, and others discovered some intriguing relationships between genetic traits and climatic and other environmental factors. They stimulated investigation into the role of natural selection in the evolution of many visible human differences. One of the most significant is skin color.

### Human Skin Color

"Throughout the world, human skin color has evolved to be dark enough to prevent sunlight from destroying the nutrient folate but light enough to foster the production of vitamin D" (Jablonski & Chaplin, 2005, p. 169).

Human skin color is a very complex trait, probably controlled by several genes. Skin color comes mainly from a pigment called *melanin* produced by cells in the skin (called melanocytes).[3] Variations in melanin produce different shades of skin, from deeper to more lightly pigmented skin. Hemoglobin, which gives blood cells their red color, also affects skin color, particularly in people without much melanin (Relethford, 2005). The red in their blood tends to show through the surface of the skin, giving their skin a pinkish color. Just as black, brown, yellow, or red doesn't really describe the skin color of the major races, neither does white.

Everyone, except albinos, produces melanin. Skin color illustrates the short-term ability of the body to adjust to local conditions without genetic change. Tanning, like sweating and shivering, is an adaptive, physiological capacity. All melanin-producing humans can tan and tanning is the body's short-term physical response to stressful environmental conditions.[4]

But the population differences we see in skin color today are mainly the result of evolutionary processes that took place over time, thousands of years ago. Skin color represents a striking example of how natural selection produces human variability in response to different geographic and climatic conditions.

*Mapping the Distribution of Skin Color*

Human skin color, as C. Loring Brace and others showed, is distributed in a clinal fashion. To illustrate, if you were to walk from Northern Europe to the tip of Africa you would see people with differing amounts of melanin in their skin. Travel from the tip of Southern India through the middle of India to the farthest northern state of Kashmir, and you would find a similar gradient of skin colors from heavy production to very little melanin. The reverse spectrum would appear going from Northern Korea through China, Southern China, Vietnam, to Malaysia and Indonesia. Even if you were to simply walk from Equatorial Africa to the southern tip of Africa, looking at the indigenous populations, you would see skin shades going from darker to lighter.

Why is this the case? All humans have the capacity to produce melanin because it is adaptive for them to do so, whether short term or as an evolutionary adaptation. Human skin is a "built-in sunscreen" (Jablonski & Chaplin, 2005, p. 169). It reduces our exposure to ultraviolet (UV) radiation. We synthesize melanin in response to UV radiation. Physiologically, too much UV can destroy skin cells, but humans produce different amounts.

Anthropologists today attribute the differences we see in skin color primarily to past adaptations of populations to varying levels of ultraviolet radiation in different microclimates. Scientists believe it would take thousands of years for even adaptive mutations to accumulate through natural selection. So these adaptations occurred long ago, as populations inhabited different geographic regions of the world.

Clinal maps of skin color show the close relationship between skin color and latitude or distance from the equator. Populations with more melanin tend to be closer to the equator. Those with less melanin tend to be farther from the equator, closer to the North and South Poles. For maps, see http://anthro.palomar.edu/adapt/adapt_4.htm or select Physical Appearance at www.pbs.org/race/004_HumanDiversity/004_01-explore.htm.

Scientists have long known that ultraviolet radiation is strongest at the equator and diminishes as one moves away from the equator. Because too much UV destroys the skin cells and can cause skin cancer, the first theory was that darker skin evolved to protect against UV rays. And as human populations settled areas farther from the equator, selection pressures relaxed. Lighter skin allowed for sufficient vitamin D production where UV rays were less strong.

Current explanations are a bit more complex and go back farther in time (Jablonski & Chaplin, 2005). They start with humans, some one to two million years ago, living in Africa near the equator. And they begin with hair loss. Anthropologists point out that only humans are relatively hairless and have varied skin colors. In contrast, our closest primate ancestors, the chimpanzees, are covered with hair and have pale skin, although it is darker in hairless areas exposed to the sun.

Anthropologists believe we humans lost our hair as we became upright, gained larger brains, and traveled longer distances. Humans had to stay cool and protect the brain from overheating. The evolution of sweat glands on the surface of our body, along with the loss of most hair, was our adaptive solution to the heat and cooling problem.

Once we lost our hair, we faced the new problem of protecting our skin from the damaging effects of sunlight, particularly UV rays. This is where melanin, the natural sunscreen, comes into play. Melanin filters the harmful effects of UV in two ways: through absorbing UV rays and through neutralizing harmful chemicals that form in the skin after UV radiation damage (Jablonski & Chaplin, 2005). Scientists reasoned that through natural selection, humans with higher concentrations of melanin came to predominate.

Melanin apparently does more than protect us against skin cancer. Jablonski and her colleagues pointed out that skin cancer tends to occur in older people, after they have stopped reproducing. Hence, skin cancer would have little evolutionary impact. That is, skin cancer wouldn't affect reproductive rates of differently shaded individuals. Instead, new evidence suggests that darker skin color evolved to protect against the effects of UV on the essential B vitamin called folate.

## The Role of Folate

Folate (from folic acid, a necessary nutrient) plays an important role in reproduction. Folate is essential for the synthesis of DNA in dividing cells. Folate deficiency in pregnant women can cause severe birth defects in offspring. It also can severely depress sperm production in males.

Exposure to UV radiation apparently breaks down folate, causing folate deficiencies. Current explanations for the evolution of darker skin, then, focus on the adaptive benefits of melanin for preventing the breakdown of folate. In short, scientists believe that individuals with darker skin, in UV intense environments, located close to the equator, were protected against folate deficiency and hence had higher reproductive rates than paler-skinned folks.

Anthropologists know that modern humans evolved in Africa about 100,000 years ago. So they assume modern humans, through natural selection, evolved dark skin as an adaptation to the high levels of UV radiation near the equator.

But how did variation in human skin color shades arise? Modern humans migrated to other parts of Africa and then out of Africa. As humans moved away from the equator, UV radiation decreased. This reduced selective pressures for darker skin and allowed individuals with less melanin to survive and reproduce. But that was not the only factor. UV rays have some positive benefit.

## The Significance of Vitamin D

Scientists have long recognized the importance of vitamin D for human well-being, especially the ability of our intestines to absorb calcium. This allows for normal development of the skeleton as well as the immune system. Vitamin D deficiency can produce rickets and other skeletal diseases. Among these are deformed pelvises, which can interfere with successful childbirth. Thus vitamin D deficiency can affect both the fertility of women and the survival of their offspring.

UV rays do have some positive effect. They initiate the formation of vitamin D in the skin. Indeed, the sun has been the major source of vitamin D throughout human history, although some foods (such as cod liver oil) provide significant amounts of vitamin D.[5] In tropical areas, while darker skin blocks UV, the amount and intensity of sunlight guarantees that enough UV will penetrate the skin to provide sufficient amounts of vitamin D.

But what happens when humans start migrating to areas farther from the equator, where the sunlight is less intense and even virtually absent much of the day? As humans moved away from the equator, the risks of UV decreased and the risks of vitamin D deficiency increased. By the time one reaches Finland or Sweden or Siberia, the UV problem is far outstripped by the vitamin D factor (at least thousands of years ago).[6]

Scientific evidence now suggests selection for lighter skin (reduced melanin production) allowed sufficient UV to penetrate the skin to stimulate vitamin D production. In short, lighter skin was more adaptive in latitudes farther from the equator. As we go farther from the equator, ancestral populations exhibit lower levels of melanin.

Natural selection, environmental factors (specifically, UV exposure), and the need for both folate and vitamin D have combined to produce the variations in skin color we see today. But as Jablonski and others point out, these selective forces operated long ago, and over thousands of years.

Meanwhile, for the past several hundred—even thousands—of years, people have been migrating (or have been forcibly taken) to geographical regions that are quite different climatically. Africans from equatorial regions sometimes ended up in areas like Boston or Canada and the British ended up in India, West Africa, and the Caribbean! As a result, humans increasingly relied on cultural rather than biological adaptations, such as clothing, shelter, and dietary changes or dietary supplements to handle the UV and vitamin D issues.

The people of the West Bank of the Red Sea, in East Africa, have inhabited the region for approximately 6,000 years. They have darkly pigmented skin and long, thin bodies with long limbs. Both are excellent adaptations for high intensity UV and heat/cooling issues (see the next section). In contrast, more recent migrant populations on the Eastern Bank of the Red Sea, the Arabian Peninsula, have been in the region for scarcely 2,000 years. They have primarily adapted through cultural means—clothing that fully protects the body and tents that provide portable shade (Jablonski & Chaplin, 2005).

Other recent population shifts, partially due to colonialism and globalization, have affected disease rates. Skin cancer is more common among lighter-skinned people of European ancestry living in areas of prolonged sunlight than among other native populations. Another problem is diseases associated with vitamin D deficiency (e.g., rickets, pelvic deformities) among darker-skinned people living in northerly latitudes such as England, Canada, Sweden, and the Northern United States (Relethford, 2005).

Skin color, then, is an example of human genetic adaptation. But cultural adaptation can trump biology. We can add vitamin D to food to augment natural sources. And we can wear clothing, visors, hats, or apply sunscreen to protect against harmful UV rays.

The evolution of skin color provides further ammunition for the argument that race is biological fiction. Skin color is an example of real human biological variation. But variations in skin color are not correlated with conventional racial categories. Skin color and race are two different phenomena![7] Skin color, like many other physical variations, can be explained as an adaptation to the environment through natural selection. Race is a cultural invention and a misreading of biology.

**Body Size and Shape as Partial Responses to Climatic Conditions**

Other visible human differences, like body shape, may also reflect natural selection. Humans, like other animals, have evolved biological mechanisms for dealing with climate-related stresses, including heat stress and heat loss. Humans evolved in East Africa, in hot climates, traveled widely, and needed cooling mechanisms for survival. The capacity to reduce excess heat through sweating is a major biological capacity all humans possess.

This capacity was enhanced, in the evolution of modern humans, through the loss of virtually all body hair and an increase in the number of sweat glands throughout our skin. This distribution of sweat glands provides our evaporative cooling system, essential for human survival.

Can sweating and other heat-related needs help explain variations in body types? Scientists seem to think so. All human populations have about the same average number of sweat glands (approximately 1.6 million). However, human groups vary in size and body shape. Body heat is mainly lost at the surface. Thus the more surface, the more heat loss.

Smaller bodies (of similar shape) have more surface area relative to volume than do larger bodies. Hence smaller bodies lose heat more rapidly; larger bodies conserve heat longer.

But body shape, including limbs, also affects surface area and heat loss or retention. The more linear the body, the greater the surface area. The rounder the body, the less surface area. Applied to humans, this means that people with relatively longer torsos, heads, arms, legs, fingers, and more surface area lose heat rapidly. And those with rounder bodies are better at conserving heat.

When scientists examine the distribution of human body size and shape by climatic zones, they find a general correspondence. Overall, populations in tropical and subtropical areas tend to be smaller and/or have more elongated body shapes and the longer limbs (including fingers and toes) that tend to be adaptive to hot climates. Populations living in colder climates tend to have rounder shapes, shorter limbs, and/or be larger in size. For illustrations, see http://anthro.palomar.edu/adapt/adapt_2.htm.

Head size and shape show similar adaptations. Cranial measurements were one basis for racial classifications in 19th- and 20th-century racial science. More recent research shows that head shape corresponds directly to climate. Groups living in colder climates tend to have wider skulls (relative to length) than populations residing in hotter climates (Relethford, 2005).

Nose size and shape may also reflect adaptations to climate. Human noses are quite variable but studies have found a relationship between the average nasal index (see chapter 1) and both average temperature and average humidity. Populations in colder and drier climates tend to have narrower noses than in hotter and more humid climates. Apparently, high, narrow noses are better at warming air than lower, wider noses and are adaptive in cold climates. High, narrower noses are adaptive in drier climates because they have more internal surface area that can be used to moisten air (Relethford, 2005).

Population differences in human body size and shape, then, may reflect past adaptations, through natural selection, to different climatic zones. For maps of nose shape and head size, see Physical Appearance at www.pbs.org/race/004_HumanDiversity/004_01-explore.htm.

On the other hand, there is a lot of variability within and between populations living in the same climatic zones. Environmental factors, including diet and nutrition, have a major impact on body size and perhaps even shape. The human adult body is quite plastic! An individual's weight can go from 140 to 210 pounds by moving from one country to another!

Significantly, none of these population differences correspond to traditional North American macroracial groups. Looking at head shape, Germans, Koreans, Central African forest dwellers, and Greenland Eskimos have very similar head shapes (average cephalic index of 77–83%). Yet they are from different races, using conventional U.S. racial categories.

As for body shape, we find relatively long-limbed individuals in Kenya, Afghanistan, South India, and Greece. We find large and small bodies in Europe, large and small bodies in Asia, large and small bodies in Africa. We find very wide and very narrow noses among Africans, as well as a broad range of noses among Asians and Europeans. Of course these are huge, diverse continental regions. But other regions, such as South Asia, are equally variable.

**Natural Selection and Invisible Human Variation: The Sickle-Cell Variation**

Modern evolutionary approaches to human variation help us understand less visible human variation, such as in the blood. Earlier we described the hemoglobin sickle cell found throughout West Africa, the Mediterranean, and South Africa. Anthropologists like Frank Livingston were trying to understand how such a harmful trait, causing severe blood anemia, could become common in so many populations. He hypothesized that it had some selective advantage.

Livingston examined the geographic distribution of the sickle-cell trait around the world. He noticed that the sickle-cell gene tended to be found in areas known to have malaria. Was there perhaps a relationship? Looking next at the geographic distribution of malaria, he found a striking correspondence between higher frequencies of the sickle cell (S allele) and higher incidence of a particular form of malaria.[8]

Subsequent research has established that having only one (versus two) copies of the mutant sickle cell conveys an adaptive advantage. That is, individuals who inherit the sickle-cell version from both parents are at a distinct health disadvantage and often die from anemia. But those with one normal and one sickle-cell allele have increased resistance to malaria without being anemic. Their survival rates are highest. They die neither of malaria nor sickle-cell anemia.

In malarial environments, then, the evidence suggests strong selective pressure for this particular mutation. This has produced the high frequencies of the mutant sickle cell that we see in certain populations. Maps showing the *malaria–sickle-cell relationship* can be found at http://anthro.palomar.edu/synthetic/synth_4.htm, and at the Mukherji lab website, www.sicklecellinfo.net/who_suffers.htm.

Scientists continue to explore selective advantages in malarial environments of other blood type variants and diseases like smallpox (see Kottak, 2005). Malaria is still one of the major infectious diseases in the world. Evolutionary roots of diseases, like Tay-Sachs, that are concentrated in particular populations, are also being investigated.[9]

Even relatively mild genetic-linked health problems that vary across populations may have partial roots in natural selection. One example, introduced in chapter 2, is the persistence of the enzyme, *lactase*, allowing *milk digestion* into adulthood. Groups living farther from the equator have less access to sunlight and hence vitamin D, which could decrease calcium absorption and bone growth. They would benefit from an ability to digest milk as adults since lactose increases calcium absorption.

Another factor may be heavy reliance on dairy farming, as with the Finns, Swedes, and the Swiss. And while most West Africans are lactose intolerant, the one pastoralist (cow-herding) group in the region, the Fulani, can digest milk as adults (Relethford, 2005).

These and other studies clearly demonstrate the lack of correspondence between what we have conventionally called races and biological variation at the population level. Even within the same region of Africa, different populations exhibit different patterns of biological variation.

The idea of races as stable, biologically distinct human groupings is a fiction, a cultural invention. A striking illustration is the case of sickle-cell anemia, long considered an African American racial disease. The maps of sickle-cell populations show that within Africa, it is found in only some populations. And it is found outside of Africa, in parts of Europe, the Mediterranean area, and South Asia. Once again, there is no correspondence between North American racial groupings and this very significant biological variation.

### Human Biological Variations Due to Other Evolutionary Forces

How do we explain other biological differences historically associated with race? Scientists are exploring possible selective advantages of different eye shape, hair form, and other variable human population traits. But not everything is due to natural selection. Other evolutionary forces affect the frequencies of traits in populations.

One is called *genetic drift*.[10] Some genetic forms become more or less frequent in the next generation for reasons having nothing to do with their selective or reproductive advantage. Often it is simply statistical "chance." A small group breaks off from a larger group to start a new community. By chance, one version of a genetic trait in the larger population (e.g., hitchhiker's thumb) doesn't appear in the subgroup. Or, by chance, a rare form in the larger population (e.g., red hair) appears in much higher numbers in this small group.[11]

This is often seen in small isolated populations (e.g., island groups or small agricultural villages in New Guinea and South America). But French Canadians in Quebec illustrate this same process. Today there are 1 million French-speaking people in Quebec, but their ancestors represent only 8,500 founders who migrated to Canada during the 16th and 17th centuries. These French Canadians were a nonrandom, small sample of the original French population. By chance, they carried much higher frequencies of several harmful alleles for diseases, such as cystic fibrosis (Jurmain et al., 2003).

In the case of genetic drift, then, any changes in population gene frequencies over time are random. Populations may acquire distinctive characteristics, such as red hair, purely by chance!

**Gene Flow and Population Variation**

*Gene flow* refers to the exchange of genes between groups. Humans have been on the move for most of our existence as a species. True, we settled down long enough to produce environmentally related traits. But individually, in small groups, for both brief and longer periods of time, we have been interacting, sexually, with our close and more distant neighbors. It is this intermating that has produced extensive gene flow between populations.

Our interactions have taken many forms—migration, trade, and, in recent human history, warfare, conquest, slavery, colonialism. The warlord Genghis Khan and his armies conquered the people living in China and in Eastern Europe in the 14th century, spreading their genes along the way, often through force. The Spanish conquistadors mated with native peoples of Latin America and Mexico during the 15th and 16th centuries.

Slavery produced extensive and primarily involuntary mating between African female slaves and their European male masters. The genetic impact can now be traced. Using data on blood groups, scientists estimate that the proportion of non-African genes in the gene pool of African Americans in Northern and Western U.S. cities such as Oakland, New York, and Detroit is between 20 and 25%. It is somewhat lower in the Southern United States (see Jurmain et al., 2003, p. 91).

And in the 20th century, the two world wars, the Korean War, and the war in Vietnam brought U.S. genes into contact with other gene pools. Clearly, individuals do not have to remain physically in a population for their genes to remain in its gene pool. Once introduced, genes stay even if individual contributors depart.

Despite some coercive mating, human contact has been mainly amicable, and mating between populations has always been a significant strategy for human survival (see chapter 8). Many cultures require young people to marry outside their own group. Such marriages have social, economic, and political benefits. But "marrying out" also produces gene flow across populations, increasing variability within the local gene pool.

Gene flow doesn't introduce new genetic material into the species but it does alter the gene pools of specific populations. It produces new combinations and permutations of genetic traits. We can see this today in multiracial and multiethnic offspring.

The sickle-cell allele, mentioned earlier, was probably not present in the United States prior to the African slave trade. And gene flow, through intermating between African Americans and European Americans, is partially responsible for lower sickle-cell frequencies among African Americans compared to Africans in malarial regions.

Gene flow between populations, in the long run, reduces difference between groups, making them less distinctive, more similar (Relethford, 2005). Indeed, gene flow and intergroup mating have been essential to our species. No human groups were reproductively isolated long enough to develop a genetically distinct path, a unique and distinct species. Gene flow, over time, creates one large gene pool. So while gene flow can introduce new variability *into* a population, it is not a major explanation for contemporary variations *between* populations.

### Nonrandom Mating and Cultural Factors

Nonrandom mating due to cultural and social factors can also affect the genetics of populations. Some individuals contribute disproportionately to the gene pool because of their status. Some societies restrict mating between higher and lower ranked groups. High status or powerful, dominant individuals, usually males, often have access to many women. It can occur during warfare. We will be discussing these cultural and social forces in more detail in part 2.

How does all this relate to race? Once again, we've shown how much human biological variation exists at the individual and population level. But this genetic diversity can often be explained by modern evolutionary theory. Natural selection, working in particular environmental contexts, seems to explain many variations, including the most racialized of all human traits, skin color. Similar factors, along with more random processes like genetic drift, may explain other so-called racial traits.

But we've also seen that the genetically distinct populations we've identified bear little resemblance to traditional racial groups. Most racial traits are variable *within* each major racial category. Knowing one's racial identity or how one is racially categorized in the U.S. tells us very little about human biology.

## KEY CONCEPTUAL POINTS

- Old approaches to human biological variation focused on classification, human subdivisions, or types, called races.
- Modern approaches to human biological variation use genetic and evolutionary theory to explain human variation at the individual and population levels.
- There are some genetic differences between populations, but these populations are much smaller groups than what are popularly termed races.
- Both geography and the environment work with natural selection to influence the genetic structure of human populations. This helps to explain some racial markers, such as skin color, body shape, and the sickle-cell gene as well as milk tolerance.
- Other genetic population differences may reflect more random processes, like genetic drift or cultural processes.
- Gene flow between populations produces new permutations, increases local population variability, and has kept us one species.

## KEY TERMS (ITALICIZED AND BOLDED IN TEXT)

| | |
|---|---|
| adaptation | macroevolution |
| clinal approach | melanin |
| evolution | microevolution |
| fitness | milk digestion |
| founder's effect | mutation |
| four evolutionary forces | natural selection |
| gene flow | population |
| genetic drift | reproductive fitness |
| lactase | sickle-cell trait |

## TEACHING ACTIVITIES

*Objectives:*
- Understand the relationships between geography, environment, and human biological variation for several traits.
- Learn how to test an hypothesis.

*Additional Information:* Mainly high school and older though some are adaptable to middle-school students. Interactive. Students will need some way to measure skin color, body type, head form, nose shape; clinal maps, blank maps (see also earlier chapters).

Several activities ask for geographic origins of students' ancestors. Ancestry can be a sensitive issue. Some students may not know, such as those adopted, not living with family, or whose roots may be somewhat clouded. One alternative is to have students interview other people with known ancestors (adults or other students) or to work in groups using only one "volunteer" from the group. The exercises would work as well this way.

### Activity Plan 1: Ancestry and Skin Color

*Procedure:*
Step 1. Students analyze skin color on their inner arm (see chapter 1). If a spectrometer is available, actual measurements can be taken. Otherwise, simply have students compare (lining up by shades, for example). If the class is too homogeneous, add pictures such as those at www.pbs.org/race/002_SortingPeople/002_01-sort.htm.

Step 2. Students examine clinal maps on skin color (see Web sources in text). Discuss the meaning of these maps.

Step 3. Discussion. Is there a relationship between student family ancestry (geographic roots) and skin color? What other evolutionary factors (e.g., gene flow or migration) could be at work?

### Activity Plan 2: Body Type and Geographic Ancestral Location

*Procedure:*
Step 1. Students measure their body types and explore the relationship

of body type to climate described in this chapter. See also the Palomar College website (http://anthro.palomar.edu/adapt/adapt_2.htm). Or students can develop their own measures of the relationship between body size, body proportions, and climate. Rather than the whole body, students can measure the ratio of the length of their fingers to their hand width. Or they could compute the ratio of their arms to their total height. Or they could measure their nose, using the nasal index or some other measure they develop.

Step 2. Using a world map that shows climatic zones and body types, students compare their body type or other body feature and see where it "fits" geographically. Is this where their ancestors came from?

Step 3. Discussion. Are results consistent with the "climate" hypothesis of body types? If not, why not? Could your ancestors have come from a different region, earlier in time? Could culture be a more important factor in survival, these days, than natural adaptations to climate? How does your body type (or body parts) compare to those of family members, especially older family members? Have any changes occurred?

**Activity Plan 3: Facial Size, Shape, and Geographic Ancestral Location. Does Natural Selection Hypothesis Apply?**

Follow the same procedures as above except measure head shape using calipers, if available. Otherwise, use "cephalic index" or other student-developed measures.

**Activity Plan 4: Milk: Lactose-Intolerance and Lactase Persistence**

Step 1. Students assess their tolerance for milk if not done earlier (chapter 2). They could ask family members about their tolerance as well.

Step 2. Students examine maps of the distribution of adult milk tolerance (lactose). These maps are available online at www.mcdonald.cam.ac.uk/genetics/khindex.html. See also the chart for different populations referred to in chapter 2. In what geographic and climatic areas of the world is lactose tolerance highest? Lowest? Evaluate climate and other environmental factors as well as food sources and dietary practices.

Step 3. Students map their tolerance for milk and their ancestry. They can do this for other family members, especially older generations.

Step 4. Discussion. Do the results fit the climate hypothesis? The dairy farming hypothesis? What else might account for lactose tolerance or intolerance?

### Activity Plan 5: Gene Flow Illustration

*Objective:* Students will understand the rapidity with which a new gene can spread through a population through mating.

*Other Information:* Time: 5–10 minutes.

*Materials:* Glitter or something that will stick to student hands but can be removed with washing. The glitter represents genes from one stranger outside the community. You could use two or three different colors to represent different genes.

*Procedure:*

Step 1. Instructions. Students (Ss) are to imagine that the teacher (T) is a stranger to the community. To meet people, T will go around and shake hands with Ss. Since people like to interact, once their hand is shaken, they will shake hands with three others Ss. No one whose hand has been shaken can participate more than once. Eventually, everyone will be contacted.

Step 2. T spreads on enough glitter so that it will "spread" when another hand is shaken. T begins by shaking hands with three students in class. The glitter should stick to hands of students but not be perceptible.

Step 3. Students proceed as outlined above, shaking hands with three other Ss. It takes very few rounds for everyone to be contacted once.

Step 4. Students examine their hands and see how quickly the "glitter" has spread. This graphically illustrates how few "handshakes" it takes for a new gene (or an STD) to spread through a population.

## Activity Idea 1: Genetic Drift and Gene Flow Illustration

For an activity that uses dried beans to illustrate these two processes, see Scott Smith's activities at www.sjsu.edu/faculty_and_staff/ faculty_detail.jsp?id = 1472.

Students can also explore genetic drift using tutorials at http:// anthro.palomar.edu/synthetic/default.htm.

## Activity Idea 2: Sickle-Cell Anemia

Explore sickle-cell anemia in more depth at the Mukherji lab, www. sicklecellinfo.net/index.htm.

## Activity Idea 3: Other Adaptations

Explore other population-level biological adaptations to environments using tutorials at http://anthro.palomar.edu/adapt/adapt_3.htm.

## Activity Idea 4: Lactose Tolerance

For additional information and research on adult milk tolerance, see www.mcdonald.cam.ac.uk/genetics/khindex.html.

## ENDNOTES

1. *Population* usually refers to a breeding population, the group that intermates, but the concept is difficult to apply to humans. Geographical or political units often serve as the population unit in actual studies (see Relethford, 2005).

2. The terms *macroevolution* and *microevolution* are often used to distinguish the scale of biological changes over time and the magnitude of the impact. For Relethford (2005), "Microevolution consists of changes in the frequency of alleles in a population from one generation to the next. Macroevolution comprises long-term patterns of genetic change over thousands and millions of generations, as well as the process of species formation" (p. 69). Yet these distinctions are rather artificial. As Kottak (2006) notes, "Macroevolution is simply the result of a lot of microevolution operating over a long time period" (p. 77). The same basic processes are involved, what is called the "modern evolutionary synthesis."

3. All humans have approximately the same number of melanocytes. But the amount of melanin produced varies. Melanin production is thought to be controlled by three to six genes (loci), each with at least two alleles. Neither allele is dominant.

Alleles code for more or less production of melanin. Each gene has an "additive" effect. The number of loci and alleles allow for a virtually infinite range of combinations and hence a continuous spectrum of skin colors. Carotene, along with hemoglobin and melanin, influences skin color (Jurmain et al., 2003).

4. Immediate tanning occurs within a couple of hours and disappears within 24 hours after exposure. Repeated exposure produces more delayed tanning, beginning within 2–3 days and reaching a maximum after 19 days, which can last as long as 9 months (Relethford, 2005, p. 194).

5. The Inuit are darker than many groups living in northerly latitudes. Jablonski and Chaplin attribute this to their relatively recent migration to the Americas (approximately 5,000 years ago) but also to their diet, rich in vitamin D from fish and cod liver oil.

6. Jablonski and Chaplin divide the Earth's surface into three vitamin D zones: tropics, subtropics and temperate zones, and circumpolar areas 45 degrees north and south latitude. The latter zone normally does not have enough UVB to initiate vitamin D synthesis and people tend to be very pale and burn easily. Those in the midregion have insufficient UV only about one month a year and hence tend to "tan." Those in high UVB synthesize vitamin D all year (Jablonski & Chaplin, 2005, p. 171).

7. Recall that indigenous populations of Southern Africa (San) and Equatorial Africans (Bantu peoples) vary substantially in skin color, reflecting natural selection and distance from the equator.

8. Malaria is still one of the major infectious diseases in the world. At least one million deaths a year are attributed to malaria (Relethford, 2005).

9. Tay-Sachs has received much attention. Marks suggests the mutant gene had a selective advantage in the TB-conducive conditions of overcrowded Eastern European Jewish ghettoes (Relethford, 2005, p. 95). Some researchers are investigating the fertility advantage for women of one sickle cell. See Relethford (2005, p. 173) for some new data on fertility rates for African American women in Mobile, Alabama, and in Costa Rica.

10. Genetic drift is "the random change in allele frequency from one generation to the next" (Relethford, 2005, p. 84). Random change refers to the absence of natural selection.

11. This is called *founders effect.* These concepts are based on probability theory. We know small samples can be quite different from the population as a whole. Over time, nonrandom traits can accumulate in a population, especially if they are neutral. Some harmful traits may also accumulate over time (Jurmain et al., 2003).

# CHAPTER 4

# More Alike Than Different, More Different Than Alike

## CONCEPTUAL OVERVIEW

This chapter brings together ideas from earlier chapters. We have shown that scientific reality often contrasts with what our culture has taught us about human biological variation. Most of us have grown up thinking that races are significant, universal, subdivisions of the human species. Historically, we were taught that noticeable variations, like skin color and eye shape, were somehow linked to other invisible but more significant differences in our bodies, even our behavioral and intellectual capacities.

Many people, including some racial scientists, once thought that biological differences between races were so great that interracial mating would not produce viable offspring. And not long ago, donors and recipients of organ transplants or blood transfusions had to be the same race. The racial biological gap was supposedly enormous and racial differences trumped all other human biological differences, even gender.

Science has come a long way in understanding human biological variation. We now know that racial markers, biologically speaking, represent a small and not very significant segment of human genetic variation. And compared to other species, we are not very genetically variable. This may be due to our recent common origins in Africa. Of the variability that exists, far more lies *within* than *between* racial groups. Most human biological variation lies at the individual level.

### There Is More Variation Within Than Between So-Called Races

We have seen in earlier chapters that so-called racial traits represent a fraction of visible human variability. Indeed, there are hundreds of slight variations in the different parts of our faces alone, much less our limbs, hands, feet, and other parts of our bodies.

Yet we've also discovered that much of human genetic variability, indeed some of the most significant, is inside the body, often invisible. Our blood, alone, has at least 13 different blood systems or factors. Many individual blood traits have several alternative forms, as in the ABO system. Some have as many as 40 different possible forms!

Given the 30,000 or so genes in the human genome, racial traits constitute only a small fraction of the total genetic variation within the human species. Moreover, as we saw in chapter 1, virtually none of the so-called racial traits, such as skin color or hair form, covary. That is, those who have paler skins or darker skins can have either curlier or straighter hair. For most of humanity, their racial group is unstable and depends on which racial trait you use!

It should not surprise us that when scientists finally began to systematically examine genetic variability within the so-called races, they found more variability *within* each racial group than *between* racial groups. Once we start looking, it does not take a sophisticated statistical analysis to discover how much visible diversity exists within each major racial group.

The major racial categories traditionally used in Europe and the United States tend to correspond to major continental land masses. These are geographical and climatically diverse, traversing thousands of miles, and crossing major climatic zones, incorporating highly variable ecological and environmental features. Within these geographic areas are millions of people, with diverse languages, political systems, cultures. Recalling from chapter 3 the impact of natural selection on populations living in different environments, as well as the genetic impact of other evolutionary forces, we would expect considerable biological variability among each of these traditional racial groups.

Take, for example, Whites, mainly Europeans and people of European ancestry. Europeans come in a myriad of sizes, shapes, colors, facial features, hair textures, lip sizes, heights, and body builds. This should not surprise us since Europe includes countries as far north as Sweden and Britain and Russia and as far south as Italy, Greece, and even Turkey. Geographically, Europe is not really a distinct continent but a rather artificial division of the Eurasian continent, with a line between Europe and Asia that shifts over time. In fact, the term Caucasian comes from the 18th-century racial classification system developed by the German anatomist, J. Blumenbach (see chapter 6), and originally included people from the Ukraine, Georgia, Saudi Arabia, Afghanistan, and North India.

The Asian racial category is equally huge and heterogeneous. South Asia, alone, incorporates at least India, Bangladesh, Burma, Nepal, Sri Lanka, and Pakistan. East Asia ranges from Korea, Japan, and China to Vietnam, Cambodia, Thailand, and Indonesia. India and China, each with over 1 billion people, represent a myriad of geographic regions and physically variable ethnic groups, nationalities, and languages. And then there are the almost 1 billion people in Indonesia, Malaysia, and Singapore. Moving west, it is difficult to discern the boundaries of Asia and the Asian race. Should we include the Philippines, New Guinea, and other Pacific Islands, like Fiji and Hawaii?

When we turn to the racial category of Black, we find enormous geographic and human variability. Africa, alone, has desert, mountains, oceans, tropical areas, and spans a range of latitudes, some quite distant from the equator. Africa also contains more human genetic diversity than any other geographic area in the world! The longer a population has been in a region, that is, the more ancient the population, the more genetic variability exists. This is partially because mutations accumulate over time and because it takes time for natural selection to produce variability.

Africa, as the oldest site of modern humans, is the most genetically variable of all regions (Relethford, 2005, p. 430). Africa is home to the shortest and the tallest people of the world. The Mbuti of the Congo in Central Africa average under 5 feet. The Tutsi of Rwanda average around 6 feet 1 inch. Other traits vary as well, including skin color, ABO blood systems, nose shapes, body shapes, even the frequency of the sickle cell and lactose (milk) tolerance, as we saw in chapter 3.

Our quick review of easily identifiable human variation suggests there is much variability within the major racial groups and the geographic regions they (or their ancestors) have inhabited in the past. But new advances in DNA analysis, as we saw in chapters 2 and 3, suggest there is far more human variability at the invisible level, in our DNA.

So how much of this is racial? How biologically similar are these traditional macroracial groups?

### Lewontin's Analysis of Human Biological Variation

The past three decades have produced a wealth of new and increasingly sophisticated scientific studies designed to evaluate exactly how much human biological variation is racial. Statistical analysis is used to analyze population data on selected genetic traits. The total variability in the entire data set is calculated and then the amount of variability found *within* each sample population is compared to the variability *between* populations.

Population geneticist Richard Lewontin's now-classic study (1972) was the first to apply this new approach. He focused on blood, one of the most significant forms of genetic variation. At the time of his research, there were no methods available for analyzing the underlying genetic information directly. Instead, researchers relied on the expressed form of the trait, in this case blood. Fortunately, blood samples are easy to collect and available from all over the world. Lewontin analyzed 17 different biochemical markers found in the blood, using existing studies on diverse populations. His data included information on nine blood groups and on eight serum proteins and enzymes in red blood cells (Brown & Armelagos, 2001).

Lewontin immediately confronted a major issue—how was he to define a race? What real populations, nationalities, ethnic groups, or regions would be included in each racial category? His solution was to first create a system of macroracial groupings, seven major geographical areas that roughly corresponded to distinct continents or regions of the world. A second level of analysis focused on biological variation within each of the major regions. Lewontin recognized that each geographic region was diverse and so he sampled a variety of populations from each of the seven geographic areas (see Table 4.1).

Lewontin first calculated the total genetic variability found in these 17 traits for all world regions combined. He then asked, how much of this total human variability is accounted for by the continental races, that is, by these seven regional divisions of the human species? Surprisingly, he found that only 6.3% of the total genetic variation was due to

**Table 4.1.  Populations used in Lewontin's Population Genetics Study**

| Geographical Group | Some Populations Included |
| --- | --- |
| Caucasians | Arabs, Armenians, Tristan De Cunha |
| Black Africans | Bantu, San, U.S. African Americans |
| Asians | Ainu, Chinese, Turks |
| South Asians | Andamanese, Tamils |
| Amerinds | Aleuts, Navaho, Yanomama |
| Oceanians | Easter Islanders, Micronesians |
| Australians | All treated as a group |

Source:  Data originally from Lewontin (1972), abstracted from Jurmain et al. (2003, p. 398).

the differences *between* major geographic continental regions. Approximately 94% of the total human genetic diversity occurred *within* the seven major geographical subdivisions (Jurmain et al., 2003, pp. 397–398). In short, barely 6% of genetic variation was what is conventionally called racial. The rest was nonracial, representing diversity among people within the same macroracial group!

Lewontin's second level of analysis examined the smaller ethnic or national populations within each continental region. For example, within the Caucasian category, he did separate analyses of Welsh, Basques, Armenians, and so forth. He reasoned these groups would show more internal genetic similarity than what he had found in the macroregional races. Yet, once again, he found more genetic diversity *within* each subregional population than *between* the populations! These more localized racial groups counted for only an additional 8.3 percent of the total human genetic variation.

Lewontin discovered how little of human genetic variation is racial, whether one looks at continental races or at more localized subregional populations. Even when he *added* the variability between geographically localized nationalities *and* the variability between the seven continental geographic populations, the total percentage accounted for scarcely 15% of all human genetic diversity. The vast majority of human genetic variation, the remaining 85%, was not racial, regional, or ethnic. The lesson was clear. Most of human genetic variability exists *within* nationalities, within ethnic groups, within villages, within kinship groups, and even within families.

Lewontin's evidence clearly established that traditional racial categories barely touched the surface of human biological diversity. The concept of race was biologically virtually meaningless, inadequate for describing or providing insights into human genetic diversity. Indeed, Lewontin argued that using racial classifications hindered rather than advanced our understanding of human genetic variation, and he advocated abandoning them in biological studies. "Since such racial classification is now seen to be of virtually no genetic or taxonomic significance either, no justification can be offered for its continuance" (Jurmain et al., 2003, p. 398, citing Lewontin, 1972, p. 397).

Subsequent studies have replicated these findings. A 1980 study by Latter analyzed a similar set of genetic markers but used six major geographical groups instead of seven. Latter divided each major area into four geographical regions and then created further population subdivisions within each region. This provided three levels of population structure to analyze.

Latter found that 7.5% to 10.4% of genetic variability (depending on the trait) was attributable to the major racial-type geographical groups. Of the balance remaining, 83.8% to 87% of the total variation was the result of individual differences *within* populations! The remaining 5.5% to 6.6% of genetic diversity was found in differences between smaller populations and regions.

In 1982, Nei and Roy Choudhury examined 23 blood groups and 62 variant forms of proteins for "Caucasoid," "Negroid," and "Mongoloid" populations. Only about 10% of the genetic variability was accounted for by racial differences. Ryman and coworkers replicated these findings using a slightly different set of blood and protein markers and new analytical methods, called *dendrograms,* for representing their results (Brown & Armelagos, 2001, pp. 35–36).

**Recent Studies Using DNA Analyses to Establish Common Ancestry**

Recent research provides additional insights into human biological variability. These studies have looked directly at the entire human genome, that is, all the DNA in a human. To do this, they rely on tiny variations in the DNA, what we called *polymorphisms* in chapter 2, except these are very, very tiny DNA sequences and often have no function.

These slight variations in sequences of DNA are part of our biological heritage because they are transmitted from one generation to another. Their presence reflects our common ancestry and ancestral history. Sometimes variations reflect ancestral historical processes related to natural selection, as we saw in chapter 3, when we talked about skin color and variations in blood systems, like the sickle-cell trait. Or we may have inherited these particular DNA versions as a result of other evolutionary processes.

Some variations are genetic, that is, they affect traits such as skin color, blood type, or susceptibility to various diseases. Most are not genetic. Rather, they occur in the remainder of our DNA that does not have any known biological function. In fact, as noted in chapter 2, scientists estimate that between 98 and 99% of DNA is not genetic. This is the portion that used to be called junk DNA.

New technology has allowed us to explore the remainder of this DNA, the most invisible kind (see chapter 2). Scientists have found ways to essentially cut the DNA into small pieces so that they can look directly at the exact sequence of chemical base pairs at particular points or locations. These same sequences can then be compared among different individuals. And it is now easy to collect DNA samples, using hair samples or cheek swabs.

What scientists are finding is not junk, at least not in an informational sense. In fact, this new DNA is providing extraordinary insights into exactly how similar—and how variable—we are as a species, as groups with common ancestry, and as individuals.

## Variability for Variability's Sake

With the complete identification (sequencing) of the human genome, geneticists have identified millions of DNA sequences that vary in minute ways. These sequences exist in both the mitochondrial DNA and in the larger portion of DNA in the cell nucleus.

One kind of variation is called *microsatellite DNA*. These are repeated short sections of DNA with only two to five bases. Remember that there are over 3 billion base pairs in the nuclear DNA of a human. So these are very small segments, indeed. And there are lots of them!

Some repetitions of these minute segments of DNA occur only a few times but in other cases they may be repeated hundreds of times. One type of analysis simply counts the number of repeats. For example, the DNA sequence CACACACACA contains five repeats of the CA sequence, and the DNA sequence CACACA contains three repeats. The number of repeats can be used to compare individuals (Relethford, 2005).

These microsatellites are extraordinarily variable, differing significantly from one person to another. In fact, every individual apparently has a distinctive pattern or arrangement of these repetitions, providing each of us with a unique DNA fingerprint (Jurmain et al., 2003). This enables forensic scientists to accurately identify individual human remains, whether at the scene of crimes or at major disasters, such as the 2005 hurricane that flooded New Orleans.

There are other longer sequences of DNA that are exactly alike in individuals except for a single base pair that differs. These are called SNPs (*single-nucleotide polymorphisms*). This type of variability is quite common. Scientists have identified between 1.4 and 2.1 million in the human genome (Relethford, 2005, p. 129). The presence of so many SNPs allows scientists to examine them for linkages with various traits, including traits that affect one's susceptibility to disease.

So . . . variability exists at a level previously unimagined. But virtually none has any impact on the human body, on our physical traits, whether visible or invisible. Most of our DNA is just filled with slightly different combinations and permutations with little biological significance—except that they are fascinating to study!

Because these sequences have no known biological impact, they are not subject to the process of natural selection. So these so-called *neutral polymorphisms* make excellent indicators of common ancestry. They occur in frequencies and locations that are specific to particular lineages and populations. They can be used to create ancestral trees of relatedness among individuals or different populations.

For example, *Alu* are short pieces of DNA that have a similar sequence or order of base pairs. These pieces, or rather copies of them, have a tendency to move around. Sometimes a piece will copy and insert itself, at random, into a new position on the same or on another chromosome. Usually this produces no biological impact even if there are genes nearby.

But each insertion is a unique event and the particular sequence (and its location) remains in place and is transmitted from one generation to another. So this tiny piece of DNA, with its special location, gives us a wonderful marker of common ancestry. If two people have the same *Alu* sequence at the same spot in their genome, we can infer that they share a common ancestor from whom they inherited that piece of DNA (Bamshad & Olson, 2003).

These tiny, biologically neutral, but ancestral DNA markers have given geneticists a wealth of data to mine. Estimates indicate that approximately 5% of human DNA consists of these types of elements (Relethford, 2005, p. 129). Recent work uses anywhere from a few to as many as 75–100 different *Alu* to estimate the closeness of ancestral relationships between individuals . . . and between different small populations of individuals.

Researchers are finding, not surprisingly, that populations that have been relatively isolated from each other geographically and historically show different frequencies of these DNA sequences. Individuals who have long resided in a particular region, or even separate populations within a country, tend to share particular *Alu* sequences not found in populations in other regions.

### Population Differences: We're More Different Than Alike

The type of studies described above work best with populations that are relatively isolated. The vast majority of the world, however, has been interacting rather intensely the last several thousands of years. This makes it more difficult to find population-specific DNA clusters . . . especially when one examines large populations. When geneticists examined 100 *Alu* in a sample of South Indians, they could not find enough similarities among individuals to characterize them as a distinct ancestral cluster (Bamshad & Olson, 2003, p. 82). Instead, the results reflected what anthropologists and historians have long known: that South India consists of a myriad of populations who have been mating with a myriad of other populations for a long time!

Some analyses of natural, nongenetic, inherited DNA sequences produce regional clusters of populations with shared *Alu* or DNA sequences. However, these are not biological races in the traditional sense. Nor are these genetically significant subdivisions of even national or regional populations. What we are seeing, once again, is the impact of common ancestry, of generations of mating and marrying. But the shared ancestral portion in any individual represents only a tiny fraction of the over 3 billion base pairs that make up the totality of the human genome, of our DNA.

## We Are More Different Than Alike, Even With Common Ancestors.

Recent studies, then, using modern technology to study both mitochondrial and nuclear DNA, reinforce Lewontin's initial 1972 findings. There is more variability within than between human populations. As much as 98% of human biological variation may lie within (versus between) geographic populations or races.[1]

But it is not just large-scale populations that show more variability within than between groups. Relethford (2005) found significant genetic variability among Irish populations living in different counties in the same general region. At virtually every level of analysis, whether the unit of study is an entire continent, a region, a linguistic or ethnic group within a region, small town, or village, or a large multigenerational family, with long-standing ancestral ties, we find more variability within than between groups.

One of the most exciting discoveries of the Human Genome Project is how much variability there is at the individual level, in the DNA of every person. We are all, or almost all of us, biologically unique. This enables us to do the kind of DNA analysis used in crime studies. Sometimes it is used to identify the victim, and in other cases to identify who else was present at the scene, including the perpetrator of the crime. But all involve matching DNA samples, comparing the DNA from the crime scene with the DNA of a known individual. It is the uniqueness of each individual's DNA that allows us to compare two DNA samples and say, with very high statistical probability, whether or not the two samples could have come from the same individual.

Of course, as we have already noted, virtually all of the genetic variability exists at the individual level. And most lies in the vast landscape of the DNA that is not genetically meaningful, that does not carry the instructions for making proteins and tissues, that does not, as far as we know, have a biological impact. So, from a DNA perspective, we are truly individuals.

One large-scale study (Jia & Chakravarty, 1993) examined DNA markers for 59 different populations. The authors found that up to 98.5% of the variation occurred within populations at the individual level. In the words of geneticist Michael Cummings, "These results indicate that individual variation in DNA profiles overwhelm any interpopulation differences, no matter how the populations are ethnically or racially classified" (cited by Jurmain et al., 2003, p. 398).

Clearly, common ancestry does produce similarities at the DNA level, at the genetic level, and in some physical traits. But it is a minute fraction of the total genetic variation in our species. And DNA we share with our ancestors is mainly nongenetic DNA, that is, the DNA that has no impact on our biology, behavior, or capacities. In short, ancestral groups are genetically rather meaningless!

Even when DNA sequences can be used to reconstruct ancestral populations or trees, these groups bear little resemblance to North American races. They are local geographic populations or local ethnic groups, and there are hundreds, if not thousands, of them. They do not reflect any fundamental biological subdivisions of the human species. Nor do these analyses provide any support for the assertion that common ancestry determines ones' behavioral, intellectual, or any other human capacity.[2]

## We Are All Alike Because We Have a Common Ancestor—in Africa

When we think about, it is not so surprising that most human variation occurs within small populations, within kinship groups, at the individual level. The story of our species, as we have said, has been primarily one of intermating between groups, of migration, of constant contact rather than isolation, of continuing gene flow. This is why we have remained a single species, with relatively little genetic variability compared to other species, and with most of that genetic variability found within rather than between populations.

The unity of the human species goes back to Africa. Scientific evidence has conclusively established that modern humans (*Homo sapien sapiens*) evolved in Africa, around 100,000 to 200,000 years ago. This is called the "Out of Africa" or *African replacement model* of human evolution.

Until recently, there was a rival theory, the so-called *multiregional hypothesis*. According to this theory, modern humans evolved in many different regions of the world from an earlier form, *Homo erectus*, which existed at least a million years ago. These regional populations were largely isolated from each other and evolved separately, but in parallel fashion, into modern humans at about the same time. As a result, they developed distinctive biological features that today we think of as racial differences.

Recent evidence overwhelmingly supports the Out of Africa or African replacement model over the multiregional theory. According to Pat Shipman (2005), a prominent anthropologist, fossil evidence clearly points to East Africa generally, and Ethiopia and the Sudan specifically, as the sites of the oldest modern human lineages and as the home of all of our ancestors.

In addition, analysis of mitochondrial DNA supports the Out of Africa theory. Mitochondrial DNA can be used to establish approximate ages of lineages, that is, how far back in time they go. Assuming constant rates of mutation, scientists can use the amount of variation in the mtDNA to estimate the approximate dates of origins of a population. Scientists examined mtDNA from five contemporary East African populations. Their data indicated that the oldest lineages go back some 170,000 years ago, so the earliest modern humans originated in Africa.

While these studies established the presence of modern humans in Africa, they do not preclude the possibility of simultaneous evolution in other parts of the world. Multiregionalists have argued that Neanderthal-form skeletal remains found in Europe were ancestors of modern Europeans. To test this theory, scientists compared the mtDNA from more than 2,000 people around the world with ancient mtDNA from a Neanderthal specimen, the hypothesized ancestors of Europeans, according to multiregionalists. Contrary to the multiregional hypothesis, the Neanderthal mtDNA was no more similar to modern Europeans than to any other geographical group. These findings support the theory of a single origin for modern humans, in Africa.

Modern genetics has allowed us to document and trace the migration of the human species out of Africa. We are one species that emerged in Africa and radiated across the globe, mating with each other along the way. All of the genetic diversity found in the world's population is found in Africa. There have never been any biological races, any distinct subdivisions of our species, and there are none now. All modern humans have the same biological structure and the same capacities. We have the same reproductive capacities, the same intellectual capacities, the same emotional and behavioral capacities.

Most genetic variation among humans has little to do with what we think of as racial traits and much human biological variation is invisible. There is far more genetic variation within so-called racial groups than the variation that exists between these groups. And while people with common ancestry do show some similarities in DNA sequences, these hereditary features are overwhelmingly found in the nonfunctional part of the human genome. In essence, the similarities between people of common ancestry are for the most part biologically irrelevant. Race, then, is not biologically real or meaningful. It neither accurately describes nor provides many insights into human biological variation. But if race is biological fiction, then what have we been experiencing that we call race? How are we to understand race? We turn to these questions in part 2.

## KEY CONCEPTUAL POINTS

- There is only one modern human species and it evolved in Africa. All modern human populations are subsets of this single African lineage. And there are hundreds and thousands of such populations. There are no distinct archaic races, which evolved separately, in different regions of the world.
- Racial traits represent a fraction of total human genetic variation. Knowing someone's race tells us virtually nothing about that person's biology, DNA, or behavioral or intellectual capacities.

- There is far more variation *within* than *between* racial groups
- Human biological variation exists but mainly at the individual level and in nonfunctional portions of our DNA.
- Common ancestry produces DNA similarities but mainly in the nonfunctional DNA and has virtually no genetic impact.
- Most human biological variation exists at the individual level, *within* families, kin groups, and communities. There are more differences within than between small populations.

**KEY TERMS (ITALICIZED AND BOLDED IN TEXT)**

*Alu*                                    "Out of Africa" or African
microsatellite DNA                          replacement model
multiregional hypothesis                 single-nucleotide polymorphisms
neutral polymorphisms

**TEACHING ACTIVITIES**

These activities provide a summarizing experience for students and build on material in earlier chapters. The first two draw on two teaching activities in the excellent companion website to the film *Race: The Power of an Illusion.*

**Activity Plan 1: Human Biological Variation. More Alike Than Different?**

*Objective:* Students will discover there is more variability within than between racial groups.
*Additional Information:* Go into the teaching module, "The Empirical Challenges of Racial Classification" at www.pbs.org/race/000_ About/002_04-teachers-04.htm.
*Procedure:*
Step 1. Students create a list of visible and invisible genetic traits, drawing on earlier chapters and online websites mentioned.
Step 2. Reduce list to about 10 traits (including some invisible traits) that students can describe in themselves and/or classmates and

perhaps family members. This is harder for invisible traits, like ABO blood group. Create a matrix of these traits (see the above website for samples).

Step 3. Divide students into racial groups. You can use the 2000 Census categories (see above website link). Do not force multiracials to select one category. They can create a separate "multiracial" category if they wish. If you have virtually no racial diversity, use religion or gender as the basis for groupings. Using gender groups can cause students to critically evaluate the "Opposite Sex" theory of gender (Mukhopadhyay, 2004a).

Step 4. Students assess themselves on each item on the chart of traits.

Step 5. Each group summarizes the data for their racial group (counts or frequencies/percentages). Compare groups' results. Students should discover that there is more variability within than between the groups.

Step 6. Proceed to the DNA sampling exercise (see website reference in Activity Plan 2).

**Activity Plan 2: Race and DNA: Who Am I More Alike?**

*Objective:* Same as for Activity 1.

*Additional Information:* This is the module "Comparing mtDNA Sequences to Learn About Human Variation" accessed at www.pbs .org/race/000_About/002_04-teachers-03.htmp.

Students compare how similar they are biologically using mitochondrial DNA samples. They can use this data to analyze their relative biological similarity to people of the same race (religion, ethnicity, ancestry, gender) in their classroom. Version 1, more complicated, requires collection of DNA samples. Version 2 uses existing online databases.

*Version 1:* Comparing Individual DNA Samples. Students collect their own DNA samples, following the process depicted in the film, *Race: The Power of an Illusion.* The film clip is available online. Students use swabs to collect mouth saliva and analyze their DNA vis-à-vis the worldwide sample of DNA in the database at the Cold Springs laboratory in Colorado. For more information, see the website www

.dnalc.org, Dolan DNA Learning Center, Cold Spring Harbor Laboratory, Cold Spring Harbor, NY.

*Version 2:* Comparing Mitochondrial DNA Using Online Global Samples. Students compare public sequence files from different world populations to gain an understanding of human genetic variation. For detailed information, see the website links at www.pbs.org/wgbh/nova/neanderthals/mtdna.html, "Tracing Ancestry With mtDNA" from NOVA Online.

**Activity Plan 3: Sorting Into Races**

*Objective:* Students will understand that racial classification based on visual appearance is often not possible, partially because race is a social category and we use social criteria to race people. Students will understand the distinction between self-identification and external imposition of categories.

*Additional Information.* This also comes from the *Race: The Power of an Illusion* website. It is an interactive computer-based activity, "The Sorting People Interactivity." Students will either need Web access or the teacher can download the images from the website.

*Procedure:*

Step 1. In the "Sorting People Interactivity" (www.pbs.org/race/002_SortingPeople/002_01-sort.htm), students first sort 20 pictures of people into racial categories using U.S. Census categories. In part 2, the Human Diversity Interactivity (www.pbs.org/race/002_SortingPeople/002_02-traits.htm), students sort these folks by three other traits: Skin color (four categories), fingerprints (four types), and ABO blood types. The faces light up for each version of the inherited traits. You see, visually, how different are the categorizations using these other genetic criteria. It's particularly useful for racially/ethnically homogeneous classes.

Step 2. Discuss reasons for any surprises. Reflect on the meaning of race and racial markers. Discuss nonphysical markers students may use to "race" other people like speech, clothing, social context, situational context features, hair style, material items, or body movements. This leads into part 2 and part 3, especially chapters 10 and 12.

**Activity Plan 4: The Story of Desiree's Baby**

This activity is from the website of *Race: The Power of an Illusion* at www.pbs.org/race/000_About/002_04-teachers-06.htm.
*Objectives:* Students will understand that the meaning of race is primarily social not biological. Students will be able to describe the biological inheritance of skin color.
*Additional Information.* This detailed lesson plan can be used in two ways: to introduce the social meaning of race (parts 2 and 3) and to explore the genetics of skin color. The activity begins with a short story by Kate Chopin published in 1893 entitled "Desiree's Baby." The story makes a poignant statement about racism. In doing so, it illustrates how skin color is not mainly about biology but about the meanings individuals, society, and culture give to skin color. The second part goes into greater depth on the genetics of skin color (see chapter 3).

Instructors can also introduce *culturally rooted* environmental factors that influence skin color. These include the type of work one does (farming or other outdoors activities vs. factory, computer, or other indoors work), various recreational activities, cosmetic products that can either lighten, darken, or in other ways affect skin color, and the recent popularity, among some U.S. Americans, of the tanning salon.

**Activity Idea 1: Explore Our African Ancestor—Eve**

This activity reviews the origins of modern humans models, mentioned in this chapter, at http://anthro.palomar.edu/hom02/mod_homo_4.htm. The regional continuity model on the website is similar to the multiregional evolution model in this chapter. The site also includes a "Late Breaking News" section in Modeling Human Evolution.

For more about the mitochondrial Eve theory and the inheritance of mitochondrial DNA through the maternal line on "Tracing Ancestry With mtDNA" from NOVA Online, see www.pbs.org/wgbh/nova/neanderthals/mtdna.html.

**Activity Idea 2: Exploring My Ancestry**

For more details, see the Mukhopadhyay website at www.sjsu.edu/ faculty_and_staff/faculty_detail.jsp?id = 1472.

Students explore their own ancestry (see also part 2), trying to find the home countries or regions of their biological ancestors. By family "ancestry," tell students it means where their ancestors came from before they were in the United States. Remind them that everyone except Native American Indians are relative newcomers to the Americas. That is, they have come within approximately the last 400 years. Most students will have multiple ancestral origins. Encourage them to find out the region as well as countries of their ancestors, especially since most nations are recent or their boundaries have often changed. For students whose ancestors are unknown, they could work with another student or interview someone with known ancestors (see chapter 3, Activity Information).

Students, perhaps in conjunction with part 2 activities, could map their family geographic ancestry more carefully, using information from family history interviews they conduct and from a family kinship chart they construct (see part 2). Students could focus initially on ancestors in the direct line of descent—parent-child (parents' parents, parents' parents' parents'). They will have a maternal line and a paternal line of descent at each generation. They could eventually expand their network to nonlineals (e.g., siblings of parents and grandparents, and their descendents). See the Mukhopadhyay website mentioned above for more details.

If this is done in conjunction with "The Ethnic Me" in part 2, students could also trace marriage patterns to see to what extent their ancestors married "out" with regard to region, ethnicity, religion, education, or other local social criteria that affected marriage.

Once students have some idea of a family tree, regardless of how crude or small, they can apply several of the activities in part 1 to their relatives. For example, they could literally map ABO blood types, body shapes, skin color, or nose form onto geographic origins of relatives. They could also look at environmental influences, such as the effect of diet on height, by comparing heights of different generations of their relatives.

**Activity Idea 3: Additional Resources**

Explore additional resources for teachers at the Hampshire College website, www.hampshire.edu/cms/index.php?id = 3441&PHPSESSID = 5ad9dbfc19a6879dfaad7cfb0024d58a.

## ENDNOTES

1. Some geneticists, such as Jeffrey C. Long, have criticized Lewontin's approach. For an accessible article, see Long (2004).

2. This is a controversial area of research because some geneticists persist in generalizing to macroracial groups, such as Europeans, Asians, Africans, even when their data come from much smaller regional populations (e.g., Northern Italians, Scottish, Northern Greeks, Mbuti Pygmies, Nigerian Ibos, South Indian Tamils).

# Part 2

# CULTURE CREATES RACE—INTRODUCTION

Race may be a biological fiction, as we have shown in part 1. But that doesn't mean race doesn't exist. Race is a social and cultural reality and profoundly impacts our lives.[1]

Most people recognize that race in the United States is real! And most U.S. Americans probably *experience* race as a social (rather than biological) reality. Educators (and even students) may have been introduced to the concept of race as a social or cultural *construct* or race as socially or culturally *constructed.*

But the idea that race is a human invention, a social construction, a cultural creation, is complex and difficult to communicate. There is particular resistance to the idea that race is *only* a cultural construct. Race seems so real! How could race be a pure invention?

In part 2 we identify and address some key barriers to understanding race as a cultural construct and social invention. Each chapter provides both conceptual background materials and illustrative teaching-oriented activities.

## CULTURE IS REAL

What does it mean to say that race is a cultural creation? To understand this, students must understand the concept of culture and how profoundly culture shapes reality. Culture shapes every aspect of human experience . . . what we hear, smell, taste, feel, and see. It structures our social world and social interactions. The human world is largely a cultural and social invention—but one that is very real. Race, too, is a cultural invention—but it is experientially, emotionally, cognitively real, deeply internalized in our psyche. Chapter 5 addresses the concept of culture.

Race is also a system of classification, a culturally and historically specific way of categorizing human beings. Like other human creations, classifications shape how we experience reality. Chapter 6 first traces the role of classification in human life and then focuses on the U.S. system of racial classification.

## RACE IS ABOUT POWER AND INEQUALITY

Race is not simply a cultural or psychological phenomenon. It emerged in a context of unequal power relations, as an ideology to legitimize the dominance of certain groups. Race, then, is fundamentally part of a system of stratification and inequality.

Students indoctrinated in U.S. individualism often have difficulty understanding abstract notions of a social system, social stratification, and how one's social position impacts individual experience and opportunities. Chapter 7 addresses these issues and suggests activities to help students see how systems of social (and racial) inequality function.

## RACE SHIFTS OVER TIME

U.S. racial categories, even if not universal and natural, are often seen as permanent fixtures of our history and culture. But long-standing and deeply embedded cultural inventions can be reinvented, altered, dismantled, or reconfigured to accommodate changing circumstances. We show, in chapter 7, how American racial categories have shifted over time, in different political contexts, and are continuing to do so today. We want students to realize that the future of race in the U.S. is at least partially in their hands.

## RACE IS NOT UNIVERSAL OR INEVITABLE

A long-standing U.S. assumption is that race, racial discrimination, race-based hierarchy, or something similar is a universal, pan-human phenomenon, indeed "built into our genes" as humans. Chapter 8 surveys the anthropological evidence and concludes this is one more longstanding and convenient myth.

## RACE AND BIOLOGY

In addressing race as a cultural or social invention, we must ask, where does biology fit? There is a mistaken notion that because races are not biologically real, there is no biology associated with U.S. racial categories. But race is a cultural phenomenon and biological markers of race are embedded in, shaped by, and experienced in a cultural context. Chapter 9 deals with the cultural creation of biological markers of race and how biological processes (mating, reproduction) have been manipulated to maintain the social reality we call race.

## ENDNOTES

1. Social scientists often use the terms *cultural* and *social* interchangeably. To anthropologists, cultural (*culture*) is broader and includes shared beliefs systems and other cultural knowledge. The term *social* focuses more on society, social identities, and social institutions such as the family and the law.

# CHAPTER 5

# Culture Shapes How We Experience Reality

Students often think they know what *culture* is. They've heard the word and their schools may have tried to address cultural diversity. They've attended cultural heritage celebrations, eaten ethnic foods, and experienced the music and dance of other cultures. From an anthropological perspective, however, this only taps the surface of the phenomenon we call culture.

A deeper understanding of culture is necessary if students are to grasp the meaning—and power—of race as a cultural construction. This chapter starts with examples that are deliberately socially neutral, like greeting behaviors, food, and language. Our first goal is for students to experience the power of culture in their daily lives . . . to have a minor *culture shock* when they realize they are not experiencing the world directly. We have found this a useful prelude to discussions about the idea that racial classifications and associated racial markers, like skin color, are cultural inventions rather than natural. It also prepares students to understand how racial categories act like other cultural preconceptions, affecting our perceptions of people. What we notice (e.g., skin color) and how we interpret what we see is powerfully influenced by culture.

## CONCEPTUAL BACKGROUND

### The Concept of Culture

There have been numerous attempts to define culture precisely (whole volumes) yet no single definition adequately expresses the complexity of the concept. The one thing all definitions have in common is that culture is *learned*. We are not born with a particular culture. We acquire culture as an integral part of our development within one or more human communities.

For many people, anthropology is archeology and since archeologists study culture, culture must be material artifacts. But if we think for a moment about most material things, such as a wedding ring, a Valentine's Day card, or a clock, it is clear that there is more to what makes these "cultural" than their physical form. An archeologist from Mars would have difficulty identifying that metal band around the third finger of the left hand as a "wedding ring." Indeed, the concept of a "wedding" and a "wedding ring" would require explanation.

Spradley and McCurdy (2000) define *culture* as *shared knowledge*. This moves beyond the concrete to focus on what Mukhopadhyay has called the *mental products of culture* (Hernández and Mukhopadhyay, 1985). Both definitions emphasize the intangible aspects of culture—the collective, shared understandings in our heads; the culturally rooted beliefs, theories, worldviews, and values; the meanings we have learned to associate with material objects. This culturally shared knowledge is actually stored in our brains—-as what psychological anthropologists call *schemata* or *cultural models* (see Strauss & Quinn, 1997). These schema provide interpretive guides for everyday experience.

But culture is more than mental products. Culture includes observable patterned behavior, such as greetings—hugs, handshakes, waves, kisses, high-fives, and less friendly gestures. It encompasses more elaborate culturally shared patterns such as "eating dinner" or "basketball games" or rituals such as "weddings" or "bar mitzvahs." Most of our actions—whether minute or elaborate sequences of events—are guided, without thinking, by culturally shared ways of behaving.

As we think about how much of what we do is cultural and learned, we realize that cultures create ways of grouping human beings, what social scientists call *social organization, social groups,* and *social roles.* To understand a wedding, we'd have to be familiar with how our society organizes people into groups like "families," some who live together ("husband," "wife," but not usually "aunts" or "cousins"). We'd have to know about other social creations, like churches, temples, governments, courts, and social roles like "priest," "rabbi," "best man," and "judges." Our working lives, especially as educators, are spent immersed in another cultural creation—schools—with their associated social groups—teachers, students, administrators, custodians, clerical staff . . . and rituals like "assemblies" and "graduation" and "tests."

While we are able to observe culturally shared social and behavioral products, such as hugs and schools, they are linked to and made meaningful by cultural knowledge that cannot be seen. This information—scripts, concepts, understandings, values, meanings—lies inside our heads, stored in our brains, along with other acquired information that enables us to function effectively and appropriately in our culture.

In short, we are immersed in a world of *cultural products* of all types—most which are intangible, many which cannot be observed, and all profoundly shaping how we experience reality. For this reason, Mukhopadhyay prefers to define culture simply as what human groups collectively create, recognizing that these products include material, behavioral, social, and mental products.

**Culture as a Symbolic System**

To many anthropologists, culture is first and foremost a *symbolic system*. Humans possess the ability to bestow meanings on things in the world, to take an object that has no intrinsic meaning—like a band of metal or a set of sounds ("dawg")—and arbitrarily imbue it with meaning. Individuals can create their own private and unique symbols—small children often do that, inventing new combinations of sounds to label objects or people. But culture consists of more widely shared symbols—-collectively shared meanings that entire groups of people associate with things in their world.

In the United States, a circle of gold on the third finger of the left hand ("the ring finger") means that one is "married"; a green light at a street means "go ahead," a red light means "stop." Most religions use material objects to convey religious meanings or identities: a star, a cross, a prayer rug, or even a woman's head scarf. Ethnic, adolescent, occupational, or other social groups often use clothing or greeting behaviors as markers of group identity.

As with all symbols, the relationship between the object and its meaning is *arbitrary* rather than a property of the object. A gold band does not intrinsically mean marriage. Low-slung baggy pants have no

inherent meanings. The links—the meanings—are cultural and historical creations. The object has become a symbol of something else. A
different object could symbolize marital status or peer group identity,
such as a ring in the right ear lobe.

It is not just material objects that function as symbols. Cultures also
bestow meanings on gestures and bodily movements in a way that is
quite arbitrary. Think for a second about how you greet a friend. You
might wave your right hand, you might both clasp hands, you might
give the friend a "hug" or a "kiss." All are culturally appropriate
greeting devices that also carry more complex information about you
and your relationship to this person.

They are also intrinsically meaningless gestures. A Martian could
not interpret their meaning! Nor could someone from a culture that
used other greeting gestures (e.g., stroking ears). Our culture uses, in
court, a bent vertical arm with palm facing away from the body to symbolize that one is "swearing to tell the truth." A totally arbitrary meaning has been linked to a body movement enacted in a specific social
setting.

Normally, we are unaware that most behaviors (or other symbols)
have two parts: the behavior and the meaning culture has attached to it.
Once we've learned the linkages, we internalize them and forget they
are arbitrary. The symbol becomes unified and we experience it as natural. In a new culture, however, the arbitrariness of the linkages is striking! We neither know nor can easily guess the meaning of a slap on the
back or a set of unfamiliar sounds.

Virtually any aspect of human sensory experience can function as
*meaning-carrying vehicles.* Cultures have bestowed meanings on
sounds, smells, tastes, touch, colors, shapes, and designs and on visible
human physical characteristics. The links are not intrinsic but cultural.
Whether the smell of a steak cooking on a barbecue evokes tasty
images or the burning flesh of a slaughtered, innocent cow depends on
culturally created linkages. Smell and taste have been filtered through
culture. Sight too has been filtered. The meanings of skin color, a fleshy
belly, a sharp nose, or other physical features are not intrinsic but cultural and historical creations.

Culture then can be thought of as a complex symbolic system. Language, as part of culture, exemplifies the symbolic complexity of cul-

ture. Sounds and combinations of sounds acquire, in a rather unpredictable fashion, meanings that are agreed upon and shared by users. Whether the sounds "dawg" or the sounds "perro" are used to represent a particular four-legged animal is arbitrary and a historical-cultural-linguistic phenomenon.[1] But once linkages are learned, hearing the sounds evokes the visual image almost automatically. By the time children are 5 years old and ready to enter school, they have learned at least one language, that is, one set of extremely complex and arbitrary associations between sounds and meanings.

Writing, if you think about it, is another set of arbitrary designs cultures have created to represent sounds and numbers. That's why there are so many different scripts or writing systems, virtually all mutually unintelligible—"scribbles." Yet by the time students have left the first grade, those scribbles have acquired some culturally shared meanings, such as "a," "b," "c," etc.

Early in school, children encounter one more complex cultural symbol—a "clock." In the classic analog clock, we see the concept of time represented in arbitrary objects and designs, with "hands" and "numbers" representing the units of time. But the clock also reflects a rather arbitrary division of "time." A day, which has some basis in reality, is arbitrarily divided into 24 "hours." Each hour consists, arbitrarily, of 60 "minutes" and each minute "60 seconds."

Learning to "tell time" is not a trivial accomplishment in such an arbitrary system. Moreover, children have to learn the concept of a week—that is, that there is a larger 7-day unit, consisting of 5 workdays and a "weekend." Not all cultures have a 7-day week, although small cultures with 4-day weeks are disappearing.

Culture, then, is filled with arbitrary culturally shared symbols that differ from one culture to another, and which we must learn if we are to function in our culture. Amazingly, we manage to learn them, beginning at birth and throughout childhood and adolescence, and, at a less intense pace, throughout life. And we learn them primarily through cultural immersion, not through formal education.

Because culturally shared symbols are generally learned at an early age through informal, subtle processes of cultural transmission, and widely shared by other people in one's culture, they come to be taken for granted. We assume everyone shares our cultural meanings. This is a mild, widespread, perhaps universal form of what anthropologists call *ethnocentrism*. Ethnocentrism is the tendency to assume that one's own cultural ways are normal, universal, and natural, and to judge others by one's own cultural standards. In its more extreme forms, especially in situations of unequal power, ethnocentrism can lead to cultural arrogance and to cultural domination.

Culture, because it is a symbolic system, can also lead to misunderstanding and misinterpretation in culture-contact situations. We automatically assume others share our symbolic systems, that behaviors have the same meanings. In short, ethnocentric reactions are common, normal, and predictable. To interpret other cultures correctly, one must understand their cultural symbols; one must know the meanings that others attach to objects, behaviors, sounds, designs, and other meaning-carrying vehicles.

Ethnocentric reactions can also occur within our own culture. Like any complex, large-scale society, the United States is not culturally homogenous. There are many *microcultures*, smaller cultures that reflect our diverse ancestries, national origins, religions, ethnicities, regions, occupations, educational levels, incomes, ages, genders, sexual preferences, and other aspects of our lifestyles.

Microcultures are also complex symbolic systems. When encountering someone from another microculture, it is easy to interpret his or her behavior (or other cultural symbols) through our own cultural system, leading to misinterpretation and ethnocentric reactions, including denigration of other cultural ways. This can happen when members of different racial and ethnic groups interact, especially if they live in socially isolated worlds with little opportunity for broader contact. We will see examples of this in part 3.

### The Psychological Reality of Culture: Culture Filters Reality

Many years ago, the famous linguist, Edward Sapir, wrote an article entitled "The Psychological Reality of the Phoneme." Sapir was making the point that we do not hear sound objectively. Instead, our language (or rather, the system of sounds used in the hearer's language) shapes our perception of sound. In short, we do not experience reality directly. Reality (in this case, sound) is filtered through a cultural-linguistic lens.

Building on Sapir's work, others have shown how profoundly culture can alter our perception of reality. The notion of *psychological reality*—that culture affects how we experience reality—can be extended to all aspects of culture, not just to what we hear.

Our basic senses—our sight, taste, smell, touch, and hearing—are experienced through a cultural filter. Our bodily processes—what we eat, how and where we sleep, how we handle and experience reproduction and excretion—these are not natural but culturally shaped and experienced. The impact of culture is even greater in other realms of life, in the world of ideas, values, and beliefs, and most importantly, for this book, in the social world, in the culturally created social world of race.

**Illustration: How Culture Shapes the Sounds We Hear**

All languages select a small set of sounds to use from the vast range of possible sounds the human voice can make. One part of learning a language is figuring out which sounds are significant and which can be ignored. For example, English speakers learn to hear the distinction between "w" and "v," as in "wail" and "veil," as clearly as a bell!

Speakers of other languages learn to ignore this difference. In Hindi, the national language of India, you could say either Diwali or Divali—both would have the same meaning—namely, the Hindu "festival of lights" for the goddess Lakshmi.

Just as Hindi speakers learn to "not hear" sounds that are irrelevant to their language, English speakers ignore—do not hear—sounds that are relevant in Hindi and many other languages. For example, all humans are capable of making what linguists call *aspirated* and nonaspirated sounds. Aspiration refers to the puff of air that comes out of your mouth when you say a word such as "pet" or "keg." Try holding your finger in front of your lips and see if a slight puff of air comes out when you say the "p" and the "k." It probably will, because most native English speakers automatically produce this airy form.

But there is another (nonaspirated) form of these (and other) consonants. If you are a native English speaker, it may be difficult to produce. But it's not genetic! Simply suppress the air when you say the "p," "t," or "k" in "pet" or "keg." You may have to press your lips together and swallow to keep the air from emerging. But you can do it and you will hear how it slightly alters the sound.

However, U.S. English doesn't employ this sound difference to alter the meaning of words. The meaning of table (or pet or kitchen) remains the same whether or not we suppress the air from coming out.

In every language, speakers unconsciously learn to hear or ignore certain sounds. Our perception of physical sound is altered by the language we speak. Even though we are presented with the same physical reality—i.e., sound—we do not perceive it similarly. Rather, what we perceive is structured by what our language has taught us to notice.

If this is true for sound perceptions, it is equally true for our other senses. We do not experience the world directly. We do not see everything that is out there. Our observations are filtered through our brain—through our culturally shared as well as more individualized experience. Our perception of taste, our sense of smell, our response to touch, what we visually notice, and how we interpret what we see—all our senses are subject to cultural influences.

### Culture Impacts Our Affective and Emotional Responses to Reality

Culture shapes our affective responses to reality, our desires, our values, and our beliefs about what is good and bad, desirable and undesirable, pleasant and unpleasant. Internalizing a culture creates emotional as well as cognitive patterns in the brain. Culture is emotionally real . . . the thought of eating a rat does produce a visceral negative emotional response in most native U.S. residents. And homophobia is a culturally rooted emotional response to a culturally created male fear of intimate, sexual contact with other males.

Given our deep emotional commitment to our own culture, it is not surprising that attempts to alter cultural patterns can produce resistance and psychological discomfort. Ethnocentrism is in part a positive emotional response to one's own culture and a negative emotional response to cultural difference. But situations of culture contact can produce anything from mild dismay at the "weird" behavior of "foreigners" to extreme disorientation—bewilderment, anxiety, anger, despair, hostility, and paranoia.

More extreme responses, commonly termed *culture shock*, occur when individuals are immersed in an alien culture. In the United States, many children, especially language minority and non-Anglo children, experience culture shock when they first enter public school, especially if the staff is predominantly middle-class Euro-American.

Awareness of the psychological reality of culture, including its emotional dimension, its tendency to produce ethnocentrism, and the phenomenon of culture shock can be very useful to students. First, it sensitizes them to their likely initial reactions when encountering students—and staff—from different cultural backgrounds. Cultural differences and cultural misinterpretation are a probable source of at least some student conflicts and disciplinary problems, as we will see in part 3, especially chapter 12.

Second, it makes students aware of the school as a microculture and of the possibility of culture shock. It can help children in the dominant cultural groups develop empathy toward what those from culturally different backgrounds experience within the school culture.

Introducing the concept of *cultural relativism* offers a useful antidote to ethnocentrism. Cultural relativism does not exclude the possibility of moral judgments. It first recognizes and teaches a basic respect for cultural diversity as part of the human experience. Second, it emphasizes *understanding* other cultures rather than simply making value judgments about them. It argues that cultures are best understood by viewing them in their own cultural context and from the native perspective.

The goal of this approach is cultural understanding—but that is not the same as cultural acceptance. In fact, one can understand a cultural practice (e.g., warfare, female infanticide, slavery) while recognizing its dysfunctional or negative consequences. And one can understand a cultural practice or cultural value even when it is in opposition to one's own cultural values (e.g., polygamy—multiple spouses, boxing, sexual segregation).

## KEY CONCEPTUAL POINTS

- Culture is what humans collectively create over time and includes mental, material, behavioral, and social products.
- Culture is mainly cultural knowledge and shared meanings that are intangible and cannot be observed.
- Culture is a symbolic system—cultures bestow meanings on the world of experience.
- Cultural meanings are arbitrary and vary across cultures.
- Culture profoundly affects how we experience reality: our perceptions, interpretations, emotions.
- Culture is learned mainly informally, through cultural immersion.
- Ethnocentrism is a common result of the deep internalization of one's culture.
- Culture contact can lead to misinterpretation and even culture shock.

## KEY TERMS (ITALICIZED AND BOLDED IN TEXT)

| | |
|---|---|
| cultural products | culture shock |
| cultural relativism | culture |
| culture as a symbolic system | ethnocentrism |
| culture as psychologically real | microcultures |

## TEACHING ACTIVITIES

**Activity Plan 1: Culture as a Symbolic System. Culture Shapes How We See the World**

*Objectives:* Students will be able to describe how cultural knowledge can lead us to misinterpret the behavior we observe. Students will provide examples of what it means to say that culture shapes reality. Students will understand how greetings are part of a culture's system of symbols.

*Additional Information:* All ages, including adults. "Simulated Greeting Behavior" (live or on videotape). Time required: 10–15 minutes for ritual; 30–60 minutes for discussion. Live version requires preparation time and materials. For a more detailed lesson plan and explicit instructions for a live performance, see Mukhopadhyay (2004). For access to a videotaped version of the activity, see Mukhopadhyay's website, www.sjsu.edu/faculty_and_staff/faculty_detail.jsp?id = 1472.

*Procedure:*

Step 1.  Students view a live or videotaped greeting behavior sequence in a hypothetical culture called Albatross.[2] In addition to an Albatrossian couple, several naïve students participate in the greeting rituals.

Step 2.  After the ritual, students describe (orally, written form) the Albatrossian culture, especially gender (male-female) relations and female status, as illustrated in specific features of the ritual. Students uniformly perceive it as a male-dominated culture and provide evidence from the ritual. For example, unlike men, women take off their shoes, sit on the floor, are served after the men, and the Albatrossian woman seems to be dominated by the Albatrossian man, as indicated by her frequent "bows" to him.

Step 3.  The instructor (or the Albatrossian couple) reveals this is a female-dominant culture. Women are regarded as superior to men, as reflected in numerous parts of the ritual. For example, only women are pure enough to sit on the ground, the sacred earth.

Step 4.  Discuss the Albatrossian vs. student interpretations. Note that misinterpretation occurs because students, predictably, have interpreted the ritual through a U.S. cultural lens. What does it tell us about culture, especially how it is inside our heads? And how it shapes what we see, feel, think, taste, or believe about others?

Step 5.  Prepare students for future discussions of other cultural inventions, like race. How might misunderstandings occur in cross-racial and cross-ethnic encounters? This activity also prepares students for discussion of cultural misunderstandings that might occur in school contexts.

Step 6.  Extend the discussion more explicitly to school contexts. These activities would work well with virtually all part 3 chapters.

- Ask students to apply the lessons of Albatross to an encounter with someone from another racial, ethnic, or religious group in their community or in their school (e.g., in a classroom, the cafeteria, other settings). What types of misinterpretation could occur?
- How might this lesson have a bearing on which students seem to be "smart" or "good students" or "bad students"? What specific behaviors do students use to form impressions of other students? Could "speaking out" in class be considered disrespectful in some cultures? Antisocial and competitive? How do you interpret other students' behavior?
- How might the lessons of the Albatross simulation help us to understand tensions between students of different ethnoracial, religious, or other cultural backgrounds or lifestyles? Have students discuss instances of cultural misinterpretation they've encountered.
- Have students provide examples of how people from different cultural backgrounds might have different interpretations of what they observe in students or teachers (e.g., student clothing, kissing in public, playground activities, disagreeing with the teacher in class, etc.).
- For a language arts lesson, have students describe the simulation and then discuss cultural biases in the terms used. Focus on the contrast between pure description and interpretation (e.g., the women *had* to sit on the floor). Also point out the contrast between lower-level purely descriptive vs. higher level evaluative terms (e.g., "the women were *horribly treated*" vs. "the women were *asked* to bow their head and serve the men").

### Activity Idea 1: Exploring the Concept of Culture Using School Culture

*Objectives:* Students will be able to apply the concept of culture and cultural products to their own school.

*Additional Information:* Student centered, interactive, appropriate for all grades; takes 10–30 minutes. No materials required.

*Procedure:* Students explore the concept of culture pretending they are Martians trying to understand their own school. Students provide examples of material, social, behavioral, and mental products of culture. They can explore a particular school site (e.g., library, playground, cafeteria), a single event (a dance, assembly, lunch), or school greeting behaviors (handshakes, hugs, etc). For examples of school-related cultural products, see www.sjsu.edu/faculty_and_staff/faculty_detail.jsp?id = 1472 . For a brief hands-on activity called "The Hug," see Mukhopadhyay (2006).

**Activity Idea 2: Teaching About Race**

Explore additional teaching activities in the Teaching About Race module at www.sjsu.edu/faculty_and_staff/faculty_detail.jsp?id = 1472.

## ENDNOTES

1. A few words are not totally arbitrary, such as "buzz" which resembles the sound of a bee.

2. This is an adaptation of a simulation called "The Albatross," which was circulating among multicultural education people in the 1970s (Gochenour, 1977). Although the basic ritual is similar, the pedagogical context, principles illustrated, and discussion aspects are different. A teacher-education-oriented version of this simulation and other activities for teaching about culture can be found in Hernández and Mukhopadhyay (1985).

# Culture and Classification:
# Race Is Culturally Real

Chapter 5 introduced the idea that classification is basic to human thinking and central to human language. Words are really labels for categories of things in the world, whether animals, plants, deities, subjects studied in schools, or groupings of human beings.

Chapter 6 explores culture's role in the systems of classification we use in daily life. We then examine the idea of race as a cultural and historically specific system for classifying the human world. We show that racial categories, like other cultural inventions, become deeply internalized and unconscious, and profoundly shape our perceptions of the social world.

## CONCEPTUAL OVERVIEW

### The Role of Classification in Human Life

Reality is enormously complex. Even the smallest thing, like a flower, has many elements. And each flower differs from every other flower, if only in minute ways.

This is true for the natural world of plants, leaves, flowers, soils, rocks. It also applies to humans. Even genetically alike twins differ as a result of environmental influences. Color is a continuum of an infinite number of shades, as a trip to a paint store will tell you. So is sound. Just ask anyone who has tried to play a stringed instrument, like a violin or guitar.

Humans probably could not survive without the ability to classify. Classifying is partially a device for reducing the complexity of reality, for eliminating "noise" that would otherwise make life chaotic. It helps us focus on and notice what is relevant. It enables us to create generalizations about the physical or social world and formulate general rules that we can apply to people, things, and situations. Can you imagine having to treat every human being, every classroom, object, and situation as totally unique? We would go mad!

So classification is an essential, functional part of human thought and language. It rests on categorizing and labeling some things as different and some things as alike, of separating apples from oranges, fruits from vegetables, blues from greens.

## Cultures Create Particular Classifications of Reality

Because most of reality is a continuum, without clear boundaries, there are many ways to classify reality. As individuals, we could devise numerous ways to classify any set of objects, but most of us rely on culture. Cultures have come up with diverse ways of classifying things in the natural and social world and in the world of ideas. Indeed, some anthropologists consider this a crucial aspect of culture.

Language, as a part of culture, reflects the culture in which the language is spoken. For anthropologists, language is one way of finding out how people classify and think about the world. Cultural knowledge is embedded in language.

Not surprisingly, language is one of the primary ways through which children learn the categories of their culture. This is true for racial as well as other categories. By learning a language, anthropologists argue, children learn a particular system of classification, a cultural way of noticing the world around them (see chapter 5). Racial categories subtly teach children what is important about people in their social world.

Research establishes that our systems of classification, embedded in language, shape our perceptions, thinking, and ways of acting in the world. Anthropologists once argued that language categories *determine* thought and perception. For example, some believed that people whose language did not contain verbs in the past tense could not think about the past. Such extreme views have been rejected. On the other hand, there is no doubt that cultures classify reality in different ways and that through immersion in a culture and a language, we acquire that culture's slant on reality.

## Cultural Classifications: An Array of Alternatives

Culture provides us with *classifications* in two main ways. Culture, through language, tells us what kinds of things go together or are similar if not essentially the same. That is, a word or term, such as "middle school," really represents a category and a category is a collection of disparate items that have been grouped together. There are thousands of different "middle schools" in the United States.

Second, culture, through language, provides us with a set of *classifying devices*. It gives us a set of principles or criteria for lumping together some things and for separating them from other things that are considered different. So we have criteria for classifying some schools as "middle schools" and others as "high schools," "elementary schools," or "colleges."

Cultures can vary, then, in their classification of reality in two basic ways. They can divide up the same reality into different pieces or categories. And they can use different criteria for lumping together or dividing up that reality.

*Classifying Drinking Vessels: "Cups"*

Let us take a simple example from U.S. culture, the concept of a cup.[1] The word *cup* is simply a label for a set of objects that differ dramatically in size, shape, material, design, etc.

There are subcategories (e.g., coffee cups, tea cups, and recently, soup cups!). And the category cup is part of a larger classification that includes "glasses," "mugs," "bottles," "straws" and other drinking vessels. Each of these, like "glasses," also has subcategories (water glasses, goblets, martini vs. wine vs. champagne glasses).

North Americans also tend to have similar criteria for classifying drinking vessels. How is a cup different from a glass? Many of us would answer handles—are they present or not? Other features we'd notice are the use of the vessel—for hot vs. cold liquids—and the construction material (glass vs. nonglass).

But not all potential differences are utilized in the U.S. classification system. We don't care about the color of the vessel, its cost, the type of people who use it, or even its shape, apart from handles. Should we go to another culture, even an English-speaking one such as England or India, we would find a somewhat different system. In rural India, for example, tea is often served in a "tea cup," a disposable clay vessel that lacks a handle, or in a glass tumbler that resembles what we would call a "glass." If you have students familiar with other countries, you could explore their cultural systems of categorizing drinking vessels.

The crucial point is the variability in how cultures classify things. This is because our labels, our classifications and categories, are cultural creations. They are not found in nature, even when they refer to natural objects (color, plants.)

*Color Terminology*

Let us take an example from the natural world, color. Color is a physical reality, like sound or smell. In fact, we are very visually oriented as a species, with both stereoscopic and color vision.

But not all languages have the same number of **basic color terms**. Some languages take the entire spectrum of colors and divide it into two basic types of colors (dark vs. light); others have only three or four categories. Still others, like English, have as many as eleven basic color terms (black, brown, gray, blue, green, purple, orange, yellow, red, pink, white). There is no evidence that people in cultures with fewer color categories lack the capacity to *see* color distinctions. They just break up the color spectrum into different numbers of groups. And they divide the continuum of color at different places in the spectrum. This should not be surprising, when we think about it. Color is continuous and there are no natural divisions!

Not only do languages have different numbers of color terms, but they also use different criteria to differentiate colors. In English, for example, hue (shade), brightness, and intensity are used (e.g., blue vs. green). The Hanunoo, in the Philippines, however, have developed specialized color terms based on additional features, such as whether or not a plant is succulent and whether it is wet or dry. Both affect the visual appearance of plants and are important in Hanunoo culture.

The point is that while color has a physical reality, it can be divided in many different ways, and different languages divide and label the same reality differently. Humans organize nature into culturally specific categories.

Culture—through language—categorizes all aspects of reality. We have classification systems for animals ("reptiles," "mammals"), plants ("roses," "pansies," "vegetables"), even edible items ("food" and kinds of foods—desserts, sandwiches, tacos) vs. inedible items (rats). We classify activities ("housework," "studying," "going out") and, as we saw earlier, time ("weeks," "minutes," "centuries").

## Classifications of the Social World: Kinds of People

*Kinship: What Kinds of Relatives Are There?*

Besides classifying the natural world, humans classify the social world. Classification of relatives is preeminent, particularly in small-scale societies. Indeed, the concept of "relative" or "family" is itself a way of classifying the human world. Many cultures traditionally divided the social world into two basic categories: relatives and nonrelatives.

If we speak only one language and have lived in only one country, we probably think of our kinship labels for relatives as natural. That is, we assume that everyone around the world describes their relatives using terms equivalent to "aunts," "uncles," "grandparents" and "cousins." We think of these as real divisions of relatives rather than as culturally specific ways of grouping relatives into different categories. Yet studies of *kinship terms* in other societies illustrate how many different ways cultures classify relatives.

Kinship is partially about biology—but not all biological differences are recognized in any system of kinship terms. Some of the most commonly used are gender, generation, maternal vs. paternal side of the family, relative age, "blood" (genetic) vs. relationship through marriage, relationship through a sibling vs. a direct parent-child relationship, and so forth.

Many cultures utilize more distinctions than we do and so have more labels for relatives—what we call kinship terms. For example, it is quite common to have different kinship terms for mothers' and fathers' relatives.

Standard U.S. English kinship terms, however, are few in number. Let us take the term "uncle." Think about how many biologically different kinds of relatives are lumped into this one category! We include mother's brother as well as father's brother even though they are from totally different "sides" of the family and are usually unrelated. We also throw in people who are not even genealogically connected but simply relatives through marriage. So in addition to father's brother, our uncles include "in-laws" like father's sister's husband and mother's sister's husband. The term "cousin" is even broader.

Such a classification would be inconceivable and incomprehensible in many cultures. Distinctions between maternal vs. paternal sides of the family and between "blood" relatives and "in-laws" are often crucial to social life. They can affect inheritance, marriage, household responsibilities, and political representation. Not surprisingly, these significant features are recognized in kinship terms, such as separate labels for mother's vs. father's brother and for relatives through marriage. Relative age ("elder" brother) may also be recognized.

In contrast, North American kinship terms, like "uncle," ignore virtually everything except gender (male vs. female) and being a "relative," if only through marriage. Some people in the U.S. go even farther. They extend "uncle" to a family friend with no kinship or marriage ties. And then there's "Uncle Sam"!

But U.S. Americans recognize distinctions that some cultures ignore. Most of us find it natural to have separate labels for mother and mother's sister ("aunt"). And we've already mentioned "uncle" (vs. "father"). Yet some cultures use the *same* kinship term for both types of relatives. The Tiv of Nigeria traditionally lumped father and father's brother into the same kinship category, using only one term for both relatives. On the other hand, they have separate terms for mother's brother and father's brother (Bohannon, 2000).[2]

The point, once again, is that there are innumerable ways to classify and label relatives, people to whom we are connected through common descent or marriage. All cultures ignore some potential distinctions and highlight others. The different choices they make produce the cross-cultural variability we see in kinship terms.

*Why Do Cultures Classify Kin Differently?*

But how do we explain these variations? Anthropologists have long asked this question. Is it just random? Chance? Hardly. Relatives are very important in most cultures, socially, economically, politically, religiously, emotionally. Indeed, family and kinship have traditionally been the foundation for social organization in most human societies.

Categorizing people in certain ways tends to reflect the local system of social organization, the kinds of rights and obligations allocated to different kinds of people. Labels have real meaning. The 1950s slogan "He's your uncle, not your dad" embodies Anglo-American concepts of family obligations as well as politically conservative notions of the "proper" (and limited) role of government.

Whether one is labeled a sister or a cousin or a mother affects and reflects the type of relationship you have with that person and your expectations, and in some cases, legal rights and obligations. We are supposed to and generally feel and behave differently toward mothers vs. aunts, cousins vs. sisters, parents vs. great-uncles, relatives vs. non-relatives. Culture is emotionally real and how we classify relatives shapes how we experience the social world of family.

**Race: A Cultural Classification of the Social World**

Large, complex cultures often use criteria besides kinship to divide up and categorize the social world. North American racial categories, as we have shown in part 1, do not exist in nature. They are a cultural creation, a system of classifying people, first invented by Europeans and subsequently elaborated in the United States.

The North American system relies on a few physical traits, such as skin color and hair form, as visible markers of one's racial classification. Other societies may select *different* biological traits to create races (e.g., height, nose or ear shape) or ignore biology altogether (see chapter 8).

Humans apparently have a propensity to classify other human beings, and to recognize, and often classify others, based on visible features. Indeed, some psychologists have argued that we are hard-wired to recognize physical differences in humans. That is, they suggest our brains are predisposed to recognize and then classify people using visual markers (see Hirschfeld, 1997).[3]

Certainly this ability would have been adaptive in early human societies. Recognizing age or gender variations, for example, would be advantageous for infant care, child rearing, and organizing social relationships and responsibilities on the basis of age and gender. The cognitive propensity to remember detailed physical features would help people differentiate among their own relatives, between relatives and strangers, and to develop a system of social roles based on kinship.

Some psychologists go further and suggest there is a human cognitive propensity to attach invisible meanings to visible traits, to see what is visible as evidence of a more fundamental, innate set of characteristics, to link surface appearances with a deeper or inner essence. In this view, *essentialist thought* is innate in human thinking, and racial thinking builds on this.

Yet not all cultures create social categories based on visible physical traits. Nor do all complex, stratified societies rank groups from inferior to superior based on biological traits. European and North American racial ideology, especially during periods of colonialism and slavery, influenced other cultures' ways of classifying people. In some cases, racial categories were superimposed on existing indigenous social systems. Nevertheless, even in places like Latin America and the Caribbean, local cultures neither attach the same meanings to "color" nor define race as in the United States (see chapter 8).

Race, like any other system of social classification, is a culturally specific device for categorizing people that emphasizes certain distinctions and ignores others. Its roots lie in historical and social conditions—not in nature. Race remains meaningful today because of its continuing social and economic significance in the U.S. and in the world affected by European and European American culture.

## THE EMERGENCE OF THE NORTH AMERICAN RACIAL WORLDVIEW

There is a wealth of scholarship that explores the origins and development of the American racial classification system, what Smedley (1993) calls the *American "racial worldview."* Scholars recognize at least two separate strands of thinking about race in the United States (Haney-Lopez, 1996). One might be called "folk beliefs," the ideas of ordinary people about race and other social divisions. Historians find race as a folk concept in the English language as far back as the 16th century. Between the 16th and 18th centuries, race was used interchangeably with other terms such as *type, kind, sort, breed,* and even *species* (Smedley, 1993).

Another prominent strand came from the world of science, especially 17th-, 18th-, and 19th-century European natural science. Building on European Enlightenment themes, the belief in "reason" and the perfectibility of "man," philosophers and intellectuals preoccupied themselves with systematically describing and classifying the natural world. They created a science of classification called **taxonomy**.

In the 18th century, these principles of natural science were extended to humans and the search for biological subdivisions of the human species began in earnest. The first formal definition of human races in taxonomic terms—that is, using modern principles of biological classification—was by the Swedish naturalist Carolus Linnaeus, in *Systema Naturae* (Systems of Nature), first published in 1735. Linnaeus classified humans into four subspecies, corresponding to the four major continents (Europe, America, Asia, Africa). Each was described by skin color (white, red, yellow, and dark or black). Linnaeus, like others during this time, linked character traits to anatomy. *Homo sapiens Europaeus* had white skin color, was inventive and ruled by law. *Homo Asiaticus* was, among other things, sallow, melancholy, and avaricious. *Homo sapiens Americanus* was reddish, obstinate, and regulated by customs. The most negative description was of *Homo sapiens Africanus*, black, indolent, and "governed by caprice" (Smedley, 1993, p. 164).

U.S. racial categories were most heavily influenced by German anatomist **Johann Blumenbach** (1752–1784), sometimes called the father of physical anthropology. After carefully studying Linnaeus' system, Blumenbach proposed five instead of four fundamental subdivisions of the human species. He separated out dark-skinned Africans from the African category and labeled them "Ethiopian." He split non-Caucasus Asians into two separate races. The first was the category "Mongoloid" and included inhabitants of Asia, including China and Japan. The second race was the "Malay" race and incorporated native Australians,

Pacific Islanders, and other island people in the region. Indigenous Americans remained a separate race.

Blumenbach also coined the term "Caucasian." Apparently, he was impressed by the beauty of a woman's skull from the Caucasus Mountains region, located between Russia and Turkey. He admired it because it was more symmetrical than other skulls in his collection. To him, the skull reflected nature's ideal form, the circle, and he reasoned it must have resembled "God's original creation" (Haviland, Prins, Walrath, & McBride, 2005, p. 81).

Blumenbach eventually visited the area, declaring its people the most beautiful in the world. From their beauty he inferred that the Caucasus Mountains area must be near where humans originated. He decided all light-skinned peoples from this region, plus Europeans, belonged to the same race, which he labeled Caucasians.

Blumenbach went farther. Based on the Judeo-Christian belief that humans were created in God's image, he believed Caucasians most closely resembled the original ideal humans. Other races, he argued, had degenerated physically and morally as a result of moving away from their place of origins and adapting to new environments (Haviland, Prins, Walrath, & McBride, 2005, p. 81).

These so-called scientific categories were actually social inventions that drew upon long-standing European folk and religious beliefs in hierarchy, in "superior" and "inferior" religions, "stock," peoples, languages, and cultures. But combining popular ideas and religious authority with scientific authority created a powerful ideology that quickly spread to the U.S. scientific community.

As U.S. racial science emerged, racial classification drew upon the 19th-century preoccupation with identifying evolutionary stages in everything from human language, technology, and religion to forms of marriage and kinship. Nineteenth-century scientists created grand evolutionary ladders, categorized diverse forms from "primitive" to more "advanced," and ranked the worlds' cultures accordingly. Cultural "advance," in these theories, primarily resulted from human biological—indeed, intellectual—development. Culture and biology were intertwined.

In *Ancient Society* (1877), the American anthropologist Lewis Henry Morgan identified three major stages of human evolution (cultural and biological). The earliest stages were Savagery and Barbarism (each with lower, middle, upper stages). The most advanced form was Civilization. Not surprisingly, the British (and Caucasians) topped the evolutionary pyramid, representing "Civilization" and "civilized" family forms, including monogamy (one husband–one wife).

European scientists occupied themselves with identifying the evolutionary position of societies under their colonial control. Morgan, in the U.S., concentrated on Native Americans. Physical anthropologists focused on identifying "primitive" and more "advanced" physical forms, measuring skulls and other presumed indicators of intellect (see chapter 1).

Blumenbach's racial categories dovetailed with 19th-century evolutionary theories and different races were assigned different evolutionary ranks. Although the theories were long ago discredited, labels and categories from this period persist: "savages," "barbarians," "civilized," "primitive," "advanced." And the race–evolutionary stage association remains alive in the minds of some U.S. Americans in assertions that some races are more evolved, primitive, advanced, or closer (or farther) from the apes.

Blumenbach's and Linnaeus's racial categories found their way into U.S. American law. The categories White and Black appear in legal documents during the colonial period. Racial science was appropriated to justify slavery and, later, to counter legal and other perceived threats to the dominance of elite Euro-American males. Legal debates in the 20th century over the meaning of White and Caucasian explicitly cite Blumenbach and employ other racial categories like Mongoloid (see chapter 7). This framework, including the label Caucasian, persists today in popular discourse and in some scientific writing (Mukhopadhyay, in press).

Chapter 7 discusses some dilemmas posed by Blumenbach's racial categories. U.S. naturalization laws, beginning in 1790, restricted citizenship to Whites. How was White to be defined? What about new immigrants such as Syrians or Armenians? And was White equivalent to Caucasian, as Blumenbach implied? If so, naturalization would be open to people from India.

Chapter 7 also describes the impact of population shifts on the U.S. system of racial classification. The late 19th century witnessed a surge of immigrants quite different from the predominant U.S. "Yankee" stock. Was this hodge-podge of Jews, Catholics, Irish, Greeks, Italians, and other "refuse" from the shores of Southern and Eastern Europe going to be accorded the same "White privilege" given to immigrants from England, France, and Germany?

As early as the mid-19th century, perhaps in response to the wave of Irish Catholic immigration, U.S. racial science began to make distinctions within the White race. Samuel Morton, a wealthy Philadelphian physician, divided the "Modern Caucasian Group" into six "families." He purported to show, using now discredited data on skull size, that the "Teutonic Family"(Germans, English, Anglo-Americans) was superior in intelligence to other "families": the Semitic group, the Celtic family, and the Indostanic family (Gould, 1981).

By the 1920s, eugenicists,[4] building on the work of scientists like Morton and on other popular writings, had divided European Whites into three or four ranked subraces: Nordic, Alpine, Mediterranean, and Jews (Semitics). The rankings not only asserted the inherent intellectual superiority of Nordics (and inferiority of groups such as Russian Jews), but also argued for fundamental differences in "character" and the capacity for civilization.

Arguments about the superiority and inferiority of White subdivisions played a prominent role in popular and legal arguments for restricting immigration in the 1920s. Supporters argued that the influx of inferior "Mediterraneans" would dilute the purity of the White population already in the United States.

One popular book by Kenneth Roberts, *Why Europe Leaves Home*, was typically blunt:

> The American nation was founded and developed by the Nordic race, but if a few more million members of the Alpine, Mediterranean and Semitic races are poured among us, the result must inevitably be a hybrid race of people as worthless and futile as the good-for-nothing mongrels of Central America and Southeastern Europe. (cited by Brodkin, 1998, p. 25)

Arguments for restricting immigration prevailed. Some Whites were deemed more White, or more accurately, superior Whites. Immigration

laws (and other practices) were designed to preserve the ethnic dominance of Nordics—the earliest North-Western Anglo-Saxon Protestant
ethnic groups. It wasn't until after World War II that ethnic, religious,
and racial barriers among European Americans began to dissolve and
the White racial category became more homogenized.

The U.S. system of racial classification has shifted over time (see
chapter 7), but some things have remained stable. One has been the
Linnaeus/ Blumenbach framework of major racial categories: White,
Caucasian; Black, African; Red, American Indian; and Yellow, Mongoloid or Asians.

These categories remained enshrined in U.S. institutions until the
1960s when they began to be challenged, especially in the context of
immigration and naturalization law. They continue as a conceptual
foundation for categories used in census, educational, and health statistics although these too are under scrutiny.

Race is fundamentally a social category, rooted in history and culture, rather than in nature. Sadly, remnants of these discredited beliefs
about race as biology, about superior and inferior races, about race and
intellect, and about links between biology and culture can be found in
contemporary popular U.S. American culture. Cultural categories—
and their associations—are very deeply rooted.

**Racial Classifications Are Learned: Race Is Real**

Racial categories, like other labels, are classifying devices we use to
negotiate the everyday world we live in, yet they are not natural. They
have to be *learned.*

We said earlier that learning a culture involves learning the categories of that culture. Part of the job of culture is to transmit to children
the culturally specific versions of what things go together and what
things are different. The North American system of *racial classification* is transmitted in a myriad of subtle (and not so subtle) ways. Children, through language, learn racial categories at an early age, just like
they learn other cultural systems of classification, whether of drinking
vessels, colors, or relatives.

This knowledge is reinforced by schools (see part 3). Part of the
school's job is to transmit to children the dominant cultural categories.

Children have a substantial vocabulary by age 5, so they enter school with a social classification system already shaped by their home culture and language. If this matches the racial classification system taught at school, children's existing knowledge will be reinforced.

But some children who have not learned the U.S. system of racial categories, such as immigrant children, may experience difficulty, a kind of *culture shock*. This is an example of what anthropologists call *cultural discontinuity*, contrasts between the home culture and school culture. Part 3 discusses other forms of discontinuity and how this can affect school achievement.

## Race Is Culturally Real

We experience the world in part through the categories our language gives us, without thinking about them. Once learned, racial categories, like other cultural categories, become deeply internalized, often at an unconscious level, especially for members of dominant racial groups. Racial classification becomes automatic, seems natural, as do races. For people who have grown up in a U.S. racialized world, race feels natural and normal, like a 7-day week or a 60-minute hour.

Racial categories, like other cultural categories, profoundly shape how we experience the world. We unconsciously focus on race and racial markers and ignore other characteristics of individuals. We literally perceive people racially. Racial attributes, such as skin color, become perceptually salient; they "stick out." Other racially irrelevant physical features, like ear lobes, hand, tooth, or body shape, recede into the background (see chapter 1).

When we encounter new people, we try to categorize them racially, by fitting them into our existing set of categories. Is this person Black? White? Latino? Asian? Native American? If they don't fit, we are confused, even disoriented. The categories have become real.

In short, we have learned to view people through a racial lens. Race has become psychologically real (see chapter 5). We notice (and interpret) racially marked traits in ways different from other aspects of human biological variation. Racial traits become symbols—and we are often unaware of the elaborate cultural meanings they invoke.

Racial categories, the concept of race, the racial worldview, is so deeply embedded conceptually (and institutionally) in our culture that it is hard to imagine it is a cultural creation. And race *is* real as a social phenomenon. Race—along with other social identities like gender, class, religion—impacts our lives, how we experience and act in the world, how others experience and act towards us.

The cultural and social reality of race makes it hard for many U.S. Americans to really *hear* that races aren't real biologically. They think the message is that races don't exist as a social invention. Perhaps that is because the social and cultural reality is so powerful.

## KEY CONCEPTUAL POINTS

- Classification is basic to human life, thinking, and language.
- Classification reduces complexity and allows us to generalize about the world.
- Classifications are cultural inventions, vary cross-culturally, and reflect the context in which they are invented.
- Classifications categorize some things as similar and others as different using one or more attributes.
- Color and kinship (relatives) are two examples of cultural variations in classifying "reality" that reflect cultural context. Racial classification in the United States is another.
- Classifications, while cultural inventions, are deeply internalized, feel real and natural, and shape how we experience the world.

## KEY TERMS (ITALICIZED AND BOLDED IN TEXT)

| | |
|---|---|
| basic color terms | essentialist thought |
| Blumenbach | kinship terms |
| classification | racial classifications |
| classifying devices | racial worldview |
| cultural discontinuity | taxonomy |

## TEACHING ACTIVITIES

The activities below utilize and build on illustrations in the conceptual background section. They also dovetail with chapters in part 3, especially chapter 10.

**Activity Plan 1: Color Terms**

*Objectives:* Students will be able to provide examples of the arbitrariness of color classifications.

*Additional Information:* All ages. Interactive. Materials: Numbered paint chips in a wide continuum of colors representing basic color categories: brown, blue, green, red, yellow, and so on (at least four or five sets).

*Procedure:*

Step 1. List basic color terms on board.

Step 2. Students divide paint chips into basic color categories (whole class, led by teacher; or small groups)

Step 3. Chart paint chip numbers, listing under basic color terms. Students are most likely to disagree on boundaries of color terms. Students from different cultural or linguistic backgrounds, nationalities, or genders may group same colors differently.[5]

Step 4. Discuss results and significance. Point out that reality is a continuum but language arbitrarily divides reality into distinct categories. This reinforces the concept of "continuous distribution" in chapter 1.

Step 5. Find some students fluent in another language, preferably a non-European language, and have them list their basic color terms. They may have a different number. Or there may be the same number but the boundaries between colors may differ (i.e., a chip called "blue" in English may be labeled "green" in Spanish or Tagalog). Repeat the same process above but with your non-English language speakers.

**Activity Plan 2: Classifying Relatives**

*Objective:* Students will understand that labels for relatives, like for color, are somewhat arbitrary divisions of reality.

*Additional Information:* All levels, with appropriate modifications. This activity can be linked to other chapter activities where students explore family background (see chapter 5).

*Procedure:* Overview. Students explore *kinship terms* or labels for relatives in English and in another language and culture. Kinship terms are labels used to *refer to* relatives, such as "uncle" or "sister." We may use different terms when *addressing* relatives. For example, we talk about someone being our "sister." But if we see her, we generally address her by her name ("Hi, Shana!"). We are not concerned here with the way relatives are addressed. Students should focus on the labels used when we formally *refer* to relatives, such as the label "sister" or "cousin." For further information, including sample kinship charts, consult the excellent Palomar College Cultural Anthropology tutorials, especially the two on kinship terminology, at http://anthro.palomar.edu/kinship/kinship_5.htm.

Step 1. Describe concept of kinship terms—ways of classifying and categorizing relatives (see conceptual background material).

Step 2. Show students how to construct a "kinship chart," a chart that uses symbols to represent different types of relatives. See the Palomar website listed above or any standard cultural anthropology text (Nanda and Warms, 2004).

Step 3. Students construct kinship chart of their family (including beyond their household).

Step 4. Students identify U.S. American English *kin terms* for each relative on their chart (in small groups or individually).

Step 5. Discuss which kinship-biological distinctions are ignored and which are recognized. Discuss possible reasons, including roles of various relatives, living arrangements, economic sharing. Note new categories of relatives in contemporary society, such as "my half-sister," "my mother's husband," "my father's partner."

Step 6. Compare American English kinship terms to those from another language, using either bilingual students in class or other multilingual people that students can interview, either in class or on their own.

Step 7. Summarize the key point: Cultures, through language, classify the same biological reality in different ways, reflecting cultural and historical context.

**Activity Plan 3: Classifying in Other Cultures—A Cultural IQ Test!**

*Objective:* Students will be able to recognize and cite examples of how things can "go together" in many different ways and how different cultures can select different criteria for classifying the same things. Students will recognize that most IQ tests are at least partially based on cultural knowledge that is learned and that is culturally specific. *Procedure:* Explain that most IQ tests rely on culturally shared notions of what things "go together." They partially test students' knowledge of cultural classification systems. Illustrate these points by giving students a hypothetical "test" of their aptitude and intelligence. These come from actual ethnographic data (see, for example, Lee, 1974). In each case, students select the *most different* of the set of items. These activities also could be used with chapter 11.

*Additional Information:* No materials except to chart responses. Time: 5–10 minutes. Age: all.

### Set 1. Auto, Turtle, Basket, Bird

Students generally select auto or basket using the culturally familiar categorizing device of machines vs. nonmachines or movement vs. nonmovement. At least some non-Western cultural groups, however, would see birds as most different because their culture emphasizes shape and birds are relatively angular rather than rounded in shape. Our culture tends to emphasize use or functionality. Thus correctness would be culture dependent.

### Set 2. Laundry, Beer, Clothing

Students generally, with great assurance, select beer as most different. Functionality places clothing and washing machines together. Yet, at least one culture views clothing as different because laundry and beer are both "foamy." Visual appearance is most salient. U.S. slang for beer ("suds") also recognizes the attribute of foaminess.

### Set 3. Chair, Spear, Couch

Students again select the "wrong" answer—at least from the perspective of the Ashanti of Ghana. U.S. Americans tend to emphasize *use,* thus placing couch and chair together as types of sitting devices (i.e., furniture). Ashanti apparently would see the couch as the most different because both a chair and a spear can symbolize authority.

*Set 4. Pig, Goat, Snake OR Cow, Pig, Chicken OR Horse, Cow, Pig*

This hypothetical example can stimulate discussion of alternative classifying devices. One can use edible vs. inedible animals—i.e., which are food and which are not, although it depends on which culture. Some Hindus (but perhaps not in Nepal) would find a goat edible but not a pig. U.S. Christians might view cows or pigs different from a horse.

*Discussion:* Students explore other alternative responses and what they might reflect.

**Additional Activity Ideas**

*Objective:* Students will understand that IQ tests contain much cultural information.

*Additional Information:* Samples of tests, including those listed below, are available in Hernández and Mukhopadhyay (1985) or from the Mukhopadhyay website, www.sjsu.edu/faculty_and_staff/faculty_detail.jsp?id = 1472.

**Activity Idea 1**

Use old Army IQ tests or old school IQ tests. One useful example is *The Psychological Examination in the United States Army, Group Examination Alpha, Form 5, Test.* Ask students which items measure "intelligence," which measure "achievement," and which measure "personality." This test strikingly illustrates how cultural knowledge is being tested in most so-called intelligence tests.

**Activity Idea 2**

Alternatively, use IQ tests created by members of nonmainstream U.S. cultures. One example is the Central West Virginia Cultural Awareness

Quiz (Morgan & Beeler, 1981). Ask students to discuss what it would take to do well on this test.

**Activity Idea 3**

Students can construct (in groups or individually) an IQ test that reflects knowledge specific to their peer group and generation. It can be "culturally biased" in favor of their culture. Once they have constructed the test, let students and teachers, staff, or other adults take it and have students score the exam. Discuss results. Students will probably do far better than adults.

**Activity Idea 4**

Use a current or relatively recent test of achievement, aptitude, or intelligence and analyze it for cultural bias. Include regional, religious, class, rural-urban, and gender biases as well as ethnic and racial biases.

**ENDNOTES**

1. This example owes much to the work of David Kronenfeld (Kronenfeld, 1996).

2. For more material on kinship terminology cross-culturally, see the tutorials, Kin Naming systems, at the Palomar College Anthropology website, http://anthro.palomar-.edu/kinship/kinship_5.htm.

3. *Ethos* (Vol. 25, no. 1, 1997), the journal of the Society for Psychological Anthropology, extensively reviews Hirschfeld's work.

4. Francis Galton, a wealthy Englishman, invented the term in the 1880s to describe efforts by some to "improve" the human species through selective breeding. Galton felt the "superior" races, namely the British, were declining in numbers and wished to halt this. See chapter 9.

5. To read more about how color terms were investigated, and for more ideas for student projects, see the classic study by Brent Berlin and Paul Kay (1969), *Basic Color Terms*. The book also includes a color chart based on Munsel color chips.

# Race and Inequality: Race as a Social Invention to Achieve Certain Goals

The meaning of race is not to be found in the physical features of differing human populations. . . . We must peel away the intricate layers of Western cultural history and look at the material conditions, the cultural and naturalistic knowledge, and the motivations, objectives, and levels of consciousness and comprehension of those who first imposed the classifications of race on the human community.

—Audrey Smedley (1993, p. 14)

Classification, as we have seen, is pervasive in human culture, and there are numerous ways we can classify the same set of things. So how does a particular cultural system of classification—whether of colors, time, food, or human beings—emerge?

Classifications do not emerge in a vacuum but in a cultural context. The U.S. system of racial classification developed in the context of what anthropologists call *social stratification*, that is, a system of structured social inequality.

## CONCEPTUAL BACKGROUND

### Stratification: Systems of Inequality

Contrary to popular stereotypes, most human cultures have been fairly egalitarian. Only with the rise of civilizations in the past 6,000 to 8,000 years do we find societies with significant differences in wealth, political power, social rights, and status. These are what anthropologists call *stratified societies*. Yet stratified societies have had a disproportionate influence on the world, gradually incorporating smaller scale, less powerful societies into their powerful empires, often as subordinate, lower-status groups.

Stratified systems of inequality have common features. First, they constitute what social scientists call a *social system*. A system is a set of interrelated social institutions (educational, occupational, legal, political, religious) that functions at a societal level. That is, although systems have consequences for individuals, they exist beyond the individual (see Nanda and Warms, 2004).

Within any social system there is a range of *social positions* or *social statuses*, or what we today sometimes call *social identities*. They are cultural inventions, rather than natural occurrences, and are often linked to social institutions, such as the social position of "professor," "president," "slave," and "U.S. citizen." Families also generate social positions such as husband, wife, grandmother, and uncle. We all have multiple social positions and identities, each associated with roles, rights, and obligations.

Society and individuals treat us according to their perceptions of our social position. Others may categorize us racially or ethnically in ways that do not agree with our own perceptions or choice of identities. The U.S. Census, for example, uses large ethnoracial categories, such as Asian, White, and Black, that may not reflect how people identify themselves.

The point here is that structural or institutional forms of privilege and discrimination accrue to individuals as members of a social group, rather than on the basis of their personal characteristics. In the colonial period, for example, only "free white males" who were citizens could serve on juries, regardless of an individual's qualifications. Legal, educational, governmental, and political institutions treat people differently, depending on their social group membership, including their racial classification.

**Ascribed versus Achieved Statuses and Systems**

Anthropologists sometimes use the terms *ascribed* and *achieved* (see Nanda and Warms, 2004, p. 281) to refer to alternative ways individuals acquire a social position or membership in a social group. Often your social status is ascribed (determined by birth) through your ancestry or kinship group or your gender or physical features.

In contrast, some social statuses can be achieved. That is, the status or social position is the result of actions, accomplishments, talents, choices, or valuables that can be acquired by anyone, regardless of his or her birth.

Stratified societies can be based on ascription, achievement, or some combination of both. The traditional Hindu caste system is often used to illustrate an ascribed system of social stratification. In theory, caste (*jati*) is determined by birth, cannot be changed in your lifetime, and is a prime determinant of your social rank. But European "royalty" is another example of a stratified system historically based on ascription. Access to political power and other upper-strata privileges was based on birth within the royal lineage.

Stratified systems can be based on achievement rather than ascription. In other words, there can be different strata (classes) with significant inequality, but there is social mobility between classes. Individuals born into one class can move upward or downward, at least in theory. Your social position is not determined at birth but can fluctuate during your lifetime.

The United States is frequently described (and describes itself) as a stratified society based on achievement, despite its history of racial, gender, and other ascribed structural barriers to mobility. In reality, most stratified societies contain elements of ascription and achievement. Britain is a class society with some mobility but Prince Charles acquired his "royal" (vs. "commoner") status by birth.

**Justifying Inequality: Legitimizing Ideologies**

Stratified systems of inequality are not just about wealth or control of political institutions. Dominant groups influence belief systems and often devise elaborate and complex ideologies to explain and justify their dominance.

Creation stories, one common mechanism, trace the social system to human origins or to the beginning of human social groups. The creator tends to be a deity-like figure with the creation story embedded in sacred text. In Hinduism, some sacred texts attribute the creation of the universe, humans, and the major social divisions to a primeval giant cosmic being, Purusha. In the United States, Christian biblical sources were used to justify African slavery.

Creation accounts often articulate the reasons for each group's rank and why some are inferior or superior. In the Hinduism example, each group's social rank (from higher to lower) originated in the part of Purusha's body from which it was created, from head (highest rank) to feet (lowest). But in Hinduism and most other systems, the subsequent and fundamental basis for one's social or "caste" position is common ancestry, the group into which you are born.

Stratified systems are not always based on biological characteristics (see chapter 8). There are many potential visible symbols of group membership and relative social status. Groups may have to wear different clothing, eat different foods, perform different work, or use (or not use) specific linguistic forms. Nazi Germany forced Jews to wear a visible cloth symbol that marked them as Jewish and distinguished them from non-Jews.

Occupational segregation, residential segregation ("ghettoes"), and other forms of social separation (separate facilities, restrictions on intermarriage) have been used to differentiate and mark higher and lower ranked groups. Surnames also transmit information about one's social standing.

But physical differences can easily be used to differentiate and identify members of ranked social groups. The U.S. American system of stratification utilized visible markers of ancestry to create an ideology of race, a racial worldview (Smedley, 1993) based on distinct, permanent, ranked categories of humans, created by God or nature. Racial categorization assigned individuals, at birth, to permanent, different, and unequal social strata and used racial status to regulate access to opportunities. In a society already inegalitarian, race became the dominant *legitimizing social ideology*.

## Themes in the American Race-based System of Social Stratification

The United States racial system developed in the context of at least three competing pressures:

1. A long-term policy of population expansion, fueled by a demand for cheap labor;
2. The desire of dominant groups to maintain their economic, political, and cultural dominance; and
3. The need to reconcile the reality of persistent and deep stratification with an equally persistent political rhetoric of individualism, freedom, democracy, and a meritocracy.

These competing pressures generated ambivalence about an increasingly diverse American population, particularly in the postcolonial and post–Civil War era. This helped shape attitudes, policies, and laws about labor, immigration, naturalization, social interaction, education, marriage, and definitions of Whiteness.

Race became a central organizing principle of social relations, superseding even religion. A bipolar system of White and non-White emerged in which White social status was linked to an array of political, legal, social, and economic privileges. Over time, lower-ranked European ethnic groups gradually achieved White status, if somewhat marginally. Racializing the labor force helped to mask the pervasive class stratification that has always characterized American society.

The following sections explore these themes in greater detail.

**Race as a Device to Organize and Exploit Labor**

A major theme in U.S. history is the demand for labor, first in the labor-intensive Southern plantation system and then in the growing industrial centers of the Northern states. Scholars tracing the evolution of the racial classification system argue that race functioned as a device for organizing labor in ways that benefited the dominant property owning classes (see Omi and Winant, 1994).

This process can be seen during the colonial period as the planter class began to view African labor as more desirable than other "indentured" servants of European ancestry. Slavery was extremely profitable for planters and profits from slave labor vastly surpassed those produced by free labor. According to some estimates, on the eve of the Civil War, enslaved workers (bonded persons) received annual clothing and food equivalent to $20 a year, one-fifth of what free workers required (Brodkin, 1998, p. 69).

Joel M. Sipress describes the racialization of slavery in colonial Virginia and argues that racial categories of Black and White can be traced to plantation management and labor control. He notes that Virginia colonial law at first made no distinction between African slaves and European servants.

> Both could own property and could enter into contracts. Servants and slaves ate together, worked together, slept together, and sometimes escaped together. In matters of crime and punishment, the law treated both alike. A slave was, in effect, a servant who served for life. . . .
>
> As Virginia's tobacco planters became increasingly dependent upon African labor, they began to elaborate a distinct legal status of "slave," as well as a racial ideology to justify it. Beginning in the 1660s, the Virginia colonial legislature passed a series of laws that stripped slaves of the rights, such as freedom of assembly, to which they had previously been entitled. Other laws enacted distinct forms of punishment for disobedient slaves. . . . As the legal status of slaves sank, the Virginia legislature began to write racial categories, such as "black" and "white," into law. (Sipress, 1997, p.181)

Throughout American history, racial classifications were manipulated to pit segments of the labor force against each other and to give dominant Euro-American Anglo groups a competitive advantage. The westward expansion led to the recruitment of immigrants for the newly acquired territories of the Southwest and the Hawaiian Islands.

The Treaty of Guadalupe Hidalgo, signed after the Mexican American War, initially promised full rights and federal government protection to Mexicans living in the Southwest. However, economics trumped treaty arrangements when gold was discovered in California. Fortune-seeking Anglos came in massive numbers, soon outnumbering Mexican Americans and dominating politically. Anglos passed discriminatory laws to make it more difficult for Mexican Americans to compete in mining gold. The 1855 antivagrancy act, the so-called "Greaser" act, and a foreign miner's tax of $20 per month applied to all who spoke Spanish, even if they were U.S. citizens (Bigler, 2003).[1]

Despite experience in mining, Mexican Americans were segregated in lower-skilled mining jobs, paid less than their Anglo counterparts for the same jobs, and given fewer food rations. This discrimination was increasingly rationalized in racial terms, citing natural, intrinsic group traits. For example, one mine owner said that Mexicans "have been 'peons' for generations. They will always remain so, as it is their natural condition" (Bigler, 2003, p. 212).

Here, and elsewhere, workers from different ethnic groups were pitted against each other. Building the U.S. intercontinental railroad required an enormous labor force and Chinese individuals were actively recruited to the West Coast. Anglos accused the Chinese of competing unfairly because they were willing to work for lower wages. Instead of organizing the Chinese, U.S. labor worked to exclude them from economic sectors where they competed with native-born Euro-Americans. But they were allowed to work in high-demand areas, such as the laundry business, where there was no competition from Anglo labor.

Planters in the Hawaiian Islands recruited labor from all over the world. The Japanese first came to the U.S. to work on Hawaiian plantations. When Japanese plantation workers organized a major strike in the early 20th century (1909), Filipino workers were recruited by the Hawaiian Sugar Planters' Association to help break the strike, becoming 70% of Hawaiian plantation workers by the 1930s (Benson, 2003, p. 245).

With Japanese migration to California, competition heated up between Japanese and Anglo farmers. Anglo political elites passed a series of restrictive land laws that barred aliens ineligible for citizenship from owning or leasing agricultural land. Under the 1790 Naturalization laws, only free Whites could apply for citizenship. As non-Whites, Japanese immigrants could therefore neither own nor lease land!

Social and occupational segregation along racial and ethnic lines maintained class divisions. When there was a labor shortage, immigration from Europe and Asia was promoted. Restrictions on immigration, such as in the 1920s, often coincided with lower demands for labor. Immigrant labor was segregated in particular industries and jobs, hindering native-born, usually Anglo, workers from bargaining effectively for better wages and working conditions. Immigrant labor was used to undercut labor rates and union organizing.

The primary issues were economic class issues and economic stratification. But both the propertied upper-classes and U.S. born, Euro-American workers framed the labor conflict in racial terms. Scarce jobs and exploitative labor conditions were masked by racial and ethnic competition. Native-born U.S. workers responded by supporting discriminatory practices and laws such as exclusionary immigration laws, or laws prohibiting interracial marriage. This further weakened worker unity movements and reinforced the power of upper-status, propertied groups.

## Cultural Dominance: Preserving the White Nation

The demand for labor in U.S. history produced a large and culturally diverse population. This diversity has always represented a challenge to dominant cultural groups.

Scholars point out that the United States was founded as a self-consciously White nation. The Founding Fathers agreed upon the need for a racially and culturally homogeneous nation if the "republic" was to thrive.

John Jay, coauthor of the *Federalist Papers*, writes in 1787, "Providence has been pleased to give this one connected country to one united people—a people descended from the same ancestors, speaking the same language, professing the same religion" (Stokes & Meléndez, 2001, p. xx).

Social characteristics besides race, especially wealth and being "indentured," initially affected a person's social status. Nevertheless, the first U.S. Naturalization Act, adopted in 1790, applied only to "free white persons," suggesting, as future court cases would argue, that only Whites could bridge the status of alien and become true Americans.

## White . . . and Christian

The dominant cultural group in 1790, however, was not simply White. It was also Christian, Protestant, English speaking, and predominantly of English or Anglo-Saxon origins. These were the "united people" to whom Jay was referring . . . and the predominant population of "free whites" coming to the United States.

There were, of course, two other significant U.S. populations: Native Americans and Africans. References to both groups as "heathens" suggests their non-Christian status was more significant than their ancestry. According to Sipress, "the original justification for perpetual servitude was not the 'blackness' of Africans, but rather their 'heathenism.' In the early years of the Virginia colony, a number of African slaves sued successfully for their freedom on the grounds that they had been baptized and had accepted Christianity" (1997, p. 181).

As race, rather than religion became the ideological justification for slavery, conversion to Christianity was not sufficient to change a slave's legal status. As early as 1667, Black and White racial categories appear in Virginia legislative records, reflecting the declining legal status of African slaves relative to Europeans in similar positions of servitude. Simultaneously, racial ancestry (an *ascribed* status) trumped religion (*achieved*) as a determinant of social status. And in 1667,

> ". . . legislators shifted the justification for slavery from religion to ancestry by declaring that all children born into slavery would remain slaves regardless of baptism." (Sipress, 1997, p. 181)

### Tolerance . . . among Christians

Christianity remained a significant, if not sufficient, implicit requirement for being U.S. American. The famous Maryland Toleration Act (1649) was not about tolerance for non-Christians. It required all persons in the colony to believe in Jesus Christ under penalty of death.

> That whatsoever person or persons within this Province and the Islands thereunto helonging [sic] shall from henceforth blaspheme God, that is Curse him, or deny our Saviour Jesus Christ to bee the sonne of God, or shall deny the holy Trinity the father sonne and holy Ghost, or the Godhead of any of the said Three persons of the Trinity or the Unity of the Godhead, or shall use or utter any reproachfull Speeches, words or language concerning the said Holy Trinity, or any of the said three persons thereof, shalbe punished with death and confiscation or forfeiture of all his or her lands and goods to the Lord Proprietary and his heires.[2]

Colonial Maryland is often praised for its religious tolerance, as a place where Catholics could freely practice their religion. However, the Maryland legislation addressed tolerance for Catholics at a time when Protestants were beginning to dominate numerically. The need for legislation reflects the prevalence of anti-Catholic feeling in other predominately Protestant colonies!

Relations between Protestant denominations were apparently also rancorous, prompting additional laws mandating tolerance among Protestants. The language of the law is explicit:

> Whatsoever person or persons shall from henceforth upon any occasion of offence otherwise in a reproachfull manner or way declare care call or denominate any person or persons whatsoever inhabiting, residing, traficking, trading or comercing within this province or within any ports, harbours, creeks or havens to the same belonging, an Heretick, Schismatick, Idolator, Puritan, Independent Presbyterian, Antenomian, Barrowist, Roundhead, Seperatist, Popish Priest, Jesuit, Jesuited Papist, Lutheran, Calvenist, Anabaptist, Brownist or any other name or term in a reproachful manner relating to matters of Religion shall for every such offence foreit and lose the sum of ten shillings Sterling or the value there of to be levied on the goods and chattels of every such offender and offenders. (Maryland Toleration Act, 1649)

Fines for acts of intolerance were not to be treated lightly. Individuals who could not pay fines were to be "publickly whipt and imprisoned without bail" until "he, she, or they shall satisfy the party so offended or grieved by such reproachful language."[3]

## Immigrant Challenges to the White, Christian, Anglo-Saxon Nation

Concerns over White (WASP[4]) dominance probably existed in the early colonial period, especially in Southern plantation regions with large African populations. Later population waves in the Southwest and in Eastern and Midwestern industrial centers threatened to "swallow" the native White population, especially politically, should the franchise be extended to all citizens.

Growing populations of Mexican Americans challenged old definitions of White culture. Within the Spanish territories, intermating and intermarriage with indigenous Indians had been common. Most Mexicans were "mestizos" ("mixed"), that is, of multiple ancestries. Were they to receive the privileges accorded Whites? Even "pure" 100% Spanish were considered by some upper-strata WASPS to be relatively lower-status Whites, "mongrelized" during the period when the Moors, North African Muslims, ruled Spain.

**Naturalization Law as a Barrier**

As immigration increased, the 1790 "White only" Naturalization Law was employed to prevent "alien" groups, such as the Chinese, Japanese, and later, Indians and Mexicans, from challenging the cultural and political dominance of native WASP elites. Court cases forced judges to wrestle with the definition of Whiteness.

Haney-Lopez (1996) argues that judges tended to rely on either "scientific" criteria, that is, on Blumenbach's classification of races (see chapter 6) or on popular "common sense" notions of Whiteness. There was no particular consistency to the rulings—except that they almost inevitably reinforced the existing system of class and racial stratification.

Earlier we mentioned competition between the Japanese and Anglos in California. The *Ozawa v. United States* case (1922) involved a Japan-born applicant for naturalization who had lived most of his life in the United States. He argued he was White using his own skin color, which he said was similar to most Anglos. The court circumvented the question of color by arguing that White legally meant Caucasian and that Japanese were Mongoloid according to scientific classifications. Ozawa lost the case and could not become a citizen (nor own land, nor sponsor relatives or spouses for immigration).

East Indians, mainly Sikhs from Northwestern India, started migrating to the West Coast in the late 19th and early 20th century. Their applications for citizenship presented a dilemma. Scientific classifications clearly designated Indians as Caucasian.[5] This was the argument Bhagat Singh Thind, an immigrant from India, used in his naturalization application.

The court was in a quandary. This time, however, the court rejected science, reversed itself, and used popular definitions of Whiteness. Denying Thind's application, the court declared that Indians, while Caucasian, were not White, citing such "obvious" things as his "brown skin." Significantly, the court also implied East Indians were too culturally alien (as non-Christians, linguistically, culturally) to become White, that is, to assimilate to the dominant "American" (WASP) culture.

Both cases coincided with a period of economic recession, extreme labor competition between U.S. and foreign-born workers, and political upheaval as organized labor grew and the Socialist Party gained support, partially from recent European immigrants. The Bolshevik (communist) revolution in Russia also exacerbated fears by propertied classes of the spread of a socialist revolution to the United States.

## Mongrelizing the "White" Race

Indians, Japanese, Chinese, and Filipinos were not the only challenges to U.S. American Whiteness. New waves of European immigrants threatened the "cultural" purity and political dominance of the prototypic White (WASP) nation originally envisioned by the Founding Fathers.

By the 1880s, European immigrants and their children were numerically dominant in major urban areas of the United States (Brodkin, 1998, p. 27). These new European immigrants were not Anglo-Saxon. They included Italians, Greeks, Russians, and other Southern and Eastern Europeans. Nor were they Protestant. Many were Roman and Eastern Orthodox Catholics or Jews. Many were uneducated. Some were politically radical.

What was the United States to do with these new and different immigrants from, according to some, the inferior stock of Europeans (see chapter 6)? Would they be treated like earlier European immigrants from England, Germany, and France? Were they really White? Would they be accorded the legal and social position of other Whites?

To the courts, at least, South and Eastern Europeans had the "potential" for assimilation. With proper education (formal and informal), they could aspire to "cultural citizenship," that is becoming true Americans. And . . . their labor was essential in the industrial centers of the East and West Coasts. They made up the bulk of the industrial working class.

### Restricting "Those" Immigrants: The 1920s

By the 1920s, however, economic recession had dampened the demand for foreign labor. Fears of foreign political radicalism coupled with pseudoscientific racial theories fueled native Anglo demands to restrict immigration. Laws were designed to preserve the dominance of the high-ranking "Nordic" populations (English, Germans, French, Scandinavians) while restricting lower-ranked European groups (Alpine, Mediterranean, Semites/Jews).

Immigration restrictions on those not designated White were even more severe. The 1917 Immigration Act created a "barred zone," which denied entry to people from South Asia through Southeast Asia, and islands in the Indian and Pacific Oceans. The Oriental Exclusion Act of 1924 declared all Asians ineligible for citizenship except people from the U.S. possessions of the Philippines and Guam.

Clearly, the intent was to bar East Indians and other Asians from becoming a permanent, political, economic, and cultural force in the United States. Citizenship did not simply imply voting and property ownership rights. Citizens could sponsor relatives, marry or bring wives from the home country, and produce "native-born" U.S. children (see chapter 9).

### Fears of "Race Suicide"

As early as the mid-19th century, school textbooks echoed the theme that Americans were "God's Chosen People" with a Manifest Destiny to prevail over other cultures. However, these were the "old" Americans, the Anglo-Saxon, Protestants, and among these, the "refined" propertied classes or upper strata.

As the 20th century got underway, upper-class males increasingly voiced concerns about race suicide. For one thing, immigrant women had higher fertility rates than native-U.S. women, especially upper-middle-class women. The late 19th–early 20th century witnessed a decline in the White birth rate relative to others—"down" to an average of four children per woman (Davis, 1981).

This partially reflected an emerging progressive vision of womanhood that included fuller engagement in public life, education, careers, voting rights, and control over fertility and the number of offspring. Of course, this "progressive vision" was available to only a small fraction of women, regardless of race.

Theodore Roosevelt, in his 1906 State of the Union message, criticized elite White women who engaged in "willful sterility—the one sin for which the penalty is national death, race suicide" (Davis, 1981, p. 209). Such beliefs fueled the eugenics movement, which was directed toward controlling, even eliminating, the fertility of the less "fit" while encouraging the "fittest" to reproduce. Even Margaret Sanger, despite her progressive politics, adopted eugenics language to argue for family planning and birth control, saying "the chief issue of birth control" was "more children from the fit, less from the unfit" (Davis, 1981, pp. 213–214).

The goal of maintaining White racial dominance racialized reproductive policies. One result was a racist strategy of population control that included sterilization of Black women and girls, often without their knowledge. Another was through essentially restricting elite, literate women's access to family planning information by classifying written materials as "obscenity" and therefore illegal to send through the mail.

A third strategy was to prevent the predominantly male immigrant population of non-Whites from marrying, having families, and producing offspring. This was accomplished through restrictions on naturalization, on immigration of non-Whites, and through antimiscegenation laws that prevented non-Whites males from marrying White women (see chapters 9 and 13).

### Reconciling Democracy and Meritocracy with Inequality and Stratification

Contradictions between political rhetoric and social reality have existed since the founding of the republic, when "all men are created equal" excluded (in addition to women) those of African or Native American ancestry along with the vast majority of nonpropertied Europeans.

But U.S. American political rhetoric was forged in the context of creating a unique national identity, one that contrasted with "old Europe." America was "destined" to be a democracy, a society based on achievement, unfettered by European notions of class, royalty, and rights based on one's birth. The language of the Constitution and Declaration of Independence reflects this theme, with an emphasis on individualism, freedom (from government constraint, from state-imposed religion, from aristocratic-ascribed privilege), and the pursuit of happiness.

As the United States matured and expanded, native-born U.S. Americans felt an "obligation" to spread their "superior" democracy to other parts of the world. The rhetoric of Manifest Destiny and an expansionist foreign policy brought the Philippines, the Hawaiian Islands, and Puerto Rico under the U.S. flag.

At home, it produced a policy of assimilating (into WASP culture) European populations deemed capable of assimilation. Other groups were excluded, through immigration and naturalization laws and through Jim Crow laws.

But stratification and inequality in the United States have always been pervasive, regardless of the rhetoric of freedom and equality. Elites, whether the plantation class of the South or the industrial barons of the North, have controlled enormous power and wealth, as have their descendants. In short, a *class system* existed, not primarily based on merit, but on ascription, on birth, inherited wealth and connections, and on race. The political rhetoric of democracy had to be reconciled with a class and racially stratified social system. So a rather unique ideological justification emerged . . . the notion of a *meritocracy*.

### The U.S. as a Meritocracy

A meritocracy can exist simultaneously with enormous inequality because it assumes everyone has the opportunity make it to the "top." Success, then, is dependent only on natural abilities and how hard people work (see Mukhopadhyay, 2004b). Using this logic, the failure of some groups to reach parity is a result of their own deficiencies rather than a structural feature of the social system. In short, in a meritocracy, the system is "fair," but some folks—indeed, entire groups—simply lack "what it takes" to succeed. The ideology of intrinsic, natural, permanent racial differences, the U.S. American racial worldview, reinforced this ideology of meritocracy by arguing that not all races or cultures possessed the same natural abilities or the kinds of character traits and capacities of the Anglo-Saxon, Protestant, Founding Fathers who had "built the nation." Some races were simply more capable of being Americans than others. Remnants of this ideology appear in current discussions of minority student educational achievement (see chapter 11).

## RACIALIZING INEQUALITY

> Initially invented to justify a brutal but profitable regime of slave labor, race became the way America organized labor and the explanation it used to justify it as natural. Africans, Europeans, Mexicans, and Asians each came to be treated as members of less civilized, less moral, less self-restrained races only when recruited to be the core of America's capitalist labor force. (Brodkin, 1998, p. 75)

Using race to legitimize inequality under the guise of meritocracy appears early in the colonial era, but it becomes more elaborate as race emerges as a fundamental social division of American society. The strategy of racializing Africans, of rationalizing legal discrimination, of justifying African American slavery on the basis of intrinsic, immutable race-based traits, was extended to other ethnic and racial groups. It was also used to justify the permanent lower social position of these groups.

We see this process in depictions of immigrant groups, especially working-class immigrants. Mexicans in the 19th century were characterized as "superstitious, cowardly, treacherous, idle, avaricious, and inveterate gamblers." In the famous Los Angeles "Sleepy Lagoon" case, the Sheriff's Department described Mexicans as inherently criminal and violent because they were Indians and Indians were "Orientals" and Orientals have "no regard for life" (Bigler, 2003, pp. 211–213).

The Asiatic Exclusion League argued that Asian Indians were not

White but an "effeminate, caste-ridden, and degraded" race who did not deserve citizenship (Haney-Lopez, 1996, p. 4). Filipinos, Chinese, and Mexicans were all stereotyped as violent and immoral, using as evidence their desire to date White women. Ironically, race-based immigration and naturalization laws exacerbated an already dramatic shortage of women among male immigrants.

Increasingly, issues of economic and political stratification in the United States became framed in racial terms, with negative stereotyping directed toward immigrants and non-White workers. However, it was not just the powerful and dominant ethnic groups that used race as a strategy to further their own interests.

Jobs held by immigrants were often defined as inappropriate for native workers, using racial justifications. This is seen in one worker's description of a blast-furnace job: "Only Hunkies[6] work on those jobs, they're too damn dirty and too damn hot for a 'white' man" (Brodkin, 1998, p.57).

Native White workers applied negative racelike stereotypes to immigrant workers forced into lower-status jobs. The stereotypes embodied the very traits of the menial jobs themselves. In essence, workers acquired the low-status characteristics of their low-status jobs!

There is a . . . crowd of Negroes and Syrians working there. Many of them are filthy in their personal habits, and the idea of working with them is repugnant to any man who wants to retain his self-respect. It is no place for a man with a white man's heart to be. The Negroes and foreigners are coarse, vulgar and brutal in their acts and conversation. (Cited in Brodkin, 1998, p. 57)

Marginal White groups, like the Irish, also employed these stereotypes. They manipulated their White status to obtain political and economic advantages, to keep Blacks from voting, to keep non-Whites out of labor unions, and to discriminate against and physically attack African Americans in the East and Chinese on the West Coast.

The "whitening" of Irish-Americans provides an example of a marginal social group that embraced a racial identity to advance its own interests. The Irish, who began arriving in the United States in large numbers in the 1840s, found themselves in a society whose culture and politics were already characterized by a strict racial hierarchy. To native-born Americans, the racial status of the Irish, like that of the Poles and Italians who followed, was unclear. Antebellum ethnologists spoke derisively of the "Celtic" race. To political cartoonists, "Paddy" bore an uncanny resemblance to an ape.

"Whiteness," according to historian David Roediger, served as a powerful weapon in the Irish struggle to carve out a place in a hostile American society. By asserting their whiteness, the Irish were able to claim the status of full-fledged Americans. The Irish wielded whiteness to assert control over jobs. White supremacist doctrine cemented the relationship between the Democratic Party, the party of slavery and Indian removal, and an Irish community desperately in need of political patrons. Although anti-Irish and anti-Catholic attitudes persisted, Irish-Americans were successful in their struggle to establish their identity as full-fledged white men and women. (Sipress, 1997, pp. 181–182)

Significantly, recurring negative stereotypes of lower-status ethnic and racial groups as lazy, stupid, dirty, unable to control themselves, untrustworthy, and less intelligent are the opposite pole of the idealized attributes of the dominant Anglo cultural group. The "free white American," the prototypic WASP of the Founding Fathers and their descendants, the Horatio Alger heroes in the 19th-century best-selling novels, are all smart, energetic, self-disciplined, go-getters, able to defer gratification in pursuit of their goals.

Implicitly, then, race and racial stereotypes served to justify, within the rhetoric of meritocracy, the relative social positions of racial and ethnic groups. Racial stratification, the argument goes, is merit based even though one's race is determined at birth. Races are just naturally different.

The rhetoric of race and race-based capacities and characteristics then both justifies and masks a class-based stratified society. The initial use of race to justify economic exploitation becomes an explanation of why social inequality is consistent with a meritocracy, with democracy, freedom, and a society based on individual merit. Success and wealth reflects merit. Lack of success and poverty simply reflects one's personal failings, a lack of ability. One gets what one deserves.

## Conclusion

The American system of racial classification is a historically and culturally specific *legitimizing ideology*, a complex and unique way for explaining, justifying, and perpetuating a system of social, economic, and political inequality.

Racial ancestry, bolstered by racial science (and religion), became the rationale for stratification and inequality. A race-based system of social classification became a way of maintaining the dominance of elite White groups, politically and socially, while simultaneously recruiting new populations to fulfill labor demands.

Race became a central basis for organizing labor and maintaining an economically stratified system, first in the agricultural sector and then in the growing industrial sectors. And racializing the labor force helped to mask the pervasive class stratification and structural inequality that has always characterized American life.

## KEY CONCEPTUAL POINTS

- Cultural classifications emerge in a cultural and historical context, serving certain purposes.
- Race in the United States emerged in a context of a stratified society, as an ideology to justify, maintain, and mask a system of structural inequalities based on class, national origins, gender, and religion.
- Social stratification, while not universal, is a widespread social system of ranked social groups.
- Stratified systems can be based on ascription, achievement, or both. The U.S. racial system contains elements of both despite a rhetoric of achievement (meritocracy).
- The U.S. racial system, definitions of Whiteness, and immigration and naturalization laws, have fluctuated in response to population changes, fueled by the demand for labor and the desire of the dominant social strata to preserve the White nation.
- Race has been used to exploit, divide, and weaken labor and to mask class inequality.

- Racial classifications have significant economic, political, legal, and other social consequences.
- Race in the past has masked other structural inequalities in U.S. society, such as class, gender, and religion. This may also be occurring today, as in school settings.

## KEY TERMS (ITALICIZED AND BOLDED IN TEXT)

ascribed vs. achieved status
class system
legitimizing ideology
meritocracy
social roles

social statuses (positions,
  identities)
social stratification
social system
stratified societies

## TEACHING ACTIVITIES

**Activity Plan 1: Census Activity**

*Objective:* Students discover that racial classifications (as reflected in the census) shift over time and reflect cultural and historical context (This exercise is also appropriate with part 3 chapters.)

*Additional Information:* For census materials, see websites below.

*Procedure:*

Step 1. Introduce students to the U.S. Census. Tell them they are going to analyze census categories over time. Examples of census categories at other time periods are available through websites such as http://home.att.net/~wee-monster/census.html (accessed July 17, 2006); the Historical Census Browser, http://fisher.lib.virginia.edu/collections/stats/histcensus/; and the United States Census, www.census.gov/. For a fee, there is also www.ancestry.com.

Step 2. Present students with 1790 census categories (see Table 7.1). Students first identify relevant social distinctions. For example, one census category is "free white male ages 16 and older." This indicates four relevant social distinctions: "free" vs. "slave"; "white" vs. "nonwhite; "male" vs. "female"; and age, "over 16" vs. "under 16."

Step 3. Students explore reasons why these distinctions might be relevant in 1790 to the government.

- Take the distinction between "slave" and "free," which could affect representation in the House of Representatives, based on population. But how were slaves to be counted? Were they property or legal persons? Plantation slave owners wanted all slaves to be counted to increase their states' (and their own) political power in Congress. Nonslave owners and states objected, probably for similar reasons—political power. The "compromise" was to count "free persons" as 1.0 and slaves as .6 of a person for purposes of political representation.
- Another reason to count slaves separately was probably for taxation purposes since they were legally property.
- Apparently slaves were not listed by name on the census, unlike free persons. This may reflect slaves' status as property rather than persons. And since they couldn't vote or serve on juries, there may have been no need for their formal names.
- Gender (male or female) information may reflect significant legal rights not available to females, such as the right to vote or serve on juries or be drafted. And married women couldn't sign legal contracts or own property in their own names.
- Age was probably useful for the draft, voting, serving on juries, except for slaves or free White females who both lacked full legal rights of adult White males.
- Teachers might point out that the only racial reference is to White (for males and females). Other free persons existed but their race was not specified. Nor was a racial distinction made for slaves. Why might that have been the case? See chapter 9 for some possibilities.

Step 4.   Students discuss how they would have been classified in the census. Point out that until recently, the census maker made that decision, using visual criteria. Discuss old and new self-identification methods. This is particularly relevant to chapter 10.

Step 5.   View other historical census categories and use the same procedure. For example, select a postslavery census, such as

1870 (see below) and discuss how the end of slavery is reflected in the census. For example, the category "slave" disappears and more races are listed (in addition to White, Black, mulatto, Chinese, and Indian). This activity could also work with chapter 9.

Immigration patterns and politics are reflected in questions about foreign birth and whether males (but only males) are citizens (and eligible to vote). Indicators of marital and socio-economic status, like property ownership, value of real estate, occupation or trade, and literacy also appear.

Other interesting census years, for racial categories, are 1920 and 1930.

Step 6.   Examine and discuss the 2000 U.S. Census categories. Note changes in classifications, new information, items that have disappeared. Point out that people can select their own racial and ethnic classification and, for the first time, can select more than one race or ethnicity. Category labels and numbers of categories have changed. This activity could also be used in part 3.

Step 7.   Discuss racial and ethnic classifications, student opinions, factors shaping their views, the larger societal impacts of who (and how many people) end up in each census category, or the impacts of redefining and creating new categories. Reinforce key point that categories are shifting, unstable constructions, motivated by self-interest, with significant impacts. They are under human control. This would be very useful as part of one of the change-oriented activities in part 3.

Step 8.   Connect to contemporary school issues, such as whether racial and ethnic data should be collected and if so, what categories should be used. This dovetails nicely with part 3.

**Activity Idea 1: Starpower: Experiencing a Stratified Society**

*Objective:* Students will understand the concept of a meritocracy as a legitimizing ideology in a class-stratified society. Students will experience the impact of ascribed class on achievement.

**Table 7.1.    1790 U.S. Census Data**

*Sample Census Data*

1790 Census (12 States). 2 August 1790

Total Population: 3,929,214

Note: 1790 census records exist for Connecticut, Maine, Maryland, Massachusetts, New Hampshire, New York, North Carolina, Pennsylvania, Rhode Island, South Carolina, Vermont and Virginia (Virginia schedules were reconstructed from state enumerations)

- head of household
- number of free white males ages 16 and older
- number of free white males under the age of 16
- number of free white females
- number of all other free persons
- number of slaves

*Source:* http://home.att.net/~wee-monster/census.html (accessed July 17, 2006)

*Additional Information:* This activity simulates a U.S. type system of stratification, based on the idea of a meritocracy, with some mobility, but prior group membership is the primary determinant of social, economic, and political status. The activity is highly interactive, intense, and emotional, takes at least two or three class sessions, and requires substantial preparation. However, it is well worth the effort and provides students with a visceral, direct experience of how the U.S. system of stratification works and feels! An anthropologically oriented adaptation of the original Starpower simulation, with detailed step-by-step instructions and postgame discussion, is available at Mukhopadhyay's website, www.sjsu.edu/faculty_and_staff/faculty_detail.jsp?id = 1472.

**Activity Idea 2: Ethnic Diversity in the United States**

Use Web or library sources to find data that reflect the presence of multiple, diverse ethnic groups within each major racial category (White or European; Asian; African; Native American; Hispanic). For example, names of towns (Little Italy), neighborhoods (and street names, school names) within major urban areas, civic and religious organizations, and local newspapers and magazines reveal the multiplicity of ethnic groups and their distinct identities. Census data is also revealing, such as languages spoken at home or in schools. English was not the only language used in U.S. schools. Even as English-only schools arose as part of the 20th-century attempts to assimilate Southern and Eastern Europeans immigrants, immigrants sent their children to after-school programs to learn their parents' native language.

**Activity Idea 3: Relevant Social Categories on Public Documents**

Students explore (using library, family documents, Web sources) the kinds of social categories previously used on key documents such as birth certificates, marriage certificates, hospital admission forms, police reports, school forms, real estate loan application forms, health statistics, and employment applications.

**Activity Idea 4: Build on Activities in Other Chapters**

- See Mating Choice Activity in chapters 9 or 13 and relate activity to class stratification.
- Exploring My Ancestry: The Ethnic Me. Incorporate student investigations of their ancestry from earlier chapters into this chapter. Show how, over time, distinct nationalities and ethnic identities within Europe have been lost, ignored in the public media, suppressed, or have merged through marriage. Explore in what ways European ethnic identities remain in the U.S. (e.g., Italian food, Greek ceremonies, Irish celebrations, Jewish culture). See also the Mukhopadhyay website above.

**Activity Idea 5: Online Teaching Modules**

See the companion website for *Race: Power of an Illusion*. These segments explore links between U.S. racial ideology and stratification.

- Jamestown: Planting the Seeds of Tobacco and the Ideology of Race can be accessed at ww.pbs.org/race/000_About/002_04-teachers-01.htm.
- Just an Environment or a Just Environment? Racial Segregation and Its Impacts, www.pbs.org/race/000_About/002_04-teachers-02.htm.

• The Growth of the Suburbs and the Racial Wealth Gap explores structural racism and how, through housing discrimination, the accumulation of wealth has been racialized, at www.pbs.org/race/ 000_About/002_04-teachers-07.htm. This website also contains additional historical links and resources.

**Activity Idea 6: Racial Inequality and Human Biology**

Explore the impact of racial inequality on human biology through information at the African Burial Ground Project website at www.nypl.org/research/sc/afb/shell.html.

## ENDNOTES

1. For a highly readable, complex picture of Gold Rush immigrants, see Isabelle Allende's novel *Daughter of Fortune*.
2. All quotes from the Maryland Toleration Act are found at http://odur.let.rug.nl/ ~usa/D/1601–1650/maryland/mta.htm (accessed July 17, 2006).
3. The Maryland State Archives website offers related materials free to schools at www.mdsa.net (accessed July 17, 2006).
4. Scupin (2003) and some others use the term WASP for the Northwestern European, predominantly Anglo-Saxon, Protestant, Christians that dominated the White U.S. population until the 20th century and, politically and culturally, thereafter, even today. Inclusion of other European groups in this White category is recent and, we would argue, contingent and incomplete.
5. Among other grounds, North Indian languages were part of the Indo-European language family.
6. This is apparently a reference to people from the region around Hungary.

# CHAPTER 8

# Cross-Cultural Overview of Race

How widespread is the U.S. system of racial classification? Is race a common, even universal, way for humans to classify people? This is the type of question anthropologists love to ask. Anthropology is fundamentally a comparative discipline. Social scientists need to look at all cultures, not just Western or even major non-Western societies, before making generalizations. Our *cross-cultural comparisons* must take into account small-scale, politically decentralized, nonurban, preliterate cultures, including preagricultural (foraging-gathering-fishing-hunting) societies, those based on herding and on simple horticulture. These are part of the human spectrum of possibilities and, until recently, the predominant forms. Large-scale, stratified, politically centralized, "states" with urban centers are relatively new cultural inventions (4,000 to 6,000 years ago) and industrialized nation-states have emerged only within the past century or two.

This chapter examines how different cultures classify humans and finds, once again, both variability and context dependence.

## CONCEPTUAL BACKGROUND

So . . . . are racial classifications a universal feature of human societies? The answer partially depends on what we are asking about. The U.S. racial worldview is specific to North America, although certain features can be found in other racially stratified societies (Smedley, 1993).

In chapter 6, we discussed the human propensity for classification as a way to simplify the complexity of everyday stimuli. But anthropologists reject the idea that racial classifications are automatic, universal, widespread, or even very easy to learn. In the words of Sue Estroff, "the way that race is thought and seen and experienced depends very much on who is thinking, about whom, and why" (Estroff, 1997, p. 115). Adults, as well as children, must learn new systems of classifications when placed in foreign circumstances.

## How Important Are Visible Features as a Basis for Classification?

Visible features, especially natural physical differences, may not even be a common basis for human social classification, at least prior to European colonialism. Some say the notion of race goes back to ancient Greece, to the concept of *genos*. But apparently its prime meaning is a community linked over generations through common ancestry—families, clans, and tribes (Lieberman, 2003, p. 38). Those not part of one's *genos* were designated as *barbaros* or barbarians. The word *Xenos*, in modern Greek, means foreigner and a *Xenodoheion* is a hotel (literally, a container for foreigners!).

Language and culture are significant social markers and indicate shared ancestry. In Latin America and the Caribbean, even today, most indigenous groups use linguistic and cultural features for social classification rather than visible biological traits. The Yanomama, a small-scale farming-foraging (horticulturalist) group living in Northwestern Brazil and Southern Venezuela, divide people according to those who know their language and culture (*Yanomama*) and those who don't (*nabuh*).

For indigenous groups living around Tupi, Peru, collective identity is closely linked to their language, which they call *Jaqaru,* from the words *jqi* "human being" and *aru* "speech." They refer to themselves as "Jaqaru" people. And despite European imposition of a common racial term, *indios*, or "Indians," on the diverse cultures in the region, most Native American people today still identify with and prefer to be called by their original names, such as Maya, Kumeyaay, and so on (Kephart, 2003).

Everyone seems aware that traditions in India classify people based on so-called "caste" (*varna, jati*). But language and language-related cultural forms (e.g., Bengali songs) are the basis for significant social divisions and social identities, along with religion. When people ask about one's "community," they could easily be referring to one's linguistic community, such as Bengali, Tamil, Gujrati, Punjabi, or Telugu. Indeed, major Indian states (Tamil Nadu, Karnataka, West Bengal, Punjab, and Meghalaya) are named after the main language spoken. Bangladesh, the nation ("land of Bengalis"), was the eastern part of British-ruled Bengal. Even now, Bengalis, whether Hindu or Muslim, in India or Bangladesh, feel a common identity. Hindi may be India's official national language but many Indians, especially in the South, prefer their "own" languages (Tamil, Telugu, Malayalam, etc.). India's Hindi films are known throughout the world but films in other Indian languages are a thriving industry.

Music, poetry, and other art forms are often language specific. And when it comes to marriage, language compatibility is crucial, even if the bride and groom speak multiple languages. Language is one means through which social identity is collectively expressed and transmitted to the next generation.

Even among Europeans, steeped in racial ideology, anthropologist Ann Stoler discovered that nonracial characteristics, personality traits, psychological and moral dispositions, and various cultural competencies were central to British, Dutch, and French colonial policies and definitions of who was European or White (Stoler, 1997, p. 101). In addition to appearance, specific attitudes and behaviors were associated with people from certain ethnic, caste, or class groups.

Even if visible features are socially significant, skin color is not a universal basis for classifying people. In pre-20th-century China, the basis of racial classification was body hair. Extensive body hair signified a lack of "civilization." Chinese writers described European male missionaries, with their beards, as "hairy barbarians." Some 20th-century Chinese social scientists continued to divide humans into evolutionary stages based on body hair. One survey of humanity provided a detailed classification using types of "beards, whiskers, and moustaches" (Miller, 2002, p. 17).

Even when skin color is culturally noticed—that is, used as a basis for creating named social categories—the meanings associated with racial categories differ. Brazil and other Latin American cultures illustrate this, as we shall see shortly.

## Is Difference Universally Devalued?

What anthropologists call *ethnocentrism* is widespread and normal (see chapter 5). Most people internalize and value their own cultural systems, their own ways of classifying humans, their own aesthetic and behavioral standards. Indeed, one's culture becomes part of one's personal identity and sense of normalcy. From this perspective, it is not surprising that individuals make value judgments when they encounter people from other cultures.

Mukhopadhyay recalls her first visit to India, in the early 1970s. She was riding a local bus in a rural area of northern India. A fellow passenger kept staring at her, particularly her arms. Finally he leaned over and sympathetically asked her Indian husband what kind of disease his wife had. He said he had noticed all the dark spots on her arms. The husband suppressed a laugh and politely tried to translate the concept of "freckles" into Hindi.

Yet the human ability, indeed propensity, to notice and classify people by visible traits does not inevitably lead to a hierarchical system of races. Sometimes groups exaggerate minor physical or cultural differences simply to assert their collective group ethnic or cultural identity. The region anthropologists call Melanesia (located in the South Pacific) is very diverse culturally and linguistically. Papua New Guinea alone, with a population of 3 million, has over 700 distinct linguistic groups. Most New Guineans live in small rural villages that traditionally were egalitarian and politically autonomous.

To an outsider, their cultures and languages are far less distinct than to natives. One anthropologist (Brison, 2003) found that neighboring villages described each others' language as mutually unintelligible and impossibly difficult to learn. Yet the languages are virtually identical except for slight differences in pronunciation. Moreover, the two groups intermarry, are culturally indistinguishable, and once were one village. Nearly everyone has relatives in both villages.

Apparently villages deliberately accentuate minor linguistic differences as "emblems of ethnic dissimilarity," part of a broader claim to local ethnic distinctiveness (Brison, 2003, p. 377). Brison traces this to colonial and postcolonial conditions. She argues that whether groups emphasize or de-emphasize potential differences, cultural or physical, depends on circumstances, relations among ethnic groups, and political consequences.

## Not All Differences Are Perceived as Negative or as a Basis for Social Stratification

It does not seem to be basic human nature to fear and denigrate difference. Indeed, anthropological evidence suggests that that the appeal of the exotic—or at least, variety—is not a recent phenomenon. Difference can delight and generate desire. *Homo sapiens* have remained one species partially because of the human urge to mate across social boundaries, with people from different groups and cultures. And human cultural products have traveled huge distances, through trade and gift giving, reflecting the human attraction to things different.

However, the appeal of difference is not random. Desirable differences, such as pale skin or sharp noses, are often features of powerful or high-status cultures or groups. In the U.S., cultural objects from Japan, like animation characters and "hello kitty" emblems, as well as the Japanese language, have acquired great popularity in the past decade (approx. 1990s–2005). Japanese cultural crossover into mainstream U.S. norms is not just a coincidence; it coincides with Japan's role as a global power.

## Stratified Social Groups Can Exist Without an Ideology of Race

The anthropological record shows that humans can have stratification and slavery without an ideology of race (chapter 7). Cultural groups that share the same ancestral roots but differ in religion or political orientation can oppress, even slaughter, each other, as happened in Northern Ireland, the former Yugoslavia, Rwanda, and the U.S. Civil War. In most wars, and all 20th-century wars, participants have not aligned along racial lines (e.g., WWII, despite Hitler's racist-religious ideology). The Romans and Greeks had slaves who were also Roman and Greek!

## Societies Can Have a Racelike Ideology Not Based on Biological Differences

Japan offers another permutation on the race theme. Japan is stratified by class but portrays itself proudly as culturally homogeneous. Former Prime Minister Nakasone once suggested that Japan's success in international business was due to its being *"tan'itsu minzoku,"* a term that connotes ethnic homogeneity. Yet scholars estimate that at least 10% of Japan's population is from minorities (Kottak, 2002).

The Burakumin are one significant minority, anthropologically speaking. Burakumin were the lowest group in the system of social stratification that emerged during the Tokugawa period (1603–1868). They have been compared to India's "untouchable" lower strata because they are forced to do "unclean" jobs, like killing animals, disposing of dead bodies, and working with leather, and then are stigmatized for doing these jobs!

Burakumin are viewed as innately physically and morally different and inferior to mainstream Japanese. Yet Burakumin are physically and genetically indistinguishable from other Japanese. They can and sometimes do "pass" as non-Burakumin. The markers of their low status are not visible or physical. Their social status is identifiable only through their family names, the segregated residential areas they traditionally have been forced to live in, and their occupations. Legal forms of discrimination no longer exist but old attitudes and stigma persist (Kottak, 2002).

The Greek philosopher Aristotle justified slavery on the grounds that humans were unequal even though many slaves came from other Greek city-states and looked physically similar. But dominant groups have the power to define the subordinate group as inferior as well as force them to dress and behave in ways that reinforce their supposed inferiority.

Ancient Greece linked social status to a type of inner essence, one's "soul." The idea that different groups are created to perform different societal functions apparently existed in Greek thought. Socrates, in the so-called tale of the metals, purportedly argued that a stable society required three classes. Souls corresponding with gold were designated rulers, those corresponding to silver were administrators and officials, and those to brass and iron were farmers and craftsmen (Lieberman, 2003).

Early justifications for North American slavery rested primarily on religious beliefs about ancestral relationships and past deeds rather than on race as biology. Within the European Christian tradition, St. Thomas Aquinas and others justified social stratification as part of the "divine plan" of God. Using biblical stories, slavery apologists in Europe and the United States attributed the enslavement of Africans (and in some versions, Native Americans) to their relationship to Ham, one of Noah's sons. In one version of the story, Noah accidentally encountered his father lying naked, in a drunken state. He failed to avert his eyes in time and saw his father's nakedness. This produced Noah's curse, condemning Ham and his dark-skinned descendents to a life of exile and servitude (Smedley, 1993, p. 158).

## Meanings: Skin Color and Other Physical Traits as the Basis for Social Ranking

The proximity and interaction of two cultures that look physically different does not inevitably lead to those differences becoming culturally and socially significant, nor is it a basis for inferior or superior social rank. Ancient Egyptian wall paintings apparently depicted humans of various shades of skin colors but this simply reflected variability in the Egyptian and surrounding populations.

In India, the term "varna" or "strata" is partially associated with skin color—higher *varna* are supposedly lighter. This probably reflects the dominance of Aryan-Indo-European groups from more northerly latitudes over the more southerly, Dravidian, and darker-skinned populations, living closer to the equator (see chapter 3). But skin color is only one superficial and often inaccurate indicator of ancestry and social status.

In stratified societies, skin color can be a marker of class status, even when the biological potential for melanin production is identical. Skin color is affected by exposure to the sun. In predominately agricultural societies, like India, lower-status groups were more apt to toil in the sun, as farmers or laborers, than their upper-status counterparts. Lower-status groups, then, were often visibly darker than elite groups.

For women in societies with strict sexual segregation, linkages between class status and color were even more intense. Elite women remained in family compounds, inside the home, or were fully covered, from head to foot, when they ventured into the public sphere. These cultural practices not only minimized exposure to the male gaze—but also to the sun. Lighter skin symbolized high status and, thus, became a particularly desirable trait in women.

Cross-cultural evidence, then, indicates that while visible traits are sometimes used for social classification, racial thinking and racial stratification is neither inevitable nor particularly common prior to European colonial expansion. Other contextual factors, motivations, and especially power relations play a crucial role in the emergence of race as a central basis for social differentiation and social stratification.

### Variable Contexts Alter the Meanings of Racial Systems

Context shaped racial ideologies, even in areas dominated by Europeans. Europeans shared popular beliefs about human variability and types of humans. But the term *race* as a way of classifying human groups did not appear in the English language until the 17th century; then it referred to characteristics of certain types of persons, such as dispositions or temperaments, or to a class of person, as the race of womankind (Smedley, 1993). From the 16th to 20th centuries, the concept of race and its social manifestations evolved along distinct paths, in different colonial regions, reflecting local circumstances and goals.

This is perhaps most striking in the Americas. Scholars have long contrasted the racial system that emerged in North America with the forms it has taken in Central America, the Caribbean, and South America. The North American system is bipolar and mutually exclusive, organized into two fundamental categories, White-Black or White–non-White. It is a rigid, inflexible system: one's race is usually established at birth, based on the lower racial status parent (the one-drop rule), and it is not changeable during one's life.

U.S. American racial categories are mutually exclusive, at least in their post–Civil War version when the category of mulatto disappeared. One is either White or Black, White or non-White—you cannot be both.

Color and other physical characteristics carry an enormous ideological load, linked in the racial world view to racially designated capacities, especially intelligence. The U.S. racial system establishes rigid social boundaries and barriers to social interaction through laws and other forms of coercion (chapter 9). Race is viewed as a fixed and permanent biological inheritance.

Latin American and Caribbean racial systems are more flexible, less exclusionary, and have more racial categories and a different concept of race. One's racial classification can change over time. There have been virtually no explicit race-based bars to social interaction, mating, and marriage. We can see the effects in Latin American and Caribbean populations. Most people aren't easily categorized using the U.S. system. In many Latin American/Caribbean nations, class stratification (and gender) is a more powerful and pervasive basis for social status than race. Thus an individual's racial designation can alter with a change in one's economic and social status.

Brazil exemplifies these contrasts. Like the United States, it is a large, complex society derived from a plantation slave economy that lasted until the last half of the 19th century. It continues to be racially stratified, part of the legacy of slavery. Yet, unlike the United States, Brazil never legally encoded its racial system; interracial sexual relations and marriage were widespread among Africans, Europeans, and Native Americans. This is reflected in recent population figures for Brazil. Using macroracial categories, 54% were classified as White, 40% Mulatto, 5% Black, and 1% Other (Kephart, 2003, p. 297).

In ordinary life, however, Brazilians use far more racial labels and some anthropologists have identified over 500 terms. The Portuguese word *tipo,* meaning "type," is used to classify people using a complex set of visible physical characteristics including skin color, nose shape, eye color and shape, hair color and type, and lip shape. One family can have many *tipos.* There are regional differences in *tipos* reflecting variations in the historic mix of populations.

The classification system is complex, as seen in Jefferson Fish's description of one city in the northeastern state of Bahia. Terms ranged from the "whitest" to the "blackest" *tipos.* For example,

a *loura* is whiter-than-white, with straight blond hair, blue or green eyes, light skin color, narrow nose, and thin lips. . . . A *branca* has light skin color, eyes of any color, hair of any color or form except tight curly, a nose that is not broad, and lips that are not thick. . . . A *morena* has brown or black hair that is wavy or curly but not tight curly, tan skin, a nose that is not narrow, and lips that are not thin. . . . A person with tight curly blond (or red) hair, light skin, blue (or green) eyes, a broad nose, and thick lips, is a *sarará*. The opposite features—straight black hair, dark skin, brown eyes, narrow nose, and thin lips—are those of a *cabo verde*. *Sarará* and *cabo verde* are both tipos that are considered by Brazilians in Salvador, Bahia, to be neither black nor white. (Fish, 2003, p. 277)

In another small Brazilian community, about half of the villagers considered themselves *mulatto* but within that category there were 10 to 15 different terms. Kottak (2003) found that one's racial description could alter, depending on who was talking, when, or even the time of day. Besides *branco* (white), he could be *claro* (light), *louro* (blond), *sarara* (light-skinned redhead), *mulato claro* (light mulatto), or *mulato* (mulatto). One of his informants constantly changed the term he used for himself—from *escuro* (dark) to *moreno escuro* (dark brunet) to *preto* (black).

The above example illustrates that racial descriptors are always relational; that is, they depend on who is talking to whom.[1] Apparently people also take into account social and economic factors when calculating one's "race." For example, a person wearing old clothes and standing in front of a rather ramshackle dwelling might be described as *preto* (black). Dressed up and standing in front of a middle- or upper-class house, the same person would be classified as *moreno* (brown) or even *branco* (white).

The situational context of racial classifications reflects how race is embedded, to differing degrees, in a system of social stratification. In some Caribbean societies, like Dominica, the society is primarily stratified by economic class rather than by color. The social class structure is almost totally based on wealth and there is no substantial White elite as there is in other Caribbean nations like Trinidad, Jamaica, and Barbados.

Variability within Latin America and the Caribbean is enormous due to the different colonial histories and local circumstances. Areas of plantation culture had large African populations and relatively few

Europeans, affecting mating, marriage, and future demographic patterns. Today, some countries, like Barbados, have less than 5% of their population categorized as "Mulatto/Mixed" while other countries, like the Dominican Republican have over 70% who are so categorized (Kephart, 2003, pp. 300–301).

In some countries, like Dominica, "Carib" is an important ethnic group. In others, like Barbados, a group called *redlegs* was originally laborers recruited from the British Isles. Although they were the poorest group on Barbados, they took pride in being "white" and identified, by color at least, with the European planter class. Later on, they began to mix and mate with the African populations but still retained their identity—and prejudices (Kephart, 2003).

There are also so-called maroon communities (from the Spanish word *cimarron* meaning "wild"), African slaves who escaped from their plantation and founded communities in Jamaica, Colombia, and, most significantly, in what is today Suriname. These groups have retained much of their African ethnic cultural and linguistic backgrounds, as reflected in their social categories and labels. They speak Creole languages, which combine West African sentence structure with mainly European vocabulary.

In the postslavery period, the planter class in colonies like Trinidad actively recruited Indian (and some Chinese) immigrants for agricultural work, partially to prevent Afro-Trinidadians from becoming economically and politically powerful. This strategy significantly altered the ethnic composition of the island. Today, Trinidad has approximately equal populations of African and Indian descent, along with some Chinese, Spanish, British, French, other Latin Americans, and a significant number of multiethnics. It also has Muslims, Christians, Hindus (multiple varieties and languages), Sikhs, Jews, Buddhists, and secular humanists enriching its cultural complexity!

One study of racial categories produced seven basic terms: *negro, Indian, dogla* (a mixture of East Indian and African), *mestizo, panyol* (Venezuelan), *Spanish* (i.e., European), and *white*. There were also nine compound terms: *madrasi-Indian, kuli-indian, Tobago-negro, chinee-negro, French-creole* (local, white), *clearskin-dogla, koko-panyol, half-white* (mulatto), and *local white* (Kephart, 2003, p. 301).

Some Caribbean islands, like Carriacou and Cuba, preserved early census information on African ethnolinguistic groups among the island's slave populations. Those born in the Americas were designated *creole* but apparently retained an ethnic identification with their mother's line (what anthropologists call matrilineal descent). There was a ranking among African ethnic groups and there were beliefs about the mental and physical attributes of different groups. Marriage was exogamous—that is, marriage partners had to be outside of one's own ethnic group.

On Carriacou, no one born and raised there is thought of as White. Nor do they think in Black-White terms. They apparently use some racial terms found in other parts of the Caribbean, such as red/redskin, brown/brown-skin, white, pink (i.e., albino) but as simple descriptive adjectives. For example, someone might be referred to as "the *brown-skin* one." Their significant social identities are as *Carriacou people*, aware of their African ancestry and of belonging to different African *nations* or *bloods*. They contrast African behaviors and beliefs with White behaviors and beliefs. Sharing food, for example, is what *negro people* do, in contrast with *white people* (Kephart, 2003).

**What Happens When Immigrants Come to the U.S.?**

Given that the U.S. system of racial classification is not universal, people from other cultures are often confused by our categories. At the simplest level, they find that the labels they use at home don't work here. Brazilians are surprised to find that the American term "blond" refers to hair color only. Many Brazilians of the Branca ("white") *tipo* are not considered White, often to their dismay. Ironically, they are frequently categorized as Hispanic even though they speak Portuguese and not Spanish. Jefferson Fish, married to a Brazilian woman, describes how their daughter, who is brown-skinned, can change her race from Black to *Moreno* (brunette) by taking a plane from the United States to Brazil.

Haiti, for historical reasons, is (with respect to ancestry) one of the most African of the Caribbean islands. But Haitians use both physical appearance and ancestry in their classifications. And one drop of White blood is sufficient to make one racially "white." Haiti's folk taxonomy includes a term for foreigners of African appearance that literally means "a black white" (*un blanc noir*; Fish, 2003).

More significantly, U.S. institutions demand that all groups fit within our system of racial and ethnic classification. As race and ethnicity have reemerged as significant dimensions of identity, with political consequences, immigrants (and their children especially) struggle to find their own identity within the available categories.

Immigrants from India and the Indian subcontinent have never fit American or European racial categories. In the Thind case (chapter 7), Indians were declared to be Caucasian but not White. With the emergence of the pan-Asian category in the 1970s, Indians have been recruited for the Asian category, despite its diversity of histories, cultures, languages, and political entities. Even more comprehensive is the "people of color" category—all non-Europeans (ancestrally). To many Indian immigrants, this classification as "colored" (vs. White) is quite foreign. Not surprisingly, U.S. Americans from the Indian subcontinent have been lobbying for a distinct category, one that reflects their background and sense of identity.

When Puerto Ricans first came to the mainland United States, they encountered a world of bipolar, bounded, racial categories that profoundly shaped their lives. After the Spanish American War and the U.S. occupation of Puerto Rico, immigration increased to the mainland. As the immigrant population grew, working-class Puerto Rican and Cuban women tried to organize along lines of shared interest. Perceived as an "interracial group," most meeting halls refused to allow them to meet (Bigler, 2003). Puerto Ricans inducted into the military after 1917 served in racially segregated units. American racial attitudes shaped how business and political leaders saw the potential of Puerto Rico, including as a potential state, an issue that remains unresolved today.

Immigrants from the Dominican Republic, now a major group in New York City, often find themselves categorized as African American—whereas in the Dominican Republican, anyone partly "white" is considered nonblack, usually mulatto. In the 1990 U.S. Census, however, Dominicans were forced to select Black, White, or Other. Fifty percent identified as "Other" and 25% as Black (Bigler, 2003, p. 225). Dominicans find negotiating their identity in the U.S. complex. They are shades of brown, speak Spanish, dance to a Latin/Caribbean beat, and are used to color being a physical feature not a social identity.

In essence, immigrants such as Puerto Ricans, Dominicans, and East Indians are forced into a North American racial system—they have been racialized according to the criteria of the predominately Anglo, Protestant, dominant culture. And skin color has a different meaning.

Piri Thomas's 1967 autobiography *Down These Mean Streets* describes his painful realization of what it means to be dark-skinned in the United States when he applies for a sales job. Unlike his light-skinned Puerto Rican friend who was hired on the spot, when he goes in, he is told that they will contact him when a job opening comes up. "I didn't feel so much angry as I did sick, like throwing-up sick. Later, when I told this story to my buddy, a colored cat, he said, 'Hell, Piri, Ah know stuff like that can sure burn a cat up, but a Negro faces that all the time.' 'I know that,' I said, 'but I wasn't a Negro then. I was still only a Puerto Rican'" (Bigler, 2003, p. 220).

Puerto Ricans, Dominicans, South Asians, Filipinos, Arab Americans, and other ethnic groups are beginning to rebel against the binary racial (and language) system operating in the United States. They are adopting new labels that are expressive of their own identities: Nuyoricans (Puerto Ricans in New York), Dominican Yorks, Chicanos, Mexicanos, Sanglish, Desi, Afro-Caribbeans.

Immigration presents an enormous challenge to the U.S. system of racial classification. Combined with the rapid growth of intermarriage between individuals of diverse ethno-racial-linguistic-religious backgrounds (see chapter 9), it is not surprising that the most rapidly growing census category in the United States is "Other."

## KEY CONCEPTUAL POINTS

- Race is not a universal system of social classification.
- Not all cultures use visible differences, including skin color, for social classification, nor do they rank or stratify groups on this basis.
- Skin color, when a basis for classification, has variable cross-cultural meanings.

- Language and culture are probably as important for social classification and identity as physical features.
- Cultural groups can either minimize or exaggerate differences, physical or cultural.
- Contextual factors—especially power relations—are crucial in the emergence of systems of racial classification.
- Racial systems developed along different paths in North America vs. Latin America and the Caribbean.
- The cultural specificity of the U.S. system makes it difficult for people who immigrate from other cultures.
- Immigration and ethnic and racial intermarriage is challenging the current U.S. system of racial classification.

## KEY TERMS (ITALICIZED AND BOLDED IN TEXT)

cross-cultural comparison
ethnocentrism

## TEACHING ACTIVITIES

*General Objectives:* Students will be able to describe immigrant experiences fitting into U.S. racial/ethnic categories as well as cross-cultural variations in social classification.

*Additional Information:* Many of these are applicable to part 3, particularly chapter 10.

### Activity Idea 1: U.S. Racial Categories vs. Categories in Other Cultures.

*Procedure:* Students do one or more of these (alone or in groups)

- Research the kinds of categories that appear on U.S. governmental or other institutional forms (e.g., census, educational institutions, birth certificates, and marriage certificates). For some online sources, see websites in chapter 7, including the U.S. Census.
- Look at census or statistical abstract population summary catego-

ries for a different country (e.g., India, Brazil, Canada, Germany, South Africa). Notice what categories are used and what social characteristics of people seem to be most important.

• Interview an immigrant in the U.S. (relative, student, teacher, neighbor, etc.). Develop interview questions (alone, in groups, or as a class). Questions should explore people's reactions to U.S. racial and other social classifications: how others see them, how they see themselves, how they respond to categories on official forms (school, census, birth certificates, and other documents that request ethnic-racial data).

**Activity Idea 2: Social Studies or Comparative World History Class.**

*Objective:* Use research projects to understand how history and local circumstances shape systems of racial classification. Sample research topics include:

• European Plantation Slavery System and Regional Diversity in Latin America and the Caribbean. Students (individually or in groups) study different countries. Use census data or other sources to identify racial and other relevant social categories. Compare plantation and nonplantation economies. Then look at diversity within plantation economies. Students explore historical and other conditions with diversity.

• European Colonial Impact. Look at places where there was no slavery, like Britain, India, Indonesia, and Nigeria. How have racial categories evolved there?

## ENDNOTES

1. The Brazil example also suggests microcultural variations in racial classification. U.S. African Americans do not necessarily share the same system as European Americans.

# CHAPTER 9

# If Race Doesn't Exist, What Are We Seeing? Sex, Mating, and Race

By now, if you have read part 1 showing why race is not "biologically real," you might be afraid to admit that you can identify people racially! But recognizing that races are culturally constructed doesn't mean there are no visible physical differences between U.S. racial groups. There *is* a biological component to the cultural invention we call race. But cultural processes are responsible for biology's meaning and continuing social significance in the United States.

## CONCEPTUAL BACKGROUND

So how does biology fit into all of this? Human biological variation is a fact. We are a diverse species and some of that diversity is visible. U.S. American racial groups share common ancestry, and common ancestry can produce some genetic markers or distinctive features, even though these represent a fraction of all our genetic material. So some of what we see, when we "see race," is the result of biology. However, physical markers of common ancestry can either be exploited or rendered meaningless. They can persist or disappear over time. In the United States, *cultural* processes—especially mating, marriage, and kinship practices—are responsible for preserving biological markers of race.

### Cultural Processes That Affect Biology

Part 1 described how microevolutionary forces operating thousands of years ago produced human biological variation. Some visible physical traits, such as skin color or nose shape, reflect human biological adaptations to different environmental conditions.

Major racial groups in the United States, historically, came from geographically widely separated and distinct places—West Africa, Northwestern Europe, and the North American continent. Skin color, as we know, long ago took different evolutionary paths in these regions.

But it was cultural processes—first European colonization and then the African slave trade—that brought these populations together in North America. Skin color was available as a convenient *marker* of ancestral background, social group identity, and, eventually, racial status.

Subsequent immigrant populations (e.g., East Indians, Italians, Chinese) also possessed visible, equally superficial, remnants of common geographic origins and a microevolutionary past. Sometimes it was skin tone but often it was facial features, such as eyes, nose shape, or hair. Markers, often with negative connotations, emerged in Anglo descriptions of these groups: the "shifty" eyes of Chinese, the "beaked" noses of Semites, the "greasy" hair of Mexicans, the "swarthy" faces of southern Italians vs. the blue-eyed blond "clean," "Nordic" look.

The second and most significant cultural process responsible for the continuing visible biological component of U.S. race has to do with mating and marriage. Humans have remained one species, without subspecies, because of *gene flow*, that is, constant intermating between populations (chapter 3). Prehistoric humans didn't restrict their mates to local folks but ventured outside their own groups.

Gene flow occurred through migration, temporary unions, and marriage exchanges between neighboring or even distant groups. In-group mating (***endogamy***) tends to preserve local population traits while outgroup mating (***exogamy***) tends to increase the diversity of the gene pool and the variability of subsequent generations. From an evolutionary perspective, finding mates outside of one's own population is a biological plus.

But cultures manipulate biology for cultural ends. The social advantages of "marrying out" are perhaps greater than the biological ones. Marriage creates ties between groups, establishing kinship relationships through in-laws and through new descendants. It facilitates other exchanges, material, social, and political. It also helps reduce conflict between groups. "Marry out or die out" . . . so the saying goes.

## How Cultures Regulate Mating and Marriage

Romantic love notions aside, all cultures regulate marriage and mating to some extent. The parent-child incest taboo is universal and restrictions on sibling sex and marriage are nearly universal. Beyond this, societies can either encourage or discourage mating and marriage outside one's own group.

In small-scale, nonstratified societies, people tend to marry outside their own circle. Children's marriages are arranged, sometimes at birth, in order to reinforce long-standing social relationships between families, kinship groups, villages, even regions. Spouses often do not live together and do not have sexual relations until after they reach puberty. Marriage, then, is a vehicle for social alliances.

Marriage also regulates the social group status and social identity of children born to women. Family and kinship are the core of most human societies and include many relatives beyond the U.S. *nuclear family* (mother-father-offspring). Children are essential for the continuation of this extended family, the lineage, and the social group.

Children, in human cultures, do not necessarily *belong* to their birth mothers even though it is rather clear, biologically speaking, whose body produced the child. The father and his family or the mother's family may claim the child, using culturally established arguments. These include having contributed the "seed" or sperm, paid the *bride-wealth* (gifts to the bride's family at marriage), or sharing a common ancestor with the child (the mother is my daughter). In some cultures, the child conventionally belongs to the mother's family or lineage; more often, it belongs to the father's kin group; sometimes, it belongs to both maternal and paternal sides. Regardless, children's social status and family membership is a cultural process, following culturally established practices, with cultural consequences.[1]

Societies with arranged marriages are not necessarily restrictive when it comes to sex outside of marriage. In some small-scale societies, a girl waits until puberty to have sex with her husband—but not with other males. Or a young married woman may take a male lover, especially if her husband is much older and marries her primarily to give him additional offspring. Should she get pregnant by her lover, her husband still "gets" the child.

Individual desire in most cultures, then, is controlled by an array of institutions, social practices, and laws. Families, kinship groups, local communities, religion, and the legal system all work together to regulate social interaction, to ensure that mating and marriage follow prescribed lines. The reproductive and social consequences are too great to leave such important matters in the hands of young people!

In stratified societies, upper-status groups are especially concerned about controlling mating and marriage, for they have the most to lose. Societal barriers are erected to prevent marriage between ranked social groups. Thus, British of "royal" birth are supposed to marry other royalty, ensuring that family wealth, titles, and other rights and privileges remain sole prerogatives of this elite strata.

Sexual segregation can reinforce social stratification. Sexual segregation not only reduces opportunities for male-female sexual relations but for sexual relations between different social strata. Upper-status women, especially of reproductive age, are sexually regulated, whether through "chastity belts," virginity tests at marriage, honor killings, or fears of being labeled a "slut" or "loose woman." Families often express concern for the "purity" of the upper-status family tree and lineage. Reproductively, intragroup mating does reduce genetic variability. But more important, marrying within one's own group keeps economic, political, and other social assets within the group. For high-status groups, then, restricting marriage is a way to maintain one's position.

### Maintaining Racial Boundaries in the United States

Almighty God created the races, white, black, yellow, malay and red, and he placed them on separate continents. And but for the interference with his arrangement there would be no cause for such marriages. The fact that he separated the races shows that he did not intend for the races to mix."—1967, statement of the Virginia judge who upheld his state's anti-miscegenation law. (Cited in Cruz & Berson, 2001, p. 4)

Within the United States, social control of sexuality, mating, and marriage have been crucial for maintaining a system of stratification based on race. Culture was used to shape biology in ways that served the cultural goals of high-status groups. From kinship and blood calculations to antimiscegenation laws, segregated schools, and housing discrimination, all are cultural devices that maintain racial boundaries, keep races fixed and permanent, and prevent new races from emerging, old ones from disappearing.

Cultural and legal barriers to interracial mating and marriage did not always exist in the United States. During the early colonial period, European–African and European–American Indian unions were common. Europeans and Africans lived and worked in the same households and were initially treated as similar, legally and socially.

Some historians put the number of biracial individuals in the colonies around the time of the American Revolution at between 60,000 and 120,000 (Cruz & Berson, 2001). The famous "Pocahontas exception," the marriage of Pocahontas and John Rolfe in 1614 in Jamestown, was apparently not a complete anomaly. Consistent with English traditions, the children of Pocahontas belonged to their father—that is, they acquired the legal status and social group identity of their father, not their mother.

Other interracial marriages occurred. Patrick Henry once suggested using tax incentives and cash stipends to encourage intermarriage between Whites and Indians. The shortage of Anglo women and the importance of families to Anglo farmers may have prompted his proposal.

With the emergence of race-based slavery and racial stratification, the legal system was employed to prevent interracial mating, marriage, and the growth of a racially ambiguous and, therefore, problematic population. The U.S. racial system required a set of visible markers of racial identity. During slavery, there were pragmatic considerations. Multiracial slaves could more easily escape and melt into the White or Indian population.

Multiracial individuals also challenged the ideology of racial science, with its notion of discrete, distinct, and ranked subspecies. They were constant, visible manifestations of the "continuous distribution" of human traits and lack of clear boundaries between groups (see chapter 1). Multiracial offspring also reinforced the viability of race "mixing," contrary to the "mongrelizing" concerns expressed in the rhetoric of racial impurity.

Most important, interracial mating and multiracial offspring threatened a system of social, economic, and legal discrimination based on visible markers. What if these markers disappeared? How could dominant groups identify subordinate racial groups? The failure to control interracial mating and the gradual expansion of an interracial population could, within a few generations, destroy visible racial divisions, leaving only a continuum! "Nature" had to be controlled. Racial endogamy—intragroup mating and marriage—especially among Whites—was essential to preserving racial hierarchy.

### Antimiscegenation Laws: Preserving the White Race

The word *miscegenation*, from Latin *miscere* "to mix" + *genus* "kind" (Merriam-Webster, 2003), did not appear until the 1864 presidential campaign. It apparently was invented by Democrats to smear Lincoln by saying (falsely) that he advocated interracial sex and marriage. Yet laws forbidding interracial marriage and sexual relations appeared in the 17th century. In 1661, Virginia passed antimiscegenation legislation and then added laws prohibiting ministers from marrying interracial couples. The fine was apparently 10,000 pounds of tobacco (Cruz & Berson, 2001, p. 2). These laws applied to all non-Whites (e.g., Native Americans), not just European and African Americans.

The most extreme sanctions were directed towards liaisons between White women and Black males. Initially, one major concern was how to maintain the slave status of the offspring of women. Male slave owners, in their status as males and slave owners, engaged in sexual relationships, usually illicit and often forced, with Black women, generally bonded women. Under traditional British law, however, children acquired the family and legal status of their father. If applied, children of White fathers and Black slave women would have been both "free" and White, although claims to their fathers' property would have been tenuous because they were "illegitimate" offspring. By reversing longstanding kinship traditions and specifying that children "belonged to" and had the legal status of their *mother*, this problem was circumvented.

Legislatures adopted the principle of *"partus sequitur ventrem*—the child inherits the condition of the mother" (Stampp, 1961, p. 193). This was convenient for the dominant male planter class. Children born of slave women were slaves and, conveniently, legally considered the property of their mother's owner. Slave women's offspring, then, increased the slave population of the slave owner.[2]

Once the principle that children inherit the status of their mother was established, it made European female–African male sexual relationships particularly problematic. Because virtually all European women were "free," their children would also be free. Should she have a child with an African slave, that child would be free, providing an avenue out of slavery for the children of slaves. Such children would also expand the free African American population, threatening the race-based system of social stratification. If the father was already biracial, the children might easily pass for White, destabilizing the boundaries between Whiteness and Blackness on which race-based stratification depended.

Despite sanctions, some European women apparently had relationships with African men (see Moran, 2001). Social and ideological weapons were used against these women. They were stereotyped as depraved, lustful, prostitutes, and outcasts, especially if they were poor. In 1691 Virginia required that any White woman who gave birth to a mulatto child must pay a fine or face indentured servitude for 5 years for herself and 30 years for her child. In Maryland, a White woman who married a Black slave had to serve her husband's owner for the remainder of her married life (Cruz & Berson, 2001, p. 2). Some planter-class women apparently had relationships with slave men but their elite status somewhat shielded them from public criticism.

The spread of antimiscegenation and related laws ensured that interracial relationships would not be legally sanctioned and offspring would be denied rights of "legitimate" children. In 1715 and 1717, Maryland's legislature made cohabitation between a person of African descent and a White person illegal. By the time of the American Civil War, at least five states had enacted antimiscegenation laws (Cruz & Berson, 2001).

Interracial mating (with multiracial offspring) continued, initiated primarily by White slave owners. The "mulatto" slave population increased by 67% between 1850 and 1860; the Black slave population by only 20% (Cruz & Berson, 2001). Stampp reports that according to the census of 1860, more than one-half million (about 12%) of the "colored" people in the slave states were "mulattoes." But he considers this an underestimate because census takers classified people by appearance and many people with Black ancestors looked White.

The end of slavery disrupted more than the plantation system. It threatened the system of racial stratification and race-based structural subordination. White identity was no longer linked to one's free status. The color line had to be maintained through more rigid social separation of European and African Americans.

Alabama's antimiscegenation laws were designed to achieve that end. Originally instituted in the early 1800s, the laws prohibited weddings between members of different races and punished transgressions with $1,000 fines. Interracial sex was not prohibited since this would have affected Euro-American men! But if an African American man, free or slave, raped or attempted to rape a Euro-American woman, he was legally subject to the death penalty. After the end of the Civil War, Alabama law was quickly revised to recriminalize miscegenation, but in a gender neutral way. Similar laws appeared in other states. California outlawed interracial marriages between Whites and *any* non-White in 1905 . . . and these laws persisted until 1948. Interracial marriages during this time frame, especially for Euro-Americans, were rare.

In the 1920s, at the height of racism and ethnocentrism, a new Virginia law prohibited Whites from marrying anyone with a single drop of African blood. Earlier laws struggled with definitions of Whiteness and took into account proportions of African ancestry. These new laws counted a single "drop"—any ancestor, regardless of how far back. By 1924, marriage between Whites and Blacks was illegal in thirty-eight states. This coincided with a series of strict anti-immigration laws, part of the attempt to preserve the dominance and purity of the Nordic race (see chapters 6 and 7).

As late as the 1950s, nearly half of all states had antimiscegenation laws. And the legislation had been extended beyond Whites and Blacks to include Mongolians, Malayans, Mulattoes, Native Americans, and other non-Whites.

## The One-Drop Rule

Contradictions have always existed between elite Anglo rhetoric of preserving its "racial purity" and powerful Anglo male involvement in sexual relationships, often long-lived, with African American women. The case of Thomas Jefferson has recently received much attention. But more contemporary 20th-century examples are easy to find. Senator Strom Thurmond, a staunch Southern segregationist, had an illicit relationship (and child) with an African American woman employed in his household.

Such relationships, and more importantly, the children they produced, challenged the system of racial stratification. During the slave period, all children of slave women were legally slaves, so their proportion of African ancestry became irrelevant. Yet, according to historian Kenneth Stampp[3] and more recent scholarship, the legal basis for deciding an individual's *racial status* was never uniform across states.

The 1849 Virginia code states, "Every person who has one-fourth part or more of negro blood shall be deemed a mulatto, and the word 'negro' . . . shall be construed to mean mulatto as well as negro" (Stampp, 1961, p. 195). Other states specified different proportions, such as African ancestry to the third generation, or having one grandparent (*quadroon*) or one great-grandparent (*octoroon*). In South Carolina, the Court of Appeals rejected the notion that all persons "of any mixture of negro blood" were legally Black. Instead it ruled that there must be a "visible mixture" and referred to the person's "reputation" among his neighbors for evidence on the visibility part (p. 195).

According to Stampp, in some states during slavery, anyone with African ancestors too remote to be classified as a mulatto was legally White, even though that person could still be held as a slave (1961, p. 196). There also was practical incentive to reject a "*one-drop*" approach especially for individuals who appeared to be White. If these persons blended into the White population, their small amount of African ancestry would have had little impact on the European population.

But as part of the African slave population, they would have had a "whitening" effect.

Gradually, more states moved toward *hypodescent*, rules of ancestry where the child's racial status comes from the racially lowest status parent. What this essentially does is preserve the "purity" of the upper-status group—since any one with even a single drop of "inferior" blood is automatically excluded from the dominant racial or caste group. It acts as an additional barrier to interracial marriage by stigmatizing, inevitably, the children of such liaisons, regardless of the high status of the other parent. And it creates a cultural system that ignores biology—a rigid, bipolar, bounded racial system where one is either White or Black. There is no continuum. Biology is manipulated by culture.

These culturally and socially created restrictions on mating over the past 200-plus years preserved, among North Americans of African and European ancestry, some visible physical markers of their geographically diverse ancestral roots. However, recent DNA and other studies show diversity in both the European and African populations (see part 1). Clearly, legal and social restrictions against interracial mating have not always been followed! Not surprisingly, contemporary African American populations show significant evidence of European ancestry as we saw in part 1.

### Mating and Marriage Restrictions for Other Non-Whites

Attempts to "preserve the White race" through restrictions on mating and marriage affected other populations in the United States, especially immigrant populations. U.S. naturalization laws, as we saw earlier, allowed only White immigrants to become citizens. Non-White males could not bring spouses or sponsor female relatives, exacerbating an already skewed U.S. sex ratio.

The female shortage prompted at least some non-White men to cross cultural and ethnic boundaries and pursue mates, if not spouses, from other ethnic groups. Early California reports, for example, report competition for women among Anglos and Mexican Americans, Chinese, Filipinos, East Indians and perhaps other ethnic groups. Predictably, as in the slave states of the Southern United States, Anglo males used social and legal mechanisms to limit Euro-American women's mate choices to Euro-American males. Male competitors were portrayed negatively, described as "sexually avaricious," and antimiscegenation laws were passed.

One result was low birth rates among some immigrant populations, such as the Chinese. Entire age cohorts of Chinese males remained bachelors throughout their lives. Some had sexual encounters with prostitutes, Chinese and non-Chinese. And many offspring were multi-racial.

These restrictions produced some new and interesting alliances. Chapter 7 described the controversy over whether East Indians were White. Once the courts declared them Caucasian but not White, they were ineligible for naturalization. If they married Indian wives they could not bring them to the United States. And the Asiatic Barred Zone, created by Congress in 1917, applied to India. But as non-Whites, antimiscegenation laws prevented them from marrying Euro-Americans! What were they to do?

A new ethnoracial group emerged. Many East Indian males living in the Central Valley of California ended up marrying Mexican American women, mainly long-term inhabitants of the U.S. Southwest. Sometimes called "Mexican Hindus," even though most were of the Sikh religion, they have a distinct cultural identity and place in California history (Bigler, 2003).

**The Barriers Are Falling**

World War II, the horrors of Nazism with its ideology of racial superiority, and the Civil Rights movement all accelerated the crossing of racial boundaries. Antimiscegenation laws were initially challenged in several states, and California declared such laws illegal in 1948. Other states followed suit, albeit slowly, and often against enormous resistance.

The Virginia antimiscegenation law was challenged in 1967 and initially upheld by the lower court. The Virginia judge, quoted at the beginning of this section, explicitly articulates the long-standing theme of "preserving the White race" (see chapter 7) through controlling mating and marriage.

Eventually, the Supreme Court, in the now famous *Loving v. Virginia* case, found all laws against interracial marriage unconstitutional. This ruling invalidated all remaining state laws. At that time, 16 Southern states had such laws.

Simultaneously, other segregation laws were ruled unconstitutional. Beginning with *Brown v. Board of Education* (1954), racially segregated schools were challenged. Today's students and many teachers have no memory of a time when African American children walked by closer White schools to attend more distant Black schools. Without school segregation, many Southern "neighborhood schools" would have been multiracial.

Non-Southern states didn't need formal school segregation. They simply used residential discrimination to accomplish the same ends, often formally inserting "restrictive covenants" in real estate contracts. It was not until 1963 that the Rumford Fair Housing Bill outlawed housing discrimination in California.

Racial segregation in housing is a complex subject, as seen in the film *Race: The Power of an Illusion*. One rarely discussed but significant impact of residential segregation—or desegregation—is interracial mating. Schools, as we well know, are a potent site of racial interaction, of boundary-crossing opportunities (see part 3, especially chapter 13). And as children get older, dating and mating across racial and ethnic boundaries become more likely and, to many families, more problematic.

Even self-identified progressive Euro-American families have often balked at free mate choice when it comes to race. All ethnic groups continue to have strong racial preferences (and prohibitions) when it comes to marriage. This is perhaps most intense among Euro-Americans. But other groups, such as African Americans, Filipino Americans, Vietnamese Americans, Indo-Americans, and Mexican Americans, are also race conscious when it comes to mating and marriage.[4]

Whether articulated or not, interracial mating and marriage continue to threaten racial boundaries and a system of stratification and group identity based in part on race. Perhaps it is not so surprising that, as recently as 1994, a high school principal refused to allow interracial couples to attend the school prom (see chapter 13).

## The End of Race-Based Immigration and Naturalization Policies

As the U.S. becomes a postcolonial global village, long-standing racial barriers are dissolving. By 2002, immigrants and their children constituted about 23% of the U.S. population, nearly 66 million people (Lee & Bean, 2004, p. 221). The 2000 Census included 14 different races (besides "other") and divided the "White" race into two "ethnicities," non-Hispanic and Hispanic Whites. The current three Hispanic subgroups will likely expand in the future to reflect growing diversity within this category. And there will have to be recognition of other Latinos, such as Portuguese-speaking U.S. Americans from Brazil, Portugal, or Cape Verde Islands.

Relatively recent immigrants, like Tongans, Hmong, and Vietnamese, also want their distinct identities publicly acknowledged. But so do Hawaiians, Filipinos, Puerto Ricans, and other long marginalized members of the U.S. American "family" who wish to reclaim their heritage and ancestry.

The 2000 U.S. Census, for the first time, formally acknowledges multiple racial backgrounds and identities. Census categories, like *mulatto,* existed in 1850 but disappeared by the 1930 Census. But *mulatto* did not recognize multiple and distinct racial identities but rather implied a merging of two previously "pure" strains. In contrast, the 2000 Census allows individuals to have more than one racial designation, to recognize all their ancestral strains, to have multiple identities, to be multiracial rather than "mixed."

The 2000 Census, with its multitude of racial categories and multiple racial identities, also reflects the end of former racially discriminatory immigration and naturalization laws. In 1952, the McCarran-Walter Immigration and Nationality Act stated that a person's right to become a naturalized citizen could not be "denied or abridged because of race." This allowed many longtime residents to become citizens; once naturalized, they could now sponsor other family members.

Civil Rights–era legislation fully dismantled the old immigration system designed to preserve a White Nordic (Christian) nation. By abolishing the old national quotas system, based on the racial and ethnic balance of the U.S. at the time of the 1890 Census, immigration from non-European regions dramatically increased.

The new legislation also removed prior immigration barriers on non-White spouses married to U.S. American citizens, even if their spouses were White. This affected U.S. servicemen who had married women in Japan, Korea, the Philippines, and other places with large U.S. bases during World War II and the Korean War. By the time the Vietnam War ended, these laws had been dismantled.

As culturally erected barriers to interracial social interaction fall and new and more diverse populations enter the U.S. population "mix," these groups challenge simple White–non-White dichotomies. More-over, human nature, the urge to merge, is again taking its course. If current U.S. racial and ethnic intermarriage rates continue, "multira-cial" or at least "multiethnic" may soon become the largest racial group. By the year 2050, as many as 20% (or one of every five) U.S. Americans will have a multiracial background (Lee & Bean, 2004, p. 222).

For the West Coast, the figures are much higher. California has the highest multiracial population, over 1 million. In the 2000 census, over 7.3% of Californians under the age of 18 (one out of every 14) reported a multiracial identification. The numbers are likely to increase in the future (Lee & Bean, 2004, p. 236; see also chapter 13).

If California leads the nation on this, as on many other trends, race-based stratification may become a remnant of the past. Of course, as we have pointed out in chapter 7, this will not mean the end of class-based stratification, of economic and political inequality. But we shall have to find some other basis than race to allocate and rationalize privi-lege and inequality.

**KEY CONCEPTUAL POINTS**

- Race is culturally invented but there are superficial, visible, bio-logical markers of U.S. racial groups. This is the biological com-ponent of race.
- Biological markers reflect diverse geographic origins and histori-cal and cultural processes (slavery, colonialism, antimiscegenation laws, and other institutional practices created to prevent race "mixing" and to preserve the markers of racial hierarchy and racial privilege).

- All cultures regulate marriage and mating and can use marriage to either extend the group's alliances (marrying out) or to restrict access by marrying within (endogamy).
- Endogamy is a common way upper-status social groups (including racial elites) preserve their wealth, status, and other privileges.
- The U.S. system of racial stratification developed cultural and legal mechanisms to prevent interracial dating, mating, and marriage and preserve the visual markers of race.
- The Civil Rights era dismantled much of this, including antimiscegenation laws, school segregation laws, and racially discriminatory immigration and naturalization laws.
- More U.S. Americans are crossing racial barriers and challenging old racial categories as reflected in the 2000 U.S. Census and the growing population of multiracials and "others."

## KEY TERMS (ITALICIZED AND BOLDED IN TEXT)

| | |
|---|---|
| antimiscegenation laws | hypodescent |
| endogamy | miscegenation |
| exogamy | one-drop rule |
| gene flow | |

## TEACHING ACTIVITIES (ALSO APPROPRIATE FOR CHAPTER 13)

**Activity Plan 1: Mating Activity**

*Objectives:* Students will
- Understand the role social factors (vs. individual desires) play in mate choices, especially in family preferences, cultural norms, and societal laws.
- Be able to provide examples of social criteria (group traits) vs. individual criteria (attributes of the person).
- Understand the continuing role of racial endogamy in mate/date choice.

*Additional Information:* Grades 9–12, college, and other adults. Probably requires more mature students, perhaps with dating experience.

*Time:* 30–60 minutes, depending on how much time is spent analyzing student responses. *Materials Needed:* Sheets of paper for students to write individual responses and to summarize group responses. For additional guidelines, see www.sjsu.edu/faculty_and_staff/faculty_detail.jsp?id = 1472.

*Procedures:*

Step 1. My Ideal Mate. Students list characteristics of their "ideal mate" on a piece of paper. Tell them to imagine writing an ad for a long-term mate. What characteristics or attributes would they be looking for? Give them 5–10 minutes. They should do this individually.

Step 2. My Parent's Ideal Mate for Me. Students make a separate list of the kind of characteristics or traits parents or other adult family members would look for if they were choosing a long-term mate for them. Again, have them do this individually.

Step 3. Students analyze results (in small groups or the class as a whole), beginning with their ideal mate. Ask students to look for patterns in the type of traits they listed. Do some types appear more often than others? See what students come up with. Then analyze their lists using the following framework.

Usually, student trait lists can be classified into three main categories—physical traits, personality or character traits, and common activity-interests-goals. For example, ask how many students listed physical features and if so, what kinds? You could make a list on the board, under "Physical Traits." You might discuss if some physical features have cultural elements (e.g., does the concept of "physically fit" have a cultural dimension? Is "a nice smile" really an indicator of culturally valued personality traits?). Or try to get them to be specific about what traits make someone "attractive" or what is meant by "good features" and whether these are culturally shaped notions. Point out that many seeming "physical traits," like "being fit" or having a "good body" have additional culturally shared meanings.

Ask what other types of traits besides physical traits are listed. Student lists tend to emphasize personality or character traits. So you might create another list on the board, Personality/Character traits, and have students add items that fit. You may need a third list, common activities or interests, for additional traits not covered by the first two categories.

Next, introduce the notion of individual traits vs. social characteristics of persons (see chapter 7 for a discussion of *social status* and related terms). Point out that their ideal mate traits usually refer to the individual person, with respect to physical, personality, or interests considerations. Virtually all fall into a more comprehensive category called "Individual Traits." Contrast this with the concept of Social Traits—that is, traits having to do with one's social status or group membership, whether achieved or ascribed (see chapter 7). These would include things like religion, race, ethnicity, gender, occupation, nationality, social class, sexual orientation, age, or family background. Ask for any ideal mate traits on their lists that would fall in this category (sexual orientation is often one, although unspoken; race or religion may be others).

Step 4. Students compare their own list to the list their parents/family elders would create (in groups or as a class). Notice similarities and differences. This time, ask them to use the different categories (especially the notion of social vs. individual traits) when comparing lists. Generally, they will find that their families are much more interested in social status characteristics than in individual traits, like looks or personality.

Step 5. Discuss the most common type of social status characteristics. Even in culturally diverse schools, we have found that race, ethnicity, gender, and religion are the most frequently mentioned. This provides an opportunity to discuss these "hot button" issues (see also chapter 13). What is often less vocalized but also present are economic and social status considerations, such as money, job, educational level, family background, and family status.

Step 6. Link class results to earlier chapters on class and racial stratification. Link also to other school hot-button issues, like conflict and mating/dating issues (see part 3).

*Follow-Up:* To add a cross-cultural comparative aspect and to provoke discussion and reflection on U.S. culture, introduce students to a culture with a different system of mating, marriage, and perhaps family arrangements. See modules on kinship, sex, and marriage in the Cultural Anthropology section of the Palomar College website, at http:// anthro.palomar.edu/tutorials/cultural.htm, or see films like *Maasaii Women*, *Dadi's Family*, or other films at Documentary Educational Resources. For arranged marriages, see popular films by Mira Nair or an accessible article by Serena Nanda on arranged marriages in India (2000).

### Activity Idea 1: Film and Discussion: Guess Who's Coming for Dinner?

Show film (entire or parts) as an entry into a frank discussion of parental/family concerns over who they date/marry.

1. Separate family issues from student concerns for discussion purposes.
2. Identify the range of factors such as cultural identity, racism/ethnocentrism, external pressure, other issues of cultural "endogamy," such as religion, social class, nationality, or language.
3. Discuss other pressures (other than individual preference) that affect students' current dating and marriage decisions (see also chapter 13).

### Activity Idea 2: The Ethnic Me (or, Who *Did* My Ancestors Marry?)

This explores another facet of the "Exploring My Ancestry" project mentioned earlier in this book. Here, students trace the ethnic and religious aspects of family marriage patterns, currently and in the past. This could include students interviewing family members (one to three generations removed) about attitudes toward interracial, interethnic, and interreligious dating and marriage.

### Activity Idea 3: Explore the Legal System

Explore, using Web sources, specific antimiscegenation laws, their wording, historical context, justification used, popular coverage, and challenges to the laws, if any, in court. Students could compare the debates over these laws to those over gay marriage today. Materials to do this are available through several websites. The Cruz and Berson article, cited earlier, includes excellent teaching ideas as well as other links. Access it at www.oah.org/pubs/magazine/family/cruz-berson .html.

## ENDNOTES

1. Kinship and marriage, cross-culturally, is a major research area within anthropology. See any standard cultural anthropology textbook for a glimpse into this fascinating, diverse realm.

2. According to Stampp, "The offspring of a Negro slave father and a free white mother was free. The offspring of a free white father and a Negro, mulatto, quadroon, or octoroon slave mother was a slave" (1961, p. 194). Stampp notes that not all slaves were Black and not all slave owners were White.

3. The work of Kenneth Stampp, a prominent University of California, Berkeley, Civil War historian in the 1960s, remains significant even today.

4. Religion, gender orientation, socioeconomic class, and for many immigrants, language compatibility are often additional family criteria for their children's mates.

# Part 3

# RACE AND HOT-BUTTON ISSUES IN SCHOOLS—INTRODUCTION

How do the concepts presented in parts 1 and 2 play out in the real world of U.S. schools? In part 3, our aim is to connect these concepts with race-related hot-button issues that are part of the everyday experiences and realities of students, teachers, principals, parents, and other people involved with education—especially in K–12 schools, teacher education programs, and community colleges. In some ways, parts 1 and 2 could have been the entire book, as most key anthropological ideas about race are presented there. But we felt an important piece was missing: the application of concepts to the actual experiences people have with race in schools and colleges. Thus, the chapters in part 3 include actual incidents or quotes about racial issues in schools, which are then related to the concepts presented earlier.

As a result, the chapters in part 3 include significant cross-referencing to previous chapters. Educators who want a solid footing on hot-button issues presented here will find it easier if they have read the relevant conceptual chapters in parts 1 and 2, as these will help them understand the deeper and often invisible structures and processes that underlie problems around race in schools, as well as in society more broadly.

Chapter 10 examines two contemporary hot-button issues that bear on the issue of racial classifications: school assemblies and clubs that are organized by race or ethnicity, and the issue of what to call people. The second part of this chapter explores the use of "the N word" and other slurs and racial labels. This chapter is closely tied to concepts in chapter 6, especially the idea that cultures impose classification systems on reality. The contemporary hot-button issues of how schools organize assemblies and clubs and what racial and ethnic labels students and teachers use provide readers with an anthropological view of school cultures as systems that both rigidify categories and offer potential for change.

Chapter 11 addresses the highly charged issue of educational inequality—the "achievement gap." More and more data reveal a persistent disparity in academic achievement in which Whites and Asians outperform Latinos and Blacks on standard measures. The "discipline gap," while not so openly discussed, is closely linked to the achievement gap and contributes to it by marking out Latino and African American boys for disciplinary consequences at higher rates than Euro-Americans and Asian Americans of either gender. This chapter draws on the notions of social stratification and power discussed in chapter 7.

Chapter 12 is about racialized conflict in schools; it suggests that conflicts may start out being unrelated to race, but through a process of racialization, they become seen as racial. This chapter refers to both chapters 7 and 8. The final chapter of this section, chapter 13, is about interracial dating in schools. This chapter clearly links to the discussion of U.S. antimiscegenation laws in chapter 9, the biological argument against race in chapter 1, and the explanation of the cultural basis for classification in chapter 6.

Each chapter in part 3 includes "reflective questions" that are intended to stimulate discussions in classes or workshops. In addition, each chapter includes at least one teaching activity that challenges taken-for-granted categories and ideas about race in schools or colleges, and helps students and teachers "see" how our racialized system has been constructed to maintain certain classification systems. These chapters also encourage empirical study and reflection; many activities ask students to do small inquiry projects and think about how, given their new understandings, they would change their own behavior and how things are done in their schools or colleges. In order for these activities to be most effective, teachers need to know what was presented in parts 1 and 2.

# CHAPTER 10

# Assemblies, Clubs, Slurs, and Racial Labels

Both educators and students are often perplexed by the tension between *pluralism* (recognizing, valuing, and incorporating differences) and *assimilation* (the idea that everyone can and should "melt" into the dominant culture). Nowhere is this tension more evident than in school discussions and arguments about whether and how to recognize certain groups through special events, whether schools should have clubs for particular races or ethnic groups, and when and how racial labels take on positive or negative meanings.

This chapter helps teachers and students apply their knowledge of culture as classification, presented in chapters 5 and 6, to their own school's events and clubs and to campus uses of racial labels. Specifically, this chapter will assist educators in developing students' abilities to perceive and critique the cultural assumptions that underlie existing racial divisions of clubs and special events, as well as to question the use of racial labels (including slurs) and the potential for altering such use among peers. We argue that by studying their own school's or college's classification systems, students will understand not only how deeply embedded assumptions about race are but also how the socially constructed categories of difference and diversity in their own environment came to be the way they are. The chapter will also show how students and school authorities are complicit in both making and unmaking racial categories in schools and will engage educators and students in thinking about ways they could change those categories to fit the more complex identities of real people.

## CONCEPTUAL BACKGROUND
### Assemblies and Clubs Organized by Race/Ethnicity

Ethnic assemblies and clubs have not always been part of the high school landscape. They arose in the decades following the Civil Rights

Act in 1964 and in keeping with the movement in the U.S. to "celebrate diversity" and become a more openly pluralistic society. Instead of privileging only European American accomplishments and holidays, schools began to have special events for Martin Luther King Day, Cinco de Mayo, Vietnamese Tet Festival, and so on. At the same time, in order to provide an opportunity for students who shared similar cultural background to affirm their own identities and have a "safe space" beyond the regular school day and curriculum, many schools began to create "ethnic clubs" that paralleled the "ethnic events." At large high schools and colleges, there may be literally hundreds of such clubs, some organized by ethnicity, others organized by sports interest or other hobbies.

To illustrate how assemblies and clubs can be a hot-button issue, we provide the following discussion among students in a California high school that has, for many years, held a series of noontime assemblies sponsored by different ethnic clubs on campus.[1] The school is large and ethnically diverse, with over 4,100 students who speak over 70 different home languages. The discussion below was part of a facilitated process in which students gave input on the design of a series of unifying events called "Days of Respect" that would serve as a catalyst to help racialized groups see each other as allies. In the excerpt, students are expressing what they feel and think about ethnic assemblies, which are typically brief noontime events designed to educate students about diversity and unity.

Jerri, an African American senior who is about to graduate with high honors, says to the group, "Assemblies are not the solution" [to the problem of racial stereotyping and racial conflict].

Karina, another African American girl, agrees: "Nothing happens afterwards. Students sit there and say 'ugh.'"

A boy comments that freshmen and sophomores have more negative attitudes. "The effort has to start with younger kids." He goes on to explain that the middle schools that feed into Ohlone High School don't have such a diverse population, so kids are not used to it.

Fatima, a Mexican American girl, adds, "People say assemblies are boring. . . . We're here because we care, but what about all those other students who express intolerance in assemblies?"

A ninth-grade African American boy, James, talks about his own experience in going from middle to high school: "I used to hang out with a more diverse group, but at Ohlone, it's back to the same old factions, we hang out with all the Blacks. Me and my El Salvadoran friend, we made a pact that we would not let culture divide us."

Sheila from Nicaragua says, "Assemblies are tedious; it's a waste to think you can educate people in 45 minutes."

Jerri adds, "There's too much factionalizing. It's beautiful to have so many clubs, but nobody is communicating with anybody else. Clubs tend to cater only to their own group. The educational message is lost. The same is true for assemblies."

As the dialogue shows, school assemblies and clubs organized by race or ethnicity do not always produce the desired results of affirming students' cultures and educating students about each other's history and culture. In fact, classifying special events and clubs by race or ethnicity and using the time to showcase a "race" or ethnic group can lead to students having a competitive or simply jaded view of diversity. Students and faculty members who are dissatisfied with these divisions create "contested terrain" in which the categories themselves are opened up for questioning.

An anthropological view of culture is useful in analyzing how schools divide people into races or ethnicities (or cultures). In many ways, schools are small cultures, or *microcultures* (see chapter 5). Even though they are part of the larger regional and national culture, they develop their own particular ways of doing things, as do organizations of any kind. That's why we so often hear phrases like "That's not the way we do it here." As with any culture, much of what goes on is implicit, taken for granted by people who are insiders of that culture. Anthropologist Clyde Kluckhohn once said, "The fish would be the last creature to discover water" (1949, p. 16). The same is true, metaphorically, for schools. We get so used to "the way things are done here" that we think those ways are immutable, somehow part of the landscape, like water to the fish. It seems natural, therefore, to have assemblies and clubs organized by racial/ethnic groups. Yet these groupings, like the concept of race itself, are not natural. Rather, they are socially and culturally constructed for certain purposes that are rooted in the history of the school and the community.

For example, when Ohlone High School was first established, the surrounding community was primarily White, Latino, and African American. The early assemblies and clubs in the 1960s focused on Latinos and African Americans because they were the largest and most visible minorities. As more diverse ethnic groups moved into the community in the 1970s–1980s, the school administration tried to "keep up" with the demographic changes by gradually adding other assemblies so that no one would feel "left out." Eventually the school ran out of available calendar days, and smaller groups (such as Pakistanis and Indians) were told they had to be consolidated into the "Asian" assembly.

Each school, given its particular demographics and culture, molds taken-for-granted societal categories into a local shape and design. In order to understand that design, you have to know something about the history of the local community. Assemblies and clubs are not the only extracurricular activities that raise issues of racial/ethnic classification and identities. Other extracurricular areas, such as the ethnic makeup of sports teams, and "color-blind" casting in theater productions, may also reveal these tensions.

*Reflective Questions:* What is the history behind the categories of assemblies and clubs at your school or college? What groups are included? Who is excluded? What assumptions are evident in the way your school/college organizes these events and clubs? What do you think people learn from these classifications? Is this learning explicitly taught or implicitly acquired? (In other words, do people just pick it up from the environment?)

Although the dialogue among students was a fairly analytical attempt to engage students in questioning the way separate ethnic assemblies and clubs affect the school climate, there are times when schools and individuals experience more dramatic conflicts over ethnic/racial events and clubs.

In the same high school, a conflict emerged during the final preparation for a big Cinco de Mayo assembly, organized by the Mexican American students' club, MECHA. Just days before, an African American young man had been killed in a car chase. He had fathered a child with one of the African American students and thus was considered "family" by many students. The African American students were offended that the celebratory Cinco de Mayo event, which traditionally involved music and dancing, was going to take place when they were grieving the loss of a member of their community. So several African American students confronted the Latino organizers in a courtyard, and a physical fight was barely averted by several teachers.

Eventually, they persuaded the leaders of the two groups to talk it out—first separately, with a facilitator, and then together. They reached an agreement in which the Latino students agreed to change the way their event was organized. Instead of beginning with music and dance, they would begin with a solemn address in which the speaker would acknowledge the sadness of the loss of the young man's life, and ask everyone to share a moment of silence. The initial speech would continue in a serious tone, and only later would the music and dancing take place.

In this instance, two underlying issues almost led to a conflict that would have been classified as "racial." But in fact, the underlying issues were really about respect (for a classmate's deceased boyfriend), and lack of communication (how well do members of different racial/ethnic groups socialize with each other outside of the classroom?). However, when the groups involved in the conflict perceive themselves and are perceived by others as racially different, conflicts about ordinary things like respect or lack of clear communication—both of which can also easily happen among people of the same racial group—can quickly become *racialized*; that is, they *become* conflicts about race even though they didn't start out that way.

Since assemblies and other special events are perceived as key moments when racial or ethnic identity is highlighted, conflicts over assemblies can involve complex, seldom-discussed feelings about which group is given more "air time" or status at the school. If students are given only a limited number of "slots" for their particular group to take center stage, the situation is ripe for conflict if any of the groups perceive an imbalance. Lustig (1997) described a similar conflict in a high school involving immigrant students (mainly Latino) and African American students. The African American students felt that the Latinos were more favored by the school faculty because they spoke a different language and had special dances from their regions. The "multicultural" events that were supposed to bring greater appreciation of diversity actually backfired, leaving the African American students feeling as if they didn't have "culture."

> Conflicts involving belonging or not belonging to clubs can take place at the individual level, as illustrated in another high school where Ana, a Filipina American, was told by members of the Filipino Club, "You're not a real Filipina." Club members, who were mainly first-generation immigrants, made Ana feel unwelcome. She didn't protest, but she stopped coming to the club meetings. "They don't understand," she said. "I'm just as much Filipina as they are. Even though I was born in the U.S., I'm still Filipina." The club that she thought was there to provide a safe, warm affiliation with her ethnic heritage actually turned out to be exclusionary—because the club leader had decided that U.S.-born Filipinos were not authentic Filipinos, and the club was only for "real" Filipinos.

In this case, the club's faculty advisor probably did not make it clear that the club should be for anyone with an interest in Filipino culture who wanted to join. The student leader, perhaps not fully reflecting on the effect it would have, used the club as a way to distinguish U.S.-born and immigrant Filipinos. Rather than serving as a positive place for students to explore commonalities and differences among first- and second-generation Filipinos, the student leader created a rigid—and arbitrary—border that included some and excluded others.

*Reflective Questions:* Has your school experienced conflicts over special events dedicated to particular racial or ethnic groups? If so, what were the underlying issues? Have conflicts that didn't start out being about race ended up becoming racialized? Why do you think this happened? If your school or campus has ethnic clubs, how are the borders of those clubs managed? Is everyone welcome, or are some people less welcome?

The examples we have shared all show how people in schools shape the way events and clubs are organized and which particular ethnic or racial borders will become salient and meaningful in a given school at a given time. Such shaping may be based on administrators' or students' assumptions about racial differences and is not always done with full awareness of the nuances and implications. However, in some cases, changes are made quite consciously as a strategy of *resistance* in which students or faculty members question, challenge, or transform existing categories of people.

One such instance occurred in a large high school where White students, who were actually a numerical minority, requested an assembly for White culture. After some discussion, the administrators granted the request, although the students were told that they had to call it a "European American" assembly rather than a "White" assembly, so as not to arouse suspicions of organizing by the Aryan Nation, KKK, or some other hate-based group.

Many people were convinced that even with the name change, this was not a wise idea. After all, they argued, the whole reason for ethnic assemblies was to highlight groups who are underrepresented in the curriculum. Given all the "dead white men" who dominate the history and language arts curricula, European American students could hardly claim lack of representation. But their point that in this school they were small in number did give their request more credibility. Also, the administration saw educational value in students exploring their diverse European ancestries so that the category of White would be shown to be more complex and less monolithic.

Interestingly, the first assembly turned out to be primarily a celebration of English and Celtic heritage, with little mention of Italian, Portuguese, Slavic, or other European heritages. People noticed this and in subsequent years incorporated more of the true diversity of the European American students' backgrounds. Focusing on Euro-American students' history and culture shows that pluralism is about everybody learning about themselves and everybody else; it is not only for "people of color" or historically marginalized cultures.

Another instance in which educators consciously moved beyond the stereotyped notions of separate celebrations for separate cultures was a Seder dinner in which African American and Jewish students shared the ceremony, and for the first time students saw the similarities between African Americans' history of slavery in the United States and the Jews' history with slavery in Egypt. This example shows how celebrations can be an opportunity to explore commonalities of tradition that students themselves do not initially see—probably because U.S. society has overemphasized differences rather than what we share.

Because schools play a crucial role during adolescence, a time when students are actively constructing their social identities, schools also have a responsibility to help students recognize that identity is not about choosing to be one kind of person and not another. It is not a matter of either-or choices. Everyone has multiple and cross-cutting social identities—for example, the same person can feel fulfilled as a female, Latina, Irish, volleyball player, good student, member of the drama club, daughter, older sister, and so forth. Schools have the obligation to demonstrate to students, through special events, clubs, the core curriculum, instructional practices, and so on, that identities are complex and cannot be reduced to simple, racialized groups.

*Reflective questions:* Can you imagine a different way to organize assemblies and clubs at your school or college? What message would this reclassification send to people at your school, and how would it differ from the message they currently receive?

### The "N-word" and Other Labeling Issues

How often have you or has someone you know commented on the changing use of racial labels and slurs across generations? Both students and adults often raise serious questions about this issue, pointing out that more and more young people are using slurs such as "nigger" or "nigga" either as in-group terms or even across groups.

Shifts in usage are occurring in labels that used to only be insults. They are occurring in labels for recent immigrants (such as "fresh off the boat" or "FOBs"), labels for people of multiple ethnicities (such as "mongrel" or "mutt"), labels for women and girls (such as "bitch" and "slut"), and labels for gay people (e.g., "queer," "queen," "faggot," etc.). For many people, especially older generations, such words immediately call forth their usage as hate language, used to demean or trivialize those so labeled. And yet, some younger people claim they are now used as affectionate terms, terms that show one is part of an in-group—or that they have simply lost their negative connotations. In the following excerpt, an African American high school senior discusses these tensions in the use of the word "nigga":

Just yesterday, I was appalled because I walking along, and there was this Filipino girl and Filipino guy, and they're just, talking and she's saying, Yeah, you know my nigga's coming down, and. . . . And I was like, am I hearing things? You know, she wasn't saying it in a derogatory way, but I'm like, that's not a word you throw around . . . but the only thing I can say is, they get it from us. They hear us calling each other nigga this and nigga that like it's just a pastime, and they think, "Oh, new word, new slang word" rather than knowing the history and understanding. That's why I think education is important; people really don't understand. Even people within the African American culture don't fully understand, or if they do understand, they brush it to the side, like that was then and this is now. And it's not. . . . It's ignorant. We've had that discussion in our group, where people say, "Well, it means something different now." Well, just because you say it means something different still doesn't take away the original definition of the word. If I say the F word doesn't mean F you anymore, it doesn't make it any better. Just like people calling each other, you know, bitches . . . that doesn't make it any better. . . . I don't understand it personally. But that's just me, and there are a lot of people who'll disagree with me.

*Reflective questions:* Why is this student "appalled" when she hears two Filipino students use the word "nigga" in their conversation with each other? Do you think it was okay for them to use this word? Why or why not?

Most schools have fairly clear rules and consequences about the use of racial slurs and insults. This is understandable and necessary in a school context where both young people and adults need to know what the limits are, and in particular students need to know what behaviors incur disciplinary consequences and what behaviors do not. Racial labeling and slurs hurt people, as does physical violence, and therefore schools must have policies about their use and teachers should know how to address such behavior when it occurs (see, e.g., Thompson, 2004).

However, individual educators can teach students how to study and learn from everyday behavior involving racial and other labels. Similarly, we teach children not to throw rocks at other people or property, but this does not mean that we do not teach them geology.

The process of changing a term's social meaning from negative to positive can be carried out by those originally the object of the slur or insult. This process is called *appropriation*. Writing about the term "nigga," Moses and Mukhopadhyay say "by taking a negatively charged word and appropriating it for themselves and for their *own* use, it is first neutralized and eventually comes to be used in a positive way as a 'core blackness' or authenticity that African Americans reaffirm among themselves. It is taboo for a non-African American person to use it" (1997, p. 95).

Other words that used to be and still are slurs have been similarly appropriated. Nam describes this process in relation to the word "yellow" as a slur against Asian people:

> It is the radical act of reclaiming and redefining the word yellow that thrills me. . . . "Yellow" takes on a new meaning. Old newspapers, magazines, and travelogues reveal phrases like "yellow peril," "yellow-face," and "yellowskins," which remind us of the ways in which "yellow" has historically been linked to negative stereotypes of Asians. Society has reinforced these images, pushing Asian Americans to the periphery in all areas of our culture. "Yellow" has been used to define skin color (even though Asian skin comes in a wide variety of colors and hues), and carries with it other racist assumptions. On our terms, however, the hyphenated "yell-oh" does not define or create barriers between Asian Americans. Simply put, the term "YELL-Oh" is a call to action. (2001, p. xxviii)

This excerpt illustrates not only that insulting terms can be redefined and reclaimed by the group that was originally the object of the insult, but also that the meaning attributed to words is always context dependent.

The context, or larger social situation, determines how a particular utterance functions. Thus, the same label might at one time be a slur that demeans a person as a member of a separate, racialized group (e.g., "you——s are all alike."); at other times, the same label might be used in a "scientific" way to examine data related to different groups ("——s are not performing as well in school as——s"); at other times, the same label might be used to affirm a positive sense of within-group identity ("Let's affirm the contributions of——s to U.S. society"). And finally, the same label can be used to talk about the label itself (e.g., "The term——seems to be shifting."). The only way to know what a racial label really means to speakers and listeners is to study the context in which it is used and observe how people react to it.

In addition to terms changing their meaning depending on who says them and in what context, other labels may be discarded and replaced with new terms to reflect a new social consciousness or "political correctness." Consider the changes in the past 50 years or so in the use of terms like "Negro," "Black," "African American," and "Caucasian," or the shifting usage of "illegal aliens," "illegal immigrants," and "undocumented workers."

Teacher-supervised inquiry projects about how labels and slurs are used in everyday life can reveal a great deal about the society we live in and the ever-changing cultures we construct. Labeling behavior and slurs are like a lens that helps us "see" social relations among different groups and how people use language to reinforce, contest, and change existing relations. Language-in-use is like a two-way mirror—it reflects back to us what is, the existing status quo of social relations and power dynamics.

But it also constructs those very relations as we speak. How does it do this? When we say that somebody is Latino, or African American, or White, or Caucasian, we construct for those who listen to us a social world in which these words stand for meaningful categories and contrasts. By using the words, we affirm the reality of the categories they stand for. Some people say that if we want to change the way people think about the social world around them, one thing we can do is to change the words we use to categorize and describe people. Even if that doesn't completely change the way they think, it at least raises questions, disturbs conventional ways of thinking and perceiving, and presents an alternative way to think about and use language. According to George Lakoff, "Because language activates [conceptual] frames, new language is required for new frames. Thinking differently requires speaking differently" (2004, p. xv).

Take, for example, the changes in the last several decades in gen-dered language. "Chairman" with its male bias was changed to "chair-person" or just "chair." "Stewardess" with its female bias became "flight attendant." Likewise, labels for U.S. racial and ethnic groups have also changed over time, as we saw in part 2. Terms like "Mongol-oid," "mulatto," "octaroon," "half-breed," "Negroid," "Hindoo," and "Oriental" were once common labels, often used in census catego-ries. Terms for African Americans have included "colored," "Negro," "Black," "Afro-American," and recently "African American." Sur-prisingly, the term "Caucasian" is still in use as a word meaning White or European American, but as Mukhopadhyay (forthcoming) points out, it is a relic of the old pseudoscientific racial categories invented in the 19th century.

As people become more aware of the negative connotations of such terms, or of their outmoded and inaccurate representation of reality, they can make a conscious effort to change their language. Gradually, changes take hold and become encoded in the policies of publishing companies, airlines, newspapers, schools, and so forth. Now, when we think about a person who chairs a meeting, most of us don't automati-cally think of a man. And we're surprised if someone uses the term "Negro." This is what we mean when we say that language not only reflects culture but also constructs culture.

*Reflective questions:* Can changing labels change the way we think about people? Is changing language enough to change social relations? Or must these be backed up by other actions, pol-icies or laws, or changes in economic conditions?

## KEY CONCEPTUAL POINTS

- The organization of events and clubs by race or ethnicity seems natural, but isn't. The categories reflect the school's implicit microculture and local community history.
- Racial classification systems reflected in assemblies, clubs, and

racial labels teach us to "see" race in a certain way and as important.

- They can be changed to reflect more complex identities—that is, if people want to change them and can exert enough power and influence to do so.
- Conflicts involving racial or ethnic events and clubs can reflect resistance to categories but may also reinforce group boundaries.
- Nonracial conflicts associated with racial events and clubs can quickly become racialized.
- Language both reflects and constructs the world, and can be a tool for changing social relations.
- Appropriation of negative language can be a tool for self- and group empowerment.
- The meaning of words and utterances is always dependent on broader "frames." Racial labels serve different functions depending on the context.

## KEY TERMS (ITALICIZED AND BOLDED IN TEXT)

appropriation            assimilation
microculture             resistance
pluralism

## TEACHING ACTIVITIES

### Activity Plan 1: Investigating Events and Clubs

*Objectives:* By the end of this activity students will be able to
- identify events and clubs at their school or college that have a racial or ethnic basis,
- identify and explain problems with these events or clubs in terms of who is included or excluded, and how well or poorly they reflect the actual student population,
- explain that the categories of events and clubs are not natural, and that they are created by people for certain purposes, such as compensating for past "invisibility" of minority groups,

- explain that because they are created by people, they can also be changed by people, and
- articulate what they would change about these events/clubs, and create a prioritized list of those changes.

*Other Information:* This activity requires two class sessions, about 45 minutes each, with possibility of an extension project (student survey) that continues for several weeks. Materials needed include white board, markers, chart paper, an official list of yearly special events at the school, and a list of student clubs, if they exist.

*Procedure:*

Step 1.    T (teacher) asks students to create a list of on-campus assemblies and clubs. T creates two *unlabeled* columns on the board: (1) clubs and events not ethnically or racially specific and (2) those that *are* ethnically or racially specific. T fills them in from students' (Ss) list but does not reveal the title of either column.

Step 2.    Students guess the difference between the two columns.

Step 3.    T asks students to get into groups of three or four, and tells Ss they should choose people who have the same or similar race/ethnicity as themselves. T then asks each group to discuss the following questions (each group should have a facilitator, note taker, presenter, and time keeper. Allow 15 minutes):

   a. Is there an annual event and/or club at this school that is specifically for your ethnic or racial group? What is it?

   b. Do you belong to this group or participate in this event? Why or why not?

   c. Do you know of other people who would like to be part of this group, but don't feel comfortable? If so, why do you think they are uncomfortable?

   d. Who are these events or clubs for (in other words, who benefits)? The insiders? The outsiders? Anybody else?

   e. Do you think the events/clubs that are *for* this group actually do a good job representing the diversity of this group of people? Why or why not?

Step 4.    T reconvenes class, S groups present findings.

Step 5.  T asks students if they noticed any patterns in different presentations. (For example, groups have problems distinguishing who "fits" and who doesn't, or some groups aren't represented in events or clubs, while others are . . . ).

Step 6.  T asks students: How did these come to be? Who created them? Why? Some suggestions might be "They're just natural, they represent the groups that are here," and so on. T can point out that "We heard that the groups don't fit all the people who are here, and that sometimes people feel excluded . . . so that means they are not simply 'natural.'" Eventually, T should state explicitly the main point of the lesson: that social divisions (clubs) are cultural and historical inventions, organized the way some people think human beings in this school should be classified. We could in theory have clubs for tall people, short people, people with long hair, and so forth. But we don't organize ourselves that way. Why not? And who decides? Are these events organized top down by administrators, or do students decide?

Step 7.  T asks students, if we wanted to change something about these events or clubs, could we do it? What would we have to do to change it? (T may want to discuss issues of power involved in change.)

Step 8.  T organizes Ss into groups of three or four, making sure groups are as diverse as possible, racially and ethnically. Give each group a set of questions (allow 20 minutes).

a.  What do you like about the way the school organizes events and clubs by racial or ethnic group?

b.  What do you *not* like about the way the school organizes events and clubs by racial or ethnic group?

c.  What do you think should be changed? Why? Make a list of the things your group thinks should be changed.

d.  Now, prioritize your list (first priority, second, etc.)

Step 9.  Group presenters post their priority lists on the board. T facilitates as students compare responses. Note similarities and differences, and discuss reasons for differences.

Step 10.  T asks, do you think it is possible for us to come up with one priority list that the whole class can agree on? If students feel they can, go for it. If they don't think they can (because of deep divisions on some issue), then make sure each group understands why other groups feel the way they do. This becomes an activity to either build consensus, and/or to develop understanding of other perspectives.

*Assessment Activities:* Choose one or a combination:

a. Write a reflection (one to two pages) about your thoughts and feelings about the past two class sessions.

b. Conversation with a nonclass member: Ss tell a friend, acquaintance, or parent what was discussed in the two class sessions and get their reaction. Ss write down what the person said and share this with the class. This serves two purposes—it helps students recall the main points of the class sessions and helps disseminate key concepts beyond this classroom.

*Extension Activity:* Students develop a short questionnaire to find out how other students feel about campus events or clubs. Design survey questions and pilot questions; decide who will answer the questionnaire (sampling). Administer questionnaire; analyze results; discuss results in class; share results with student leadership, faculty, and administrators. Develop recommendations for change.

**Activity Idea 1: Collecting and Analyzing Data on Racial Slurs and Racial Labels**

This inquiry-based activity involves students in studying the use of racial slurs and racial labels at their own school or college. By doing collaborative research, they will discover patterns in the way slurs and labels are used and why people use them (for example, to signal group identity, to delineate power relations, to draw a line between insiders and outsiders, etc.). They will see that racial labels and slurs reflect their school's own social structure. Finally, they will begin to articulate their position on slurs and labels and see how they can interrupt current labeling practices and propose alternatives. Requires about three class sessions of 50 minutes each, with 2–3 days in between to collect data. For a detailed plan, see the website at www.sjsu.edu/faculty_and_staff/ faculty_detail.jsp?id = 1480.

**Activity Idea 2: Explore the Teaching Tolerance Website**

This website (http://www.tolerance.org) contains many classroom activities focused on addressing racism, sexism, and other "isms" in the classroom. One can also order teaching kits and handbooks. One classroom activity is called "Facing the N Word" by Kathryn Knecht. The author explains how she handles the use of slurs in literature at www.tolerance.org/teach/. This would be particularly appropriate in conjunction with chapter 10.

## ENDNOTES

1. All school-based examples in Part 3 are drawn from original data collected by Henze, Katz, Norte, Sather, & Walker (1999). Pseudonyms are used for both individuals and schools.

# CHAPTER 11

# The Academic Achievement Gap and Equity

The notion of an "academic achievement gap" and what to do about it has been a focal point for much discussion in U.S. education in the past decades. This chapter will examine this issue by (1) presenting a short history of different explanations offered by social scientists; (2) delineating what anthropologists contribute to our understanding of this issue, (3) pointing to some issues teachers need to consider as they work toward understanding and eliminating the achievement gap; and (4) suggesting activities for students. The primary focus of this chapter is to provide conceptual background for teachers. However, we also think there is value in having students participate in studying sources of inequality in their own educational communities.

It's important to look more closely at what people mean when they talk about an *achievement gap*. In the U.S., the term usually refers to a difference in academic achievement by different populations, using standardized test scores as the main indicator. The term "achievement gap" can be used to talk about many kinds of populations, including those differentiated by gender, class, language background, and so on. For example, one can talk about an achievement gap in math between boys and girls. But the most pervasive use of this term refers to a so-called racial achievement gap—in other words, an achievement gap that is predictable on the basis of race.

Even when parents' income and wealth is comparable, African Americans, Native Americans, Latinos, and immigrants for whom English is not a first language lag behind English-speaking, native-born, Euro-American students. The evidence for the gap has been documented repeatedly by the usual measures. These include drop-out rates, relative numbers of students who take the advanced placement examination, and numbers of students who are enrolled in the top academic and "gifted" classes and/or admitted to higher-status secondary schools, colleges, graduate, and professional programs. And last but not least, there are the discrepancies in scores on standardized tests of academic achievement, on which teachers' and students' fate so heavily depend. (Berlak, 2001, ¶3)

More succinctly, "Whites and Asians are at the top, Blacks and Browns are at the bottom" (Lynch, cited in Tilove, 2003, ¶19).

The present chapter approaches the achievement gap as a present-day manifestation of inequality in U.S. schools and is closely linked to chapter 7, which provided historical background on how U.S. racial categories evolved to justify economic and social inequality. Nonetheless, it appears that racialized identities do make a difference and that statistically speaking, students categorized as Whites and Asians do outperform African American and Latino students on standardized tests and other indicators of academic achievement.

But how do we explain this gap? Are we going to try to find a biological explanation? Is it a gap based on social and cultural factors? Is it a gap that has been created by the way our society constructs and explains race?

Even the language we use to talk about this issue is loaded with assumptions. The term "achievement gap" focuses our attention on the students who fail to achieve, meanwhile obscuring or drawing attention *away from* the real problem—which lies in our social and institutional structures, historically designed to use race as a sorting mechanism (see chapter 7). An alternative term, suggested by Cammarota (2005) and others, is *opportunity gap*. This phrase locates the problem with the institutions and environmental conditions that provide opportunities for certain students and not others—opportunities that are predictable on the basis of race.

Ultimately, this chapter shows readers that the racial achievement gap is the logical outcome of hundreds of years of a racialized hierarchy in Europe and the U.S. We are reaping what was sown for us. It shows us how powerfully cultural constructions of inequality based on race have worked—to the point that even now, when most people want to undo the legacy of racism, the legacy persists.

## CONCEPTUAL BACKGROUND

This section explores why the racial achievement gap exists and why it persists despite decades of attempts to reform schools. Scholars in a wide variety of disciplines, including biology, sociology, psychology, anthropology, and economics, have advanced many different explanations. Here, we provide a brief overview of some of the major ones.

### The Biological Explanation

As we have seen in part 1, there are no biological races. However, the idea persists to this day that the racial achievement gap can be explained by positing biological (inherited) differences that make some groups more "intelligent" or more capable of abstract thinking. The most recent resurgence of this idea came in 1994, with the publication of *The Bell Curve,* by Herrnstein and Murray. The authors argue that IQ tests measure general intelligence, that these tests show that an individual's IQ is largely inherited, "that the human 'races' were differentially gifted with IQ, and that IQ is a cause, rather than an effect, of economic success or poverty" (cited in Cohen, 1997, p. 253).

As Cohen points out, "The book was well received because it spoke perfectly to American prejudices against minority groups. It justified existing inequalities, and fed cherished beliefs such as the idea that access to success was based purely on merit and open to anyone with sufficient intelligence" (p. 253). Yet this version of a biological explanation is as flawed as earlier attempts to link intelligence with race. We have seen in part 1 that "races" are not scientifically different biological categories. The individual traits that make up typical racial stereotypes (skin pigmentation, eye shape, hair texture, etc.) do not covary. Even if a trait such as intelligence were measurable by a single, culture-free test, there is no reason to expect that it would vary with other "racial" traits.

Furthermore, despite attempts to make IQ testing unbiased, it is virtually impossible to create a test that is not rooted in culture. It is not merely a matter of removing obviously culture specific words such as "escalator" or drawings that might be culturally ambiguous. The IQ tests, and all tests, are cultural in much deeper ways, including their structure and logic. For example, analogies that ask students to complete a comparison (e.g., acorn is to seed as oak is to ____) are entirely based on categorizing, and as we have seen in chapter 6, categorization is a fundamental way in which culture is expressed.

In addition to the above problems with IQ tests, scientists have also challenged the notion of intelligence as a general capacity. Howard Gardner, well known among educators for his work on *multiple intelligences*, provides convincing evidence that there are many different types of intelligence. While he fully acknowledges that the creation of separate types is his own construct—"nature brooks no sharp discontinuities" (1983, p. 70), he nonetheless suggests that it could be useful for educators to think in terms of intelligence types such as linguistic, spatial, musical, bodily-kinesthetic, and so on. Others, including Rogoff (1990) and Lave, Murtuagh, and de la Rocha (1984), draw on Vygotsky's *sociocognitive theory* to show that all cognitive activity is deeply social and situational. There is no such thing as learning that is not embedded in a social and cultural context.

In summary, then, to argue that there is an inherited, biological thing called intelligence that is devoid of cultural influence and that correlates with "racial" traits flies in the face of all scientific research in the latter part of the 20th century.

**The Cultural Deficit Explanation**

When race-based biological explanations for the achievement gap began to be discredited in the mid-1900s, a new explanation emerged that focused on culture. It began to take shape in Oscar Lewis's book on the "culture of poverty" (1966), in which he argued that poverty and unemployment among Puerto Ricans was partially the result of habits and beliefs that differed from those of mainstream U.S. culture. This "culture of poverty," however, was itself an adaptation to and emerged in the context of poverty and inequality (Mukhopadhyay & Chua, in press). While there are many different versions of cultural explanations, one that was prominent in the 1960s and still exists today is the "cultural deficit" explanation. From this perspective, certain racial groups, especially African Americans, Latinos, Native Americans, and some Asians, lack cultural predispositions and experiences that would help them succeed in school. This ethnocentric position places cultures in a hierarchy, with Western, middle-class, and usually European American people at the pinnacle of cultural development, while other groups fail in school because of "cultural deficits" (Barker, 1981).

One can easily hear such comments today. One of the authors, in traveling to different school districts around the U.S. in the late 1990s, heard the following: "They don't have concepts in the Yup'ik language" and "Children from rural Mexico are coming to school with a lot of cultural deficits; for example, they don't know what an escalator is because they've never been on one."

Anthropologists point out that the term "culture" has many meanings (see chapter 5). A useful distinction can be made between Culture with capital C and culture with a small c. The capital C denotes what is often called "high Culture"—that is, the practices and values of the elite in any culture. In the U.S., high Culture would include learning to play the piano, taking art classes, traveling widely, speaking French, and so on. Culture with a small c, on the other hand, is the everyday practices, knowledge, attitudes, and values of any group of people who share a common heritage (Kramsch, 1998). We all acquire culture as a normal part of growing up in communities, and we participate in and enact it all the time, no matter what we do.

Thus, from an anthropological perspective, saying that someone has no culture, or has "cultural deficits" makes no sense at all. Everyone acquires the culture of the communities they participated in—especially the culture of origin plus any additional cultures (such as the culture of the wider society, the culture of school, or the culture of a foreign country). We acquire as much culture as we need to behave appropriately in our social networks. When people need to participate in wider social networks or function in a foreign country, they usually are able, over time, to acquire enough of the new culture to be able to function.

When someone says that an individual or a group has cultural deficits, this can only be understood to mean "deficits" in relation to some other culture that the speaker implicitly assumes to be superior. The cultural deficit explanation for the academic achievement gap lacks scientific validity because it assumes a hierarchy of cultures, as if some cultures are just inherently "better" than others. This explanation fails to recognize the implicit power dynamics hidden behind the term "cultural deficit." For this reason, some have called it *cultural racism*—a thinly veiled substitute for the old biological racism (Barker, 1981)—although not all anthropologists agree (see Mukhopadhyay & Chua, in press).

### Poverty as an Explanation

Some people have argued that the achievement gap is not so much a function of racial identity but rather of poverty. Because African American, Latino, and some recent immigrants to the U.S. are disproportionately poor, it is often difficult to untangle the effects of racialization and the effects of poverty. But among researchers who have studied the relationship between poverty and race in school achievement, race consistently emerges as a major contributor to low achievement, even when poverty is factored out.

For example, Myers (2000) conducted a statistical study to determine whether poverty was a primary cause of the poor performance of Black students on the Minnesota Basic Standards Test. Seventy-five percent of African American students failed the math test, and 79% failed in reading, compared to 26% and 42% respectively for Euro-Americans. The findings show that being poor in and of itself is not necessarily linked to low school achievement. But being poor *and* being Black or Latino does have an impact (Skiba & Rausch, 2004).

### Tracking and Other Forms of Inequality as an Explanation

There is convincing evidence that being on the "down side" in various forms of inequality is associated with poor academic outcomes. In other words, it is not poverty in itself that causes low school achievement, but the juxtaposition of unequal opportunities both in school and in life outside of school. In Myers's study in Minnesota, success on the tests was related to how an individual had been tracked, regardless of racial group. Only 6.9% of students of color compared to 23% of Euro-American students had access to "gifted and talented" programs.

According to this study, evidence suggests that tracking and other unequal opportunities in school influence not only how well a student does on the standardized test but also academic performance generally (Myers, 2000).

The practice of *ability tracking*, defined as the sorting and grouping of students by perceived ability, can take place at various levels of organization, from whole schools being designated as "college prep" vs. regular, to within-school tracking by classes (such as honors, regular, "consumer math," etc.). Tracking can also occur within classes, for example, through assignment of students to different reading groups.

When considering the effects of tracking, it is important to distinguish between tracking that is temporary—designed to help students improve their achievement and "catch up"—versus tracking that is permanent. A well-implemented summer bridge program between middle and high school that is designed to give low-achieving students the extra boost they need to do well in ninth grade may help reduce the achievement gap. However, a tracking system that assigns low-achieving students to classes where they never receive the enrichment-type curriculum and instruction that college prep classes receive tends to relegate low-achieving students to a permanent underclass.

While school policy may claim that it is possible to "jump tracks" and go into a higher-level class the next semester or year, in practice this is almost impossible because lower-track classes typically do not prepare students for the work expected in higher-level classes, which usually involves more problem solving and critical thinking. "In this way . . . tracking is one of the means by which the race- and class-linked inequalities notable in our schools and in society at large are reproduced" (Rubin, 2003, p. 541).

In an ethnographic study of a detracked ninth-grade program in an urban, diverse high school, Rubin (2003) found that even in classrooms and schools where teachers tried to faithfully carry out the best practices of detracking, "inequalies were often reinforced rather than challenged" (p. 566). She explains this is, in part, a result of a system that attempts to isolate school practices as if they were separate from the surrounding society. She points out that "the educational reforms that created the need for detracking are rooted in systemic inequalities along race and class lines, which detracking reform alone cannot fully address" (p. 567).

Ability tracking in schools, then, appears to reflect larger U.S. economic inequalities. "The U.S. is the most unequal society of all the industrialized nations" (NOW, 2002, ¶1). We have the biggest wealth gap between rich and poor, and these economic differences are linked not only to educational achievement but also to health. Contrary to popular opinion, it is not the poorest societies that have the worst health, but rather, the societies that have the biggest income disparities between poor and rich (Wilkinson, 1997). And there appears to be a racial factor in wealth management as well. People of different racial groups starting off with similar wealth tend to diverge after only a few years. Conley (2001) explains that "financial education processes, or how one acquires, manages, and develops their financial resources" differ across racial groups in the U.S. (cited in Lucey, 2004, p. 27).

*Social reproduction theory* links inequalities in schooling with inequalities in the larger society, viewing unequal schooling as one of the primary ways in which existing relations of power and dominance (related to the labor market and economic gain) are maintained and reproduced. In other words, tracking and other inequalities in education help to continually reproduce different classes for the labor force (Bowles & Gintis, 1976).

### Students' Expectations of Academic Success as an Explanation

The inequality explanation above locates the problem of the achievement gap in our institutions, which differentially place students in challenging or "dumbed down" educational experiences. It paints a picture of students as passive victims whose academic outcomes are already determined by their location as poor, racialized people in a greatly unequal society. But this explanation fails to address *how* tracking and segregated schooling actually result in low academic achievement by so many students of color. What goes on in the students' perceptions?

According to anthropologist Fordham (1996), the "hidden" and explicit curriculum shapes student aspirations and achievements. Confronted by a stigmatized racial identity in school and an awareness that the playing field is far from even, African American adolescents express profound ambivalence about the value and possibility of school success. An African American student in Fordham's study expressed this as follows:

> "Well, we supposed to be stupid . . . we perform poorly in school 'cause we all have it thought up in our heads we're supposed to be dumb so we might as well go ahead and be dumb," he said. "And we think that most of the things we learn [at school] won't help us in life anyway. . . . What good is a quadratic equation gonna do me if I'm picking up garbage cans?" (cited in Berlak, 2001, ¶21)

Ogbu, also an anthropologist, brought a cross-cultural perspective to the issue of how students respond to different environments of inequality and equality. He looked at a similar ethnic population in two distinct social environments. Ogbu (1978) examined the Burakumin (leather workers) in Japan (see chapter 8) and in U.S. schools. In Japan, where the Burakumin are stigmatized because of their lower-class status and occupations (e.g., touching dead bodies, excrement), children of Burakumin families do poorly in school. Yet when Burakumin families migrate to the U.S., their children tend to do well in school. This suggests that doing poorly in school is not an inherent trait of Burakumin but a function of the social environment, namely their stigmatized location in Japanese social structure. In the U.S., in contrast, Burakumin children are not singled out from other Asian American children, who on the whole are stereotyped as "good students."

Student interviews and focus groups show that students who are aware of the poor resources they receive in school compared to students in middle-class and elite schools exhibit anger, frustration, shame, and a sense that they will not be able to compete in "serious" institutions (Fine & Weis, 2003).

### The Stereotype Effect Explanation

A somewhat similar explanation is that of Claude Steele, an American psychologist. Steele and his colleagues conducted experiments in which Stanford students (all presumably preselected as being successful students) were given challenging items from the GRE. Some were told that it was a test of how people solve verbal problems, and others were told that it was a true test of their abilities.

African American students who were told that the test was a true measure of ability scored significantly lower than the White students, while African American students who were not given any prior commentary scored the same as Euro-American students. For Euro-Americans, it made no difference what they were told. Steele explains that African American students know they are likely to be seen as having limited ability and that this knowledge produces extra intimidation (Berlak, 2001).

Steele called this effect "stereotype vulnerability." It suggests that, somehow, low expectations and racist attitudes and behaviors are internalized by the person who is the recipient of these expectations, attitudes, and behaviors. In a follow-up study, Steele found that the students most likely to do poorly on the experimental test were also the ones most likely to be highly motivated and academically focused. This suggests that if these students had not internalized negative attitudes based on racial stereotypes, they might have done well on the test.

*Reflective questions:* Which of the explanations for the achievement gap have you heard before? Do people at your school or college talk openly about the achievement gap? What do they say about it? Which explanations do you think seem most plausible, and why?

## What Else Should Teachers Know About the Achievement Gap?

While researchers are getting better at explaining the achievement gap, educational reformers have not been very effective at eliminating it, despite years of school reforms. We are still left with many puzzles, especially regarding teachers' roles in addressing the achievement gap. In addition to scholarly explanations, teachers need to be aware of additional dimensions to the problem.

• *Policies and How They Are Framed Matter.* The achievement gap is a policy problem in the sense that a nation that prides itself on being democratic cannot simply ignore data that show that certain groups, based on race, class, and so forth, consistently do less well in school. The achievement gap is the central tenet of the Bush administration's No Child Left Behind Act of 2002. This law attempts, through the institutionalization of accountability practices in schools, to set high standards of achievement for all children, and to hold schools that do not produce adequate progress from year to year accountable. Schools must show that all subgroups, including historically underachieving racial groups, are progressing toward higher achievement, and if they do not, those schools are designated "low performing" and must redress their weaknesses through approved professional development and curricular interventions. While it is too early to know if this will narrow the achievement gap, so far textbook companies and test makers seem to be the largest beneficiaries of the NCLB Act, as they are the ones receiving large contracts to monitor the results in each school district (Arce, Luna, Borjian, & Conrad, 2005). Thus, policies designed to end or narrow the achievement gap must be looked at critically in terms of who stands to gain the most economically.

- *The Achievement Gap Is a Systemic Issue:* One cannot isolate the systemic effects of schooling from the effects of the larger society (e.g., residence patterns, wealth distribution, health care, etc.). Therefore, the achievement gap cannot be addressed by *only* changing schools. Those who seek to address student underachievement need to look for solutions outside as well as inside schools. Post-Katrina New Orleans is an example. The public schools of New Orleans were some of the worst in the nation before the hurricane. Now that the city is ready to rebuild, unless historic social and economic conditions of some of its poorest citizens are addressed, the public school system will remain impoverished.

- *Beliefs Affect Practices, and Practices Affect Beliefs.* Teacher beliefs and expectations, which are materialized through words and actions, can have a powerful impact on young people. The stereotype effect described above is an example of how young people internalize the expectations of respected elders and the larger society. We have a lot of work to do to make sure that the messages young people hear and see from media, educators, and parents are positive and do not reinforce old racial ideologies. Even small actions can have great import; a principal might wonder, for example, whether a tutoring program targeting "Black students" will assist those students or stigmatize them (Pollock, forthcoming). Teachers and other school officials make innumerable small decisions daily with racially relevant impacts.

• *Silence Plays a Role in Reinforcing the Achievement Gap:* Many educators and parents would prefer not to talk about the "achievement gap" at all. As Pollock (2004a) points out, there is a dual standard. Race and the achievement gap are talked about openly in policy meetings, research reports, and other "high-level" discourse. But in schools themselves, among teachers, among teachers and students, and between teachers and school leaders, the gap is rarely discussed explicitly or publicly.

One result of this silence is that people adhere to a "color-blind" ideology. The color-blind ideology is no doubt well intended, or at least not intended to do harm. It is a way for teachers to recognize publicly that race is not biologically real. However, it can have an injurious effect on students because it sends the message that (a) racialized differences are "something we don't talk about here"; they are secret or dirty, something to be ashamed about; and (b) students' experiences as a result of these racialized identities are not important or worth talking about. In the extreme, students who feel harassed or targeted for race-based hate crimes have no place to go and talk about their experience and get help. In reality, "race matters"—still.

• *The Belief in Meritocracy Helps to Reinforce the Achievement Gap.* **Meritocracy,** discussed in chapter 7, is the idea that those who get ahead in the U.S. do so because of merit. They have "pulled themselves up by their bootstraps" and become successful because they worked hard and saved without seeking outside assistance from government programs such as welfare. This has been called the "myth of meritocracy" (Villegas & Lucas, 2002). Many still believe this myth of meritocracy—that anyone who is motivated and tries hard can get ahead despite racial and other barriers. This same notion of meritocracy has been extended to the area of school achievement and is equally mythical. It blames the victim, compounding the "stereotype" effect cited earlier.

- *The Notion of Equity Is Not Well Articulated.* Unlike the notion of equality, which presumes that the solution to the academic achievement gap is to treat everyone equally, providing the same books, teachers, schools, and curriculum to all students, the notion of equity assumes the "playing field" is not level, and therefore giving all students the same things will not close the achievement gap. All students do not start out with the same advantages. Some start school already "disadvantaged" because of poverty, family history, and other factors.

  In an equity-based approach, institutional actions are designed to redress these social differences. These actions might include, for example, special summer programs to help students "catch up" before they enter ninth grade or ESL and bilingual programs that help immigrants simultaneously develop academic literacy in English and in their native language. Equity is not a concept restricted to race; it can be applied to a gender gap, an economic gap, or any other group disparity in educational outcomes. Equity-based approaches are controversial, however, because some students receive resources not given to all students. This undermines fundamental ideas of fairness.

- *Macroracial Categories Mask Important Diversity:* This is especially important when talking about the "achievement gap" because using traditional large racial or ethnic category labels like "Asians" can mask significant variability among subgroups. There is a powerful stereotype in the U.S. of Asian educational achievement. Yet this is not true for all "Asians" such as the Hmong, Mien, and some Vietnamese (Lee, 1996). For the same reason, the even larger macro term "people of color" is also problematic. This term usually encompasses all people who have common experiences of oppression due to racism. However, when used uncritically, it also tends to exclude certain groups such as Chinese, Japanese, Filipinos, and South Asians—in other words, people of darker than European American skin pigmentation who are none-theless doing well in the U.S. educational system.

*Reflective questions:* Which of the above issues reinforce or com-plicate the achievement gap in your school or college? What have you already done to try to reduce the achievement gap? What more could you do?

## KEY CONCEPTUAL POINTS

- The term "achievement gap" constructs students as failures, rather than acknowledging the institutional structures that make the gap real. A more appropriate term might be "opportunity gap."
- The racial achievement gap, while real, is not based on biological capacities but on a system of social inequality and institutional rac-ism that perpetuates unequal opportunities.
- Cultural deficit explanations for the achievement gap replace biol-ogy with culture.
- Both poverty and race play a role in the racial achievement gap.
- Inequality has a psychological component. Students internalize others' perceptions of their competence and this affects their aca-demic behavior. Negative racial stereotypes, especially linked to educational or intellectual capacity, have negative educational impacts.

## KEY TERMS (ITALICIZED AND BOLDED IN TEXT)

ability tracking
achievement gap
cultural racism
meritocracy

opportunity gap
social reproduction theory
sociocognitive theory
theory of multiple intelligences

## TEACHING ACTIVITIES

### Activity Plan 1: Unequal Resources

This plan is adapted from Youth Together's unpublished curriculum. Another activity that can accomplish similar objectives is "Starpower"; a brief description is in chapter 7 with a Web link to a detailed plan.

*Objectives:* Students will be able to

- understand what people do to protect what's theirs and what happens when people work together,
- identify what inequalities of resources exist in their school/community, and
- identify what they can do about negative conditions in their school/community

*Other Information:* This activity, appropriate for high school and above, requires three or more class sessions. Materials needed include the following:

- 4 envelopes
- 4 instruction sheets
- 1 pen
- 1 pair of scissors
- 1 glue stick
- 1 ruler
- 1 pencil
- a package of multicolored construction paper (see below)

*Procedure:*

Step 1. Prior to class, T (teacher) should prepare the contents for the four envelopes. Each envelope should contain the instruction sheet plus the following: Envelope 1: one pen, two sheets of gold paper; Envelope 2: one pair of scissors, one glue stick, two sheets of white paper; Envelope 3: one ruler, one pencil, two sheets of black paper; Envelope 4: two sheets of blue, two sheets of red, and two sheets of green paper. The instruction sheet should say:

Please create each of the following items:
- a three-colored flag
- a four-ring chain
- a 3″ × 3″ gold square
- a 2″ × 4″ rectangle
- a T-shape that is 3″ high and 3″ across

Step 2. Divide the students into four groups and place them at different tables or in different corners of the room, well-spaced. Have participants leave their belongings aside. You will provide them with all they need for the activity. Tell the groups you are giving each of them a packet that includes instructions inside. When all groups are ready, ask them to open their packets and begin.

Step 3. The groups will need to work together to complete the instructions, but they have to discover that. Do not give clues if you can avoid it. Do not allow groups to use their packet envelope or instruction sheet as supplies (they can be reused). Do not allow them to get supplies from backpacks, closets, purses, and so on. If you stay in the room, you may want to take notes on what you observe. For example, how long does it take for groups to start working together? Who starts the sharing? What are the conditions placed on sharing? What do you hear people saying?

Step 4. When all groups are finished, ask them to show their finished products and explain how they made them.

Step 5. Ask the students the following questions:
   a. What happened in this activity? How did you make it work?
   b. Did you have any problems or frustrations? Explain.
   c. Although you had the same instructions, did different groups solve problems differently? Is that okay? (make note of the diversity of group responses).
   d. The name of this activity is "Unequal Resources." Does this relate to your life? In what ways do groups have unequal resources? How are they shared or protected? How does it make you feel when you have less than others? How does it make you feel when you have more than others?

Step 6. Assessment activity: Have students write in their journals about what happened in the activity and how it felt for them to have less or more than others.

Step 7. Preparation for next class: As homework, ask students to think about an example of unequal resources at their own school. Be prepared to discuss the situation in class.

Step 8. Extension: Read the information on the following website about global inequality. Discuss in class why the U.S. is the most unequal of all the industrialized nations (See http://www .pbs.org/now/politics/income.html).

## Activity Idea 1: Chairs

This activity, appropriate for secondary students and adults, is highly interactive. Through the unequal allotment of chairs per people, it is designed to simulate the unequal and crowded conditions of inner-city poverty versus the spacious, luxurious living of the wealthy. By the end of the activity, students will be able to articulate that crowded and segregated environments tend to make people lash out at those closest to them, rather than at the sources of the problem. The activity can be done in one class period, with optional (but strongly recommended) follow-up assignments. For complete activity, see the website http:// www.sjsu.edu/faculty_and_staff/faculty_detail.jsp?id = 1480.

## Activity Idea 2: The Growth of the Suburbs and the Racial Wealth Gap

Video segment and teaching activity based on the film *Race: The Power of an Illusion*. The website provides a detailed lesson plan that explores how the opportunity to accumulate wealth has been racialized, at http://www.pbs.org/race/000_About/002_04-teachers-07.htm.

## Activities and Resources for Educators

The following resources and activities are focused on equity and addressing the achievement gap.

http://www.arc.org/erase. This is the website of ERASE, which stands for "Expose Racism and Advance School Excellence." This website has a number of materials that will be useful to educators. Of particular interest is the report "Facing the Consequences" by Gordon, Della, and Kelleher, who offer recommendations for school districts to address both the racial achievement gap and the discipline gap.

http://www.justicematters.org. The Justice Matters website provides publications related to how schools can turn around the achievement gap and the discipline gap. Of particular interest is the publication by Susan Sandler and the Justice Matters Discipline Task Force, "Turning to Each Other Not on Each Other: How School Communities Prevent Racial Bias in School Discipline." This report profiles schools across the country that are models of strong communities with caring discipline approaches and that get excellent results.

http://www.racismnoway.com.au/library/recognising/index-Recognis.html. This is a website that should help teachers recognize racism in schools.

http://seattlepi.nwsource.com/disciplinegap/61966_jameslick13.shtml and http://seattlepi.nwsource.com/disciplinegap/61940_newdisci pline12.shtml. These two articles by Rebekah Denn (March 15, 2002) of the *Seattle Post Intelligencer* provide excellent starting points for faculty to discuss the achievement gap and the discipline gap. The first is titled "How One School Almost Succeeded" and the second "Blacks Are Disciplined at Far Higher Rates Than Other Students."

http://www.ericdigests.org/2004-3/gap.html. This article, "Closing the Achievement Gap: Two Views From Current Research" by Erwin Flaxman (2003), which provides a short summary of recent research by Ferguson and Ogbu, could provide a good starting point for educators to begin a discussion on the achievement gap.

http://www.ncrel.org/gap/takeon/toc.htm. This article by E. Robelan (2002) is called "Taking on the Achievement Gap." The author suggests strategies schools may use to decrease the disparity.

Page, Clarence. (2001). *Closing the Achievement Gap.* This video looks at Amistad Academy, a public charter school for mostly poor fifth through eighth graders who often enter performing at lower-than-average levels but leave performing on par with students from wealthier areas. Available from the PBS website http://www.pbs.org/closingtheachievementgap.

# CHAPTER 12

# Racial and Racialized Conflicts

In this chapter, we present the hot-button issue of racial or racialized conflict as an entry point for teaching students to understand why racial or racialized conflict emerges. Our aim is to provide teachers with tools to help students analyze the genesis of conflicts that have a racial component to them. We have already briefly discussed conflicts over assemblies, clubs, and racial slurs in chapter 10. This chapter develops a more comprehensive understanding of racial conflict.

As with other chapters, we assume that life in schools and colleges provides ample opportunities to use real incidents and issues as "teachable moments." Rather than waiting for a time in the planned curriculum to teach about race, you can jump in with a lesson or unit at the point where student interest is evident.

## CONCEPTUAL BACKGROUND

What do we mean when we say a conflict is "racial"? Sometimes conflicts are obviously racially or ethnically based because we see evidence that race or ethnicity is used as a resource for creating conflict. For example, if someone uses a racial slur, talks about "those Filipinos" in a hostile way, or physically attacks a symbol of ethnic group affiliation such as a Sikh student's turban, it is pretty obvious that the conflict has something to do with racial, ethnic, or religious prejudice. Similarly, if a girl refuses to date someone because she says she doesn't like that person's race or ethnicity, it's clear that attitudes and beliefs about the other group are involved. But not all conflicts that end up being characterized as racial start out that way. As we pointed out in chapter 10, some conflicts become racialized. For example, if two people get involved in an argument because one stepped on the backpack belonging to the other, the initial argument is not racial. Race becomes involved, however, when those two people (or onlookers) make it racial, calling attention to the fact that the two people are of different "races." The conflict then becomes not only about a person stepping on a backpack but also about the underlying tensions between their two "races."

It's important for students to realize that ethnic and racial differences do not *have* to lead to conflict; there is nothing inherent about ethnic or racialized differences that requires people to be in conflict. Anthropology's cross-cultural perspective is useful for understanding this point. For example, in Brazil until recently, race was considered relatively unimportant in whether people were successful. The more salient issue was class. Similarly, many Caribbean islands cultures such as Cuba and the Dominican Republic do not recognize racial or ethnic differences in the way U.S. Americans are conditioned to see race (see chapter 8). Despite diverse heritages (indigenous Americans, African, Asian, European), they tend to identify as Cubans or as Dominicans first, and not solely as members of discrete racialized groups within their country.

What makes U.S. society more prone to ethnic and racialized conflict? As explained in chapter 8, first race has to become associated with stratification, which then leads to inequalities in resource distribution, economic or political competition, and prejudice or discrimination based on race. For example, in the U.S. case, European men who had sex with Native American or African slaves did not accept them as legitimate children, and thus these children did not become legitimate heirs. The U.S. system created a permanent, intergenerational underclass that included anyone with Native American or African ancestry; the Brazilian system, on the other hand, created a society that allowed more mobility. In Brazil, the freed offspring of master and slave became plantation overseers and foremen and filled many intermediate positions in the emerging Brazilian economy (Kottak, 2005). The comparison between multiethnic populations in the U.S. and Brazil illustrates one way in which inequality became more "fixed" and more racialized in the U.S. than it was in Brazil.

One way to create or maintain inequality is for governments to enact laws and policies that create or enforce segregation by race. When people lack meaningful contact and knowledge of individuals of another race or ethnicity, they tend to develop stereotypes about the other group (sometimes called "othering" in postmodern and critical theory); lines of difference become hardened and, in this environment, conflicts develop more easily because there is less of a personal basis for communication, friendships, and understanding.

New Orleans provides an historical example. Before Louisiana was sold to the U.S. by the French in 1803, there was a more racially tolerant and integrative society in which French men had Creole and mulatto wives and mistresses, and multicultural social interactions were more commonplace. That all changed when the United States took over the territory and people were prohibited by law from interracial fraternizing. We can still see the legacy of that segregation in the way both race and class interfaced in New Orleans in the aftermath of Hurricane Katrina in September of 2005. We saw in the media how people who did not have cars—primarily poor people, old people, and people of African American descent, predominately women—were left behind.

*Reflective questions:* How do you define "racial conflict"? Do you think conflict is inevitable in a diverse society? Why or why not? Does your community or school experience racial conflict? If so, what do you think is the underlying cause? Can you think of diverse communities with no racial conflict? If so, what makes that possible?

## THE "ICEBERG" MODEL OF CONFLICT

How do the dynamics of inequality and segregation play out in contemporary schools and colleges? The same principles that operate in society as a whole also operate in schools. If we look at schools as *microcultures*, we can see the same dynamics. When teaching students about how and why racial conflicts arise, it's important to convey the idea that conflicts have histories, just like medical symptoms have etiologies. One has to understand the roots of conflict, not just the triggers that set it off at a given point in time. The *iceberg model of conflict* (see Figure 12.1) can help students conceptualize the development of

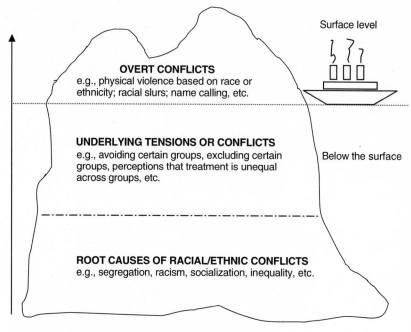

Surface level

OVERT CONFLICTS
e.g., physical violence based on race or
ethnicity; racial slurs; name calling, etc.

UNDERLYING TENSIONS OR CONFLICTS
e.g., avoiding certain groups, excluding certain
groups, perceptions that treatment is unequal
across groups, etc.

Below the surface

ROOT CAUSES OF RACIAL/ETHNIC CONFLICTS
e.g., segregation, racism, socialization, inequality, etc.

*Overt conflicts:* Physical fighting or the use of racial slurs.
This stage of conflict is exposed and easy for others to detect
because you can see it, hear it, or read it.

*Underlying, latent, or potential conflicts or tensions:* The people affected
by these conflicts and tensions may or may not be aware of them;
for example, when people are excluded from participation in a
group because of culture, ethnicity, language, etc., they may feel
uncomfortable and hurt, but may not recognize it as a form of
racial tension. Such conflicts or tensions may remain hidden
indefinitely or surface later as overt conflicts.

*Root causes of racial/ethnic conflict:*
• segregation, which allows for the development and maintenance of stereotypes
  about other groups with whom one has little actual contact
• institutionalized racism and individual racial prejudice
• socialization in which parents and other adults consciously or unconsciously
  transmit to children negative information about other groups
• inequality, in which power, status, or access to desired goods
  and services are unequally distributed among groups

**Figure 12.1.    The Iceberg Model of Racial or Ethnic Conflict**

Adapted from: Henze, R., Katz, A.; Norte, E.; Sather, S.; Walker, E. (2002). *Leading for Diversity: How
School Leaders Promote Positive Interethnic Relations.* Thousand Oaks, CA: Corwin Press, p. 50

conflict. Schools that do a good job at addressing the root causes of conflicts and paying attention to the subtle tensions that precede an overt conflict tend to have fewer overt, violent kinds of conflict. Conversely, schools that are constantly "putting out fires" may never address the underlying sources of those fires.

However, because each school has a different microculture from other schools, some schools with multiethnic student bodies are relatively free of ethnic and racial conflicts, while others are deeply troubled by racial and ethnic hatred and violence. Why is this more prevalent in some schools than others?

Research points to two explanations. One is that the knowledge, skills, actions, and attitudes of those in leadership roles make a big difference. In other words, even when the community surrounding the school is ridden with ethnic or racial conflict, the school can be an oasis of safety and hope. Henze et al. (2002) portrayed in detail what proactive school leaders, including teachers, principals and other leaders, do to create these schools. Especially critical is the notion that proactive leaders create positive conditions for interaction and understanding among diverse groups. They try to address underlying issues such as segregated and unequal programs or classes, and they try to ensure that students are educated about racial and other kinds of diversity, not only through extracurricular activities such as multicultural assemblies but also in the required curriculum. Books such as this one can help educators embed in-depth explorations of race and diversity in social studies, science, and life skills curricula.

Another explanation is that in some schools there is less inequality among the different groups to begin with. For example, if students of different ethnic groups are basically from middle-class households, chances are there will be less conflict than if some students are from poor and working-class homes while others are from middle- and upper-income homes. As we noted in chapters 7 and 11, income and resource disparities among students are easily observed and so set the stage for conflict. Scarcity—of resources or goods, of partners that are seen as desirable—will often lead to more competition. When conflict in schools does arise out of ethnic or racial differences, it is usually triggered by real or perceived inequalities in material or social resource distribution, or because one group's values, beliefs, and cultural expressions offend or stigmatize another group (Kreisberg, 1998).

In Los Angeles in the spring of 2005, riots between students broke out at Jefferson High School, a large urban, predominately Latino high school that had been a predominately African American, poor and working-class community only a few decades ago. African American students (roughly 10% of the student body) interviewed for National Public Radio said they felt that they were being ignored by both teachers and administrators. They complained that because they were not bilingual, most resources were used up by immigrant students who were not necessarily even American citizens. (See Teaching Activity for more information).

Table 12.1, based on a study of 21 schools across the U.S., identifies issues that triggered racial or ethnic conflicts in those schools.

**Table 12.1. Issues That Can Trigger Racial/Ethnic Conflicts in Schools**

A. Distribution of material or social resources:

Distribution of *academic expectations* through tracking and other means of demonstrating what is expected of different groups

Distribution of *staff positions* based on race/ethnicity

Distribution of *disciplinary referrals or consequences;* e.g., high referral rate for African American and Latino males

Control of *territory* on or off campus; may be gang related

Distribution of *power* (decision making, voice, etc) based on ethnicity or race

Distribution of *assemblies* and other celebratory events

Inclusion or exclusion of multicultural perspectives in *curriculum*

Distribution of *time and schedules*

Distribution of *financial resources*

Distribution of *respect*

Distribution of *sports opportunities*

B. Values, beliefs, and cultural expressions:

*Talking about race/ethnicity* versus belief that we should all be color-blind

Appropriate or best *instructional methods*

*Staying within group versus mixing with others* (includes dating issues)

Use of racial slurs within or between groups (e.g., "*nigga*" or "*nigger*")

Culturally appropriate ways to *discipline* students

Use of *languages* (English and others)

Expression of *religion* in schools

*Assuming preferences or dispositions* based on race/ethnicity

Cultural differences in *clothing*

*Source:* Adapted from R. Henze, A. Katz, E. Norte, S. Sather, and E. Walker, *Leading for diversity: How school leaders promote positive interethnic relations* (Thousand Oaks, CA: Corwin Press, 2002).

## When Frustrated, People Tend to Strike Out at Those Closest to Them

Ironically, in societies where segregation occurs in a context of great inequality, as in the U.S., people at the lower rungs of society tend to have conflict with each other rather than between the lower and upper classes. In large cities in the U.S., for example, there is a higher incidence of "Black on Black" and "Brown on Black" violence than there is between White and Black, White and Latino, and so forth. Why?

Simply put, under conditions of poverty and frustration at shrinking resources, it is easier to strike out at whomever is nearby, in the same neighborhood, than to look for the underlying sources of your problems. During the Los Angeles riots in the aftermath of the Rodney King assault, it was African Americans and Korean immigrants who fought each other. The Korean immigrants had established themselves as owners of "mom-and-pop" stores and other small businesses in South Central Los Angeles, primarily in African American neighborhoods. As in many urban areas, there was existing tension because immigrants had moved in and taken over businesses that were frequented by primarily African American customers. The immigrants were also, as a group, slightly better off economically.

But the immediate cause of the problem wasn't between African Americans and Koreans, but rather the behavior of the four White policemen who brutally beat Rodney King, a Black man, after a car chase, and in their subsequent acquittal. The root of the problem was in the institution of law enforcement in Los Angeles that dated back at least to the Los Angeles Riots of 1965 and in the U.S. justice system. Because of the history of racial stratification in this country, the penalty for violence against poor Blacks and Latinos is often less than it would be if the same violence were perpetrated on middle-class White people. Although this disparity in treatment is no longer legally sanctioned, it remains in practice.

This pattern of people lashing out not at the source of their oppression but at whomever is within striking distance is also played out in schools. Segregated schooling in which poor and minority students are isolated from the mainstream and provided with substandard schools creates conditions that make violence possible.[1] Students in crowded, badly maintained schools with high teacher turnover rates and poorly prepared teachers are more likely to turn their frustration and anger toward each other, not toward the policies and policymakers that allow such conditions to exist. (See also teaching activity in chapter 11.)

> *Reflective questions:* Can you think of situations in which people have taken their frustration out on those closest to them, rather than on more distant people or institutions that may be responsible for those problems? Why do you think this happens? How does racial segregation and stratification by class and race affect who has conflict with whom?

## Culture Influences How We Interpret Behavior

In chapters 5 and 6, we showed how culture shapes what we perceive and how we interpret behavior. Our culturally preconditioned ways of seeing and understanding play a key role in the interpretation of conflict. For example, we saw in chapter 11 that there is a wide "discipline gap" that is racial as well as gendered. African American and Latino boys tend to end up being suspended or expelled at a much higher rate than other racial groups. One of the reasons this happens is that there is wide variation in teachers' and administrators' decisions about what kinds of behaviors to count as conflict. Most schools have "menus" of choices that teachers and administrators can use to refer a student to the principal's office for disciplinary action. A common category is "defiance of authority."

However, different individuals will have quite different perceptions of what counts as defiance of authority. For some, it may be merely talking loudly in the classroom. For others, it may be restricted to directly insulting the teacher. Because many categories of referrals are quite open to interpretation, teachers' immediate judgments come into play—judgments that are partially based on the teachers' own cultural norms. In the end, students may be referred to the principal's office not so much because of what they say but because of the way they speak and the fact that their communicative norms differ from those of the dominant culture of the school and the classroom, in which sitting still, being quiet, and working independently are valued (see chapter 6 for a discussion of "cultural dissonance").

In the following excerpt, Mr. Aguirre, an assistant principal in a large high school, discusses these cultural differences in the interpretation of behavior:

> There are also a lot of stereotypical things. And the best example I could say is today, the African American students tend to speak loudly and in high tones and maybe sometimes animated. And staff here takes that oftentimes literally as a threat. And so, as soon as they see it they write down in a report, "I was threatened by this person." But when I talk to them—look, it's just mannerisms and things like that. And without that understanding—yeah, on paper you can write anything and make it sound like something is a real serious threat, but it just turns out to be a real verbal back and forth and nothing serious. But, it's gotten to the point where I know students have gotten into real serious trouble because a teacher insists on calling it a threat. . . . So, there's a lot of the institutionalized way of thinking in terms of discrimination and race that's still going on here.

Another category of referrals is "fighting." But what constitutes a fight? This, too, is open to culturally shaped interpretations. A security officer in Seattle reported that African American boys are more likely to engage in "play fighting" than non-African Americans. School officials who don't understand this will tend to overreport fighting.

Sometimes, students engage in what looks to the outside eye like conflict, but is in fact staged as a way to gain respect or admiration from peers. The people involved actually have no intention of really fighting. Arriaza (2003) documented this **symbolic fighting** at a middle school that went from having many physical conflicts to one in which students, both males and females, often postured but avoided actual physical fights: "Symbolic fighting becomes, therefore, a metaphorical strategy that students use to negotiate their personal space within their friendship groups, gain respect from the larger group, and go through the rituals of growing up in school" (p. 11).

It's important to remember that the generalizations above do not apply to all African American students. As we saw in chapter 5, culture is what we learn in communities; we are not born with a particular culture. It is the community students grow up in and the community they identify with, rather than the ascribed race, that shapes students' communicative behaviors. Just as there are many non-African American students who speak more loudly than the norm in school, there are also many African American students who are quiet and deferential in school.

Open-ended categories such as "defiance of authority," "disruptive," and "fighting" create an opportunity for racist and culturally biased assumptions to play a role in disciplinary decision making. One way to interrupt this tendency is to better prepare teachers to be aware of culturally based behaviors and to be more cautious about jumping to the conclusion that a student is being "defiant" or "disruptive" just because the teacher finds the behavior irritating. Another way to intervene is to make the categories themselves less "squishy"—that is, more grounded in observable behavior and less open to interpretation (Denn, 2002b).

*Reflective questions:* How do you know when two people are fighting versus pretending to fight? When someone is threatening you or another person? What cues do you pay attention to? How is this selective filtering and interpretation affected by your cultural background?

### The Degree of Personalization Makes a Difference

As we noted earlier, the emergence of racial conflicts is often rooted in segregation, which leads to superficial or stereotypical understandings of those perceived as "different." Because many schools are large and depersonalized, and because teachers often don't live in the neighborhood where the school is located, teachers often are unfamiliar with the students' parents and communities. In one large high school, writes Pollock (2004a), new staff members were actually given a "bus ride through the ghetto" so they would see the impoverished neighborhoods some students came from. While this might have been well intentioned, it "framed 'blacks' as the school's most needy population" (p. 196) and ignored other neighborhoods and students. Teachers who know their students' communities well and view them as potential sources of local knowledge that can be used to build bridges with school knowledge tend to be more effective, engaging students and getting them to see the relevance of school to their own lives (González, Moll, & Amanti, 2005).

*Depersonalization* or lack of familiarity with students' communities can pave the way for easy acceptance of stereotypes of students as "violent," "gangbangers," "aggressive," and so forth and makes it easier for teachers to refer students to the principal's office. Teachers may also be afraid to confront students on their behavior because they fear physical retaliation. This results in letting unacceptable behavior pass, thereby lowering behavioral standards for the whole school (Pollock, 2004a) or increasing administrative referrals for incidents that teachers who felt safer would address directly with the student (Noguera, 1995).

## Conclusion

Students may have an idealized notion that all social conflict should be eradicated. Teachers should point out that social conflict is a normal part of human existence in communities, but it doesn't have to be destructive, and it doesn't have to be racial. When people are educated to express their frustration, anger, or hurt with words rather than with physical attacks, and when schools provide support systems to help people resolve conflicts, there is tremendous learning potential. People can develop a better understanding of each other and the issues that made them behave as they did. In essence, people who learn to talk about their conflicts develop empathy and understanding for the other perspective, even if they ultimately "agree to disagree." This is particularly true in the case of tensions between people of different races or ethnicities, as well as gender, class, sexual orientation, religious, and other kinds of differences. Social conflict, if handled well, helps us all to learn and grow.

Applying anthropological perspectives to conflict in schools and colleges can help students and teachers view conflict in a comparative way, recognizing that not all societies that are racially diverse have racial conflict. The particular way that racial conflict has evolved in the U.S. grows out of our history and is socially constructed, not natural or universal. Recognizing this point can be very empowering to both students and teachers because it allows us to consider how we might change the underlying structures of racial inequality in order to construct our society differently—and thus make racial conflict not inevitable but rare or nonexistent.

## KEY CONCEPTUAL POINTS

• Ethnic and racial differences do not inevitably produce conflict; peaceful multiethnic societies exist in other parts of the world.

- Racial and ethnic conflicts are often triggered by real or perceived inequalities or stigmatized cultural patterns.
- Segregation leads to superficial or stereotypical understanding of "other" groups, which in turn can result in conflicts based on miscommunication.
- Conflicts have a history, and learning that history helps educators and students address the roots of ethnic/racial conflict instead of just reacting to the most immediate or overt conflicts.
- When frustrated, people tend to strike out at other powerless people close to them.
- The interpretation of conflict is susceptible to wide cultural variation, and some conflicts may be "symbolic." That is, the students involved may appear to be ready to fight but in fact they are posturing for an audience of peers as a way to gain respect.
- Depersonalization facilitates easy acceptance of antiauthority student stereotypes and excess disciplinary referrals. But depersonalization can also make teachers fearful of confronting students on inappropriate behavior.
- It is impossible to eradicate all social conflict, but conflict can provide an opportunity for learning.

## KEY TERMS (ITALICIZED AND BOLDED IN TEXT)

depersonalization                           symbolic fighting
iceberg model of conflict

## TEACHING ACTIVITIES

### Activity Plan 1: Understanding Racial Conflict

*Objectives:* Students will be able to
- explain how nonracial conflicts can become racialized,
- identify trigger issues that are often the justification for racial or ethnic conflict,
- distinguish overt conflict from underlying tensions and root causes that might lead to overt conflict, and
- develop recommendations for healing racial/ethnic violence in their school or community.

*Other Information:* This activity is appropriate for secondary students or adults. It requires approximately two to two and a half sessions of about 50 minutes each. Materials needed include overhead transparencies and poster-making supplies for students.

*Procedure:*

Step 1.  Session prior to activity: Students (S) do a journal entry on the following prompt:

Write a one- to two-page journal entry about a time when you were involved in, witnessed, or knew about a conflict that was related to the people's race or ethnicity. Change names to protect people's identity (so you don't spread gossip). Be prepared to share your story with other classmates and the teacher.

Teacher (T) collects and reads journals before next class, making notes on how many students wrote about overt (vs. underlying) conflict, name calling as the beginning of the incident, incidents that didn't start out as racial, but ended up that way. T should also note which "trigger issues" (see Table 12.1) appear to be involved most often and which groups appear in conflicts most often.

Step 2.  Next class: Tell students you read their journals and say something positive about them. Introduce the activity. Say they are going to learn about what causes racial conflicts and come up with some ways to use this knowledge to help prevent these conflicts.

Step 3.  Return student journals. Using the iceberg model of conflict (Figure 12.1) as an overhead projection, T asks Ss what an iceberg is. Ask if they know the expression "that's just the tip of the iceberg"? Explain if necessary. Then, explain the iceberg model of racial/ethnic conflict, giving examples of each "layer," as indicated in Figure 12.1. Emphasize that racial conflict is not inevitable or universal. By changing the underlying conditions that allow racial conflict to arise, we can make racial conflict less likely.

Step 4.  Recognize students who wrote about overt conflicts vs. underlying tensions or root causes, and if more overt ones, ask students why (because it's more obvious, easier to detect, can be reported to a teacher or principal, etc.). But just because we can see or hear or read it (graffiti may be overtly racist!), does that mean there are no deeper issues?

Step 5.    Place students in diverse pairs (based on ethnicity, gender, religion—depending on the mix you have in class). Tell them to read each other's journals and then ask each other the questions below. Remind them of the need to respect each other while doing this exercise, since some people may have very personal and important things to share.

The reader asks the writer:

- How did you feel when you were writing about this conflict? (This question is important because some students may write about painful experiences and they need to have an opportunity to have someone listen to how they felt or feel.)
- Where would you place this conflict in the "iceberg model"? Why?
- What do you think is the root cause of this conflict?

If there's time, ask at least one student to volunteer to read his or her piece. If some wrote about underlying conflict or root causes, try to get them to read as well.

Step 6.    Make an overhead transparency of the "trigger issues" presented in Table 12.1. Use transparency to elicit the following information: Can you find a trigger issue on this list that is similar to the one you wrote about? T checks ones students wrote about. T asks Ss: Are there any other trigger issues you can think of that are not on this list?

Step 7.    T asks Ss: Did anybody write about a conflict that didn't start out racial, but ended up that way? If so, ask one student to read his or her entry. If no one has an entry on this point, read the one from chapter 10. Ask the class to come up with reasons why a nonracial conflict becomes racial. What happens to make it racial? List stages or steps on the board. For example:

- Two people of different racial or ethnic groups have an argument or misunderstanding.
- Other people see or hear this.

- Friends of each person come to give support.
- If each person mainly has friends who are of the same race or ethnicity, it can quickly begin to appear as if the conflict is racial (in other words, people will assume that the conflict started because someone expressed racial prejudice or slurs).

Step 8.  Did anybody write about a conflict over dating? Ask for S volunteers to read their journals, if they are not too private. Ask whether problems with gender sometimes overlap with racial or ethnic conflicts. For example, at the high school level, what happens if a girl refuses a date with someone of a different race or ethnicity? Does that mean the girl is racist? Or does it mean that she just doesn't want to date that individual? Can a boy pressure a girl to date him by saying she's a racist if she refuses? Do boys or girls ever pressure girls not to date someone of a different race?

Step 9.  Note any journal patterns regarding which groups are in conflicts and discuss reasons with students and root causes.

Step 10. Ask Ss to read the mini-case below; have Ss (in pairs or groups) answer discussion questions.

At Jefferson High School in Los Angeles, conflict and violence between Latino and African American students has been increasing in the early 21st century. While the students may see these confrontations as primarily based on a racial or ethnic dislike for each other, the conflicts are really about a lot of things, including the following:

- Twenty-five years ago Jefferson High School was predominately Black and today it is predominately Latino.
- Both groups tend to be poor and live in poor neighborhoods with high unemployment rates; their parents compete with each other for low-paying jobs.
- Jefferson High School was built for 1,500 students; in 2004, it had over 4,000, so there is a lot of overcrowding and the sharing of old equipment.
- The majority of students do not speak English as their first language, so a lot of resources go toward ESL courses,

leading African Americans to believe they are not getting equal resources or attention.

- The high school has been grossly underfunded for decades.
- The tensions from the local neighborhoods are brought to the high school campus and are often played out in the lives of the students.
- School officials have been complaining that this situation was going to blow up for years.

   a. Draw an "iceberg model" of the conflicts at Jefferson High, identifying root causes, subtle or underlying tensions, and overt conflict.

   b. Discuss who is responsible for these conflicts. What can be done to address the underlying or root causes of these conflicts?

Step 11. Assessment: Ss do a group change-oriented project (in class or as homework). Students should now be able to identify strategies to address root causes of racial conflict. T. tells them they will now show the results of their learning by making "Recommendations for healing racial/ethnic violence." Organize students into groups and ask them to create posters of their group's recommendations for healing racial violence. The recommendations can be specific to the school or the community they live in, or more generalized. They can also be targeted to a certain issue in their school or community. The assessment should be based on how well they incorporate key concepts, such as the trigger issues, and the distinctions between overt conflicts, underlying tensions, and root causes. If possible, the teacher should try to get the posters displayed in a public area so that others will be able to see and discuss them.

## ENDNOTES

1. Even though racially segregated schooling was declared illegal in 1954, de facto segregation still exists. Most schools draw students from the immediate neighborhood, and most communities are residentially segregated. "White flight" from inner cities also leaves behind mostly Blacks, Latinos, and other people with no choice but to send their children to inner-city schools.

# CHAPTER 13

# Interracial Flirting and Dating in Schools

How is the social construction of race manifested in the kinds of choices and pressures young people experience when they consider who is an attractive partner? A partner for a long-term relationship? A partner for marriage? Building on the content of chapter 9, this chapter takes up these questions in the context of contemporary schools, especially high schools in the U.S.

In chapter 9, we showed how cultures regulate mating and marriage either by discouraging marriage outside their group or by encouraging it. In the U.S., the prevention of interracial dating, mating, and marriage was one way that the visible differences we call "race" were preserved, both by legal measures and by social pressures. By marrying and having children with someone of your own ethnic or racial group (***endogamy***), it is likely that your children will look somewhat like you and your spouse, and you and your family will thereby fit the physical features that make people of your ethnic or racial group look similar. In this respect, we can say that culture creates race. In other words, the culture of mating and marriage, by imposing restrictions on whom you can mate with or marry, preserves a group's physical similarity and screens out people of a different ethnicity or race whose genes would introduce some minor and superficial physical differences. As we saw in chapters 8 and 9, endogamy was used in U.S. history as a way to maintain racial stratification in which Euro-Americans were the dominant group.

This chapter focuses on the contemporary school context in which young people navigate "fluid, intermingled, and often conflicting" cross-currents of peer group, familial, and institutional pressures regarding what type of person to date, or whether to date at all (Hemmings, 2004, p. 5). Dating, as we noted in chapter 12, is one of the "trigger issues" that can lead to racial conflicts in schools. The goal of this chapter is to articulate how the social construction of race in the U.S. influences the conflicts and dilemmas which young people experience about flirting, dating, and mating. We focus on how cultural norms influence students' choices or pressures to date (or not date) certain people. But we also highlight the concept of resistance, showing how young people are currently changing or "bending" the status quo of race relations (Pollock, 2004b). Ultimately, this chapter should help teachers guide students to see how particular struggles around dating people who are of a different "race" are part of the larger social construction of race.

## CONCEPTUAL BACKGROUND

Students experience conflicting pressures about dating both within and beyond school. However, the typical coeducational school in the U.S. provides an important source of potential "mates." Thus, in addition to the potential of schooling to provide formal or informal instruction about these important human desires and needs, schools are also places where relationships are formed, developed, and perhaps consummated through sex, commitments to date only one person, engagements, births, and so forth.

Proms are one of the most institutionalized and public ways in which society's attitudes about interracial relationships are played out. Though many people believe that color doesn't make any difference in love, in some parts of the country, stark color lines still exist. In February 1994, the White principal at Randolph County High School in Alabama called an assembly of seniors and juniors.

The school's student body was 62% white and 38% black. Holand Humphries, who had been principal for 25 years, asked if anyone was planning on attending the prom "with someone who was not of the same race." When several students indicated that they were planning to do just that, the principal threatened to cancel the event. The junior class president, ReVonda Bowen, whose father is white and mother is black, asked the principal what his order meant for her. The principal allegedly replied that Bowen's parents had made a "mistake" and that he hoped to prevent others from doing the same.

Community condemnation was swift. Parents organized demonstrations and called for a boycott of classes. In response, about one fifth of the high school students did not attend classes for several days. Although the principal withdrew his threat of canceling the prom, he was suspended with pay by a four-to-two vote from the local school board. Bowen's parents filed a civil rights lawsuit for the degrading comments their daughter endured. Even still, there were some white parents who applauded the principal's strict approach, and Humphries was reinstated two weeks later. (Cruz & Berson, 2001, pp. 4–5)

Something similar happened in Georgia even more recently. In 2002, Taylor County High School held the school's first-ever integrated prom. But in 2003, African American students learned that a group of Euro-American students was planning a "Whites only" prom at a private club (Williams, 2003). The White students went ahead and held the separate prom, although later, a more inclusive event was held, which some of the same students also attended (Hightower, 2003).

Perhaps these instances will seem extreme to people in other parts of the country. The South, after all, is the region with the deepest legacy of slavery. But the South is also a part of "us," and the history of race relations in the South is part of our collective history. Proms, according to Best (2000), "are a central part of the larger process of schooling, in which kids make sense of who they are and where they are" (p. 137). Through the negotiations over music and other decisions that must take place as proms are organized, either by the school or by the students themselves, racial, class, and other identities are reinforced and sometimes challenged. Proms are fraught with inequality, with some paid for by the school; others paid for by students themselves. Some students cannot afford to attend; others simply refuse to go because they do not see a place for themselves in the prom, often cast as a reflection of White privilege.

*Reflective questions:* If proms could still be separate in Georgia in 2003, what does that mean for people in other parts of the U.S.?

How does the social construction of race still affect young peoples' preferences to date or marry across racial lines in the U.S.?

## The Use of Language Both Reflects and Constructs Social Reality

First, it is important to examine the problems with the very terms we are using here—terms like "interracial" and "mixed." Unfortunately, the English language has not yet developed widely accepted terms that can easily and quickly convey the complexity of our incredibly comingled human history. Both terms assume that races are real biological entities with clear boundaries, and that people must be one or the other, or some type of "mongrelized" version (mixed). Terms like "interracial" and "mixed" assume that there are people who are not "mixed" and who must therefore be "pure." Given the intermating among populations that has occurred since human history began, the idea of such purity is absurd!

Young people are challenging these terms more and more, even as they struggle with the rigid systems of classification that are imposed on them. A common question heard on middle, high school, and college campuses today is "What are you mixed with?" (Pollock, 2004b). While this question still uses the term "mixed," it also succeeds in normalizing mixture as the default condition; that is, it assumes that the addressee *is* mixed with at least two or more entities. This stands in stark opposition to earlier uses of the term mixed which implied impurity or deficiency—a status to be ashamed of, akin to the term "mongrelized."

What are young people really saying when they say they are "mixed" or talk about "multiracial marriages"? Usually, what they mean is that the partners look physically different in terms of skin color and other superficial markers of race, and that they have different cultural backgrounds. For instance, a marriage between two "White" people, one Jewish and one Protestant, probably would not be called "interracial" these days (though in the past it might have). However, a marriage of two people of the same religion, but different skin colors, would probably be called "interracial."

It is clear that the old biological boxes based on superficial physical features like skin color and hair texture are still being used today to delineate and police the boundaries of marriage and dating, but they are no longer taken for granted. Young people challenge the old categorizations every day through the use of terms like "Latinegra" and "Japapino" (Pollock, 2004a) and through questions that assume that everyone is mixed. They use language to not only reflect social reality but also to challenge that very system and begin to construct a new social categorization system. This back and forth, strategic use of old as well as new ways of categorizing groups of people is what Pollock calls *"race bending."* It is a great example of the cultural and shifting nature of classification systems, and how people can change them to suit various purposes (see chapter 6).

However, we have to remember that the young people who are practicing race bending do not (yet) have any institutional power to do away with the old classifications. Significant change will require broad institutional leadership as well as grassroots efforts and natural language change. In other words, change has to be both bottom up and top down.

*Reflective questions:* What terms do you hear in your community or school that describe people with complex ethnic backgrounds? Who uses these terms? Are they institutional terms that appear on official forms, or informal terms that are used to challenge traditional race categories? What does the term "interracial relationship" mean to you?

## A GENERAL TREND TOWARD MORE INTERRACIAL MARRIAGES

Although people still, by and large, tend to initiate and maintain relationships with people of similar characteristics (Lee & Bean, 2004), demographic studies point to an increasing trend toward interracial marriage as well as cohabitation. In fact, interracial cohabitation rates are higher than marriage rates (Ford, Sohn, & Lepkowski, 2003).

Current trends (see chapter 9) suggest that the old color lines may be disappearing and that sometime in the future, we will have a society in which race no longer matters in love and marriage. But statistics that lump everyone together should be interpreted with caution because they do not explain *why* these trends are occurring, nor do they specify variations within the general trend.

## Historical Relations of Inequality Shape the Degree of Stigma Attached to Interracial Relations

Discussions about interracial relationships tend to be framed as a matter of Black and White, ignoring other racialized groups such as Latino, Asian, and Native Americans. This tendency to interpret interracial as "between Black and White" probably harkens back to our history as a nation of White Europeans, Black slaves, and indigenous people. As seen in chapter 9, through both legal and social mechanisms, Black/White marriage became the most stigmatized marriage in the U.S. even though antimiscegenation laws affected all non-Whites. Only since the 1970s and 1980s have other interracial relationships received scholarly attention (Moran, 2001).

Do the rising rates of intermarriage mean that all groups are crossing the "color line" with increasing frequency? The answer is a resounding "no!" Social scientists have found that U.S. racial groups differ in their rates of intermarriage (Ford et al., 2003). Some have a higher rate of intermarriage than others. For example, European Americans and African Americans are the most likely to marry within their racial group, with about 93% of marriages being endogamous. Asians and Latinos marry within their racial group about 70% of the time, and American Indians do so only 33% of the time (Lee & Bean, 2004, citing Harrison & Bennet 1995; Waters 2000). Furthermore, when Asians and Latinos marry outside their group, they usually do so with Euro-Americans. Trends among younger Asians and Latinos indicate that intermarriage rates are increasing, especially with Euro-Americans. This suggests that these groups accept intermarriage to Whites, and that Whites also see Asians and Latinos as suitable marriage partners. However, Moran (2001) provides the following caveat:

> Because marriage is an avenue to white privilege, a non-white partner must earn this opportunity through extraordinary effort. Only the most talented and deserving nonwhite can win the affection of even an average white person. Because race matters, upward mobility through marriage is limited to the privileged few and leaves the color line largely intact. If race were not an important social boundary, perfectly ordinary

nonwhites could marry perfectly ordinary whites and experiment with forging new identities (p. 115).

Racial boundaries, partially for historical reasons, seem more prominent between Blacks and Whites than any other U.S. groups. Legal proscriptions such as the one-drop rule of hypodescent, the ban against miscegenation that lasted until 1967 in 16 states, and the whole history of slavery, has made the Black-White racial gap much more salient and difficult to cross via intermarriage than the Latino-White or Asian-White racial divides (Lee & Bean, 2004). In addition, immigrants often bring with them a different set of racial categories, with different meanings, than those in the U.S. (Arriaza, 2004). For this reason, Latino and Asian immigrants and their children tend to view intermarriage more flexibly and fluidly. They have not completely bought in to the U.S. racial paradigm.

Lee and Bean see two potential implications of this increased flexibility. If Asians and Hispanics see themselves and are seen as racialized minorities with an ascribed racial status (see chapter 6), then it is likely that the softening of boundaries they are experiencing will also eventually take place in Black-White relationships; according to this view, it is only a matter of more time before all proscriptions against intermarriage are erased. The term "people of color" seems to have arisen in this context. It symbolizes the alliance and solidarity of Asians, Latinos, and American Indians with Africans Americans as a unit, and implicitly opposes them to "White."

However, another view is that Asians and Hispanics are becoming less racialized, following the path of earlier White ethnic groups who eventually "melted" via intermarriage to the point that ethnic differences no longer mattered when considering partner preferences. In this view, Asians or Hispanics have simply not yet had time to join the social and economic mainstream. This is a more pessimistic view for African Americans because it suggests that improvements in the situation of Latinos and Asians do not necessarily predict similar improvements for African Americans. This could lead to a new color line. Instead of the old Black-White line, we could end up with a Black–

Non-Black divide, which "would be a disastrous outcome for many African Americans" (Lee & Bean, 2004, p. 239).

### School Integration and Interracial Dating

Schools used to be segregated racially. This meant that potential mates a student might meet in school were going to be of the same race, and usually, the same socioeconomic class, because schools, especially in the North, were neighborhood based, and residential segregation based on economic status was and remains the norm. So schools didn't become sites where interracial mating and dating was even an issue until school integration took place.

With the end of segregation (*Brown v. Board of Education*, 1954— not that long ago!), schools had to accommodate an influx of racially diverse and economically diverse students—primarily Black and White, since this was prior to large-scale non-European immigration. To accomplish integration, students in large-city school districts were bussed from distant neighborhoods. But little else was done to ensure that Black and White students got to know each other. It was assumed that simply placing them in the same schools would suffice to develop positive interracial relationships (Fine, Weis, & Powell, 1997).

Some support for the notion that community affects partner choice, including the likelihood of choosing partners of a different ethnic or racial group, is found in a national study of adolescents by Ford et al. (2003). The authors note that partner choice seems to be affected by whether that community is residentially segregated, as well as how accepting the community is of interethnic or interracial dating. They suggest that the immediately local community may constrain adolescent partner choices even more than adult partner choices because adolescents often are less mobile than adults.

Despite the good intentions of school desegregation, so-called integrated schools remain quite segregated within—due to tracking and other ways in which segregated groupings continue, for example, in sports. Thus, actual opportunities for diverse students to get to know one another on a personal level may be less available than is commonly assumed. This in turn constrains potential choices of partners.

## The Strategic Nature of Race Talk

When students are interviewed about their own attitudes and beliefs about interracial dating, a wide range of results is possible. It turns out that the topic of interracial dating is highly sensitive to context. The responses one gets depend on how the questions are asked and in what circumstances. Asking students about the relevance of race to their dating preferences often results in students denying that race is important at all. Interviewers may think they are getting accurate information about what students really believe, but such talk is often constructed for strategic purposes—that is, to create a certain impression with the interviewer or the others who may be listening in (Pollock, 2004a).

People will usually say what they think is socially desirable at the moment, in that context. Given the ideology that in the U.S. race shouldn't matter, it is not surprising that students will often produce the socially desirable answer. In addition, public statements about interracial dating may differ from private beliefs (Yon, 2000).

One way to mitigate the problem of the "socially desirable answer" is through ethnographic studies of young people in their schools and communities. *Ethnography*, a cultural anthropological approach to doing research involving fieldwork, immersion in a culture, participation-observation, and an emphasis on "native" perspective, is a particularly rich vehicle for understanding how students are "navigating the crosscurrents" of interracial relationships. Several ethnographic studies in recent years have included a focus on interracial dating (Best, 2000; Hemmings, 2004; Yon, 2000).

*Reflective questions:* In your school or college, are some types of interracial relationships more stigmatized or encouraged than others? In what ways does your school or college limit (subtly, explicitly) your potential partners? What other peer pressures are there? Can students in your school or college date anyone regardless of race? How could you conduct research on this issue to get at people's real beliefs and behaviors rather than "socially desirable" answers?

**"Cross-currents" Students Might Need to "Navigate"**

Students who are trying to sort out the multiplicity of opinions and pressures that surround interracial dating might hear the following messages from parents, other family members, and other young people:

- *Sticking to Your "Own Kind" Is Better Because Greater Understanding Is Possible.* Crossing boundaries by engaging in interracial relationships invites trouble and misunderstanding because cultures are different. In statements of this kind, "culture is imagined as acting upon people and setting the terms for who can belong and who cannot" (Yon, 2000, p. 109). By saying that it's preferable to date someone of your own culture, avoiding people of other races becomes an "innocent by product, a kind of racial coincidence. Cultural compatibility regularly leads to the selection of a spouse who happens to be of the same race" (Moran, 2001, p. 125).
- *Dating Someone of Another Race Will Create Conflict in the Family.* Students may be told that if they marry across racial lines, their children and grandchildren will suffer society's lingering prejudice. While students may or may not directly worry about their future children's experience of prejudice, they are often pressured by adult family members' concerns. According to Root (2002), White family members often fear the loss of privileged status, while other ethnic groups' families may fear loss of cultural identity through assimilation.
- *Love Knows No Color.* In other words, love will overcome any racial or cultural differences (Yon, 2000). This statement, while representing an ideal of a "color-blind" society, is also very real to many people. Young people in particular often fervently advocate this position. However, as noted earlier, public statements of this kind may not reveal private feelings about particular relationships.
- *Interracial Relationships Can Start Out Being About Love, but Can Quickly Become Racialized.* An African American girl in Yon's study (2000) gave a particularly telling example of this, pointing out that if she were in a relationship with an African

American man, "Your man might slap you around the ears; that happens. But you know if a white guy raises his hand to me, well, it's like slavery all over again" (p. 110). The same behavior, which in the first instance is abusive and degrading, takes on additional meaning in the second situation, becoming a racialized (as well as gendered) act of abuse.

- *Try to Find Someone of Our Own Race but With a Lighter Skin Tone.* The preference to date people of lighter skin tone within one's own racial group, reminiscent of the *pigmentocracy* in the Caribbean, is called *shadeism* among some young people today (Yon, 2000). These preferences are heard in phrases like "nice skin" and "nice hair." In a high school class on Filipino American Heritage, Filipinas were discussing the pressures they felt from their older female relatives to maintain the lightest complexion possible so that they would be more "attractive" to potential husbands. Efforts to maintain a light skin tone even included bleaching the skin in some cases (Henze, 2001).
- *Girls of the Other Group Are "Easier"; Boys of the Other Group Have Bigger Penises, or Are More Sexually Aggressive.* Sexual stereotypes in our society have become attached to certain racial groups and genders. In Yon's study (2000), female African Americans claimed that African American boys went out with White girls because they perceived them as "easier" than Black girls. Espiritu (2001) found that Filipino families counsel their daughters not to be like White girls who "sleep around." The myth of Black male hypersexuality is well known, and also cultivated by some of the rappers. Asian women are said to be "hyperfeminine" (Moran, 2001).
- *If You Date Someone of Another Race, You Are Betraying Your Race.* This is heard particularly among African American women, some who argue that when African American men date White women, they devalue Black womanhood (Edwards, 2002). This argument may be related to high rates of death and imprisonment among Black males in this country, which makes it difficult for African American women to find eligible African American men. Also, because African American women have higher educational levels than African American men, marrying a same race partner

may mean choosing someone with a lower educational level or job status (Moran, 2001).

• *Stay with Someone of Your Own Religion—or Class.* While these messages are not explicitly about race, they often end up being racial messages due to the racial stratification of class in the U.S., and due to the tendency of religious congregations to be organized along racial and ethnic lines.

With such a multiplicity of messages coming at young people, from all kinds of sources—parents, peers, the media—it is no wonder that young people struggle to sort out their own beliefs and actions with regard to dating across racial lines. Given this broad range of messages, it would be normal to feel conflicted or ambivalent. But young people are not merely acted-upon, passive recipients of these conflicting messages. They are also active agents who daily transform these messages into new meanings that better fit—at least for the moment—their reality.

*Reflective questions:* Which of the above messages do you or your students hear in your community or school? Who is sending these messages? Are the messages consistent, or conflicting? How do you respond?

**Homosexual Relationships and Race**

So far, we have been assuming heterosexual relationships. What about homosexual relationships that cross ethnic or racialized boundaries? Do gay partners experience the same racialized dynamics as straight partners? According to one young man who identifies as Cuban and Black, tensions related to race and ethnicity are just as common in gay relationships as in straight ones. This may surprise some people because they expect people in the gay community to be very accepting of others given that they have had to struggle to be accepted themselves.

The first time I ever was excluded from someone's list of dating possibilities based upon my cultural backgrounds was about a year ago. I had just recently come out, and to celebrate my newfound pride in being gay, I wanted to share it with someone special—a boyfriend! Being that I was only 17, I didn't have access to many gay people besides those who worked with me at the mall. There was no place that I could meet guys like myself, so I started to meet them online (as do many gay teenagers). I talked to one guy for three days. We had a lot in common, but once we exchanged pictures he had an immediate problem. He said that he only dated other white guys. That hurt a lot and it was the first time that I ever felt like I wasn't good enough for someone to be with because of the color of my skin. ("Nickolas," 2005)

Nickolas attributes the prejudice he experienced to two things—people's tendency to want to be with others who have similar background and experiences because it makes them feel more comfortable, and secondly, to the degree of openness to other cultures and ethnicities in your family of origin.

Although it may be true that same-sex partners encounter the same pressures and conflicts regarding interracial relationships as straight people do, communities and families differ greatly in their acceptance of openly gay children. Marlon Riggs' video, *Black Is Black Ain't* (1994) describes his own journey of gaining acceptance as a gay man in a Black community ridden with homophobia. In communities that are less accepting of homosexuality, gay people tend to stay "in the closet" more and are therefore not available as potential partners in interracial relationships. Any statistical analysis of the rates of interracial relationships among gay men and women would be questionable for this reason; societal prejudice and homophobia have already skewed the data.

**Conclusion**

As young people continue to meet, flirt, date, have sex, and marry (not necessarily in that order), will the old color lines fade, as some suggest? The research points toward two different conclusions. Interracial marriage is becoming more commonplace among all ethnic and racial groups, but it is increasing at a very slow rate among Blacks and Whites. Segregation by both class and race still limits our ability to meet and marry someone of another race, and young people are still faced with conflicting messages from family and the media about what type of person is acceptable as a mate. Because of these conflicting messages, and the importance of sexuality in adolescence and young adulthood, interracial dating is clearly a hot-button issue that teachers and students should examine together. As the next generation grows up, they have the potential to make race less or more meaningful in partner selection, and in doing so, they act as cultural agents shaping race.

## KEY CONCEPTUAL POINTS

- Mating and marriage are culturally regulated, explicitly and subtly, to preserve and strengthen the group (see also chapter 9).
- Terms such as "interracial" and "mixed" are themselves misnomers, implying there are "pure" races that then are "mixed." This is biological fiction.
- Young people frequently engage in "race bending"—both the strategic deployment of traditional race labels and creative use of new words and phrases to challenge old models.
- Interracial marriage in the U.S. is increasing but not all racial groups intermarry at the same rates. Black–White boundaries remain partially due to the legacy of history and class-based racial stratification.
- Despite school integration, there is still considerable within-school segregation.
- It is difficult to gather valid data about students' beliefs, values, and practices regarding interracial dating.
- The social pressures young people feel with regard to dating interracially are varied and often conflicting.
- Interracial homosexual relationships involve similar racial dynamics as in straight relationships.

## KEY TERMS (ITALICIZED AND BOLDED IN TEXT)

endogamy                              race bending
ethnography                          shadeism
pigmentocracy

**TEACHING ACTIVITIES**

**Activity Plan 1: Creating and Enforcing Racial "Purity"**

*Objectives:* Students will be able to
- explain that culture creates norms of what is an ideal mate, and that these norms are reinforced through parents, peers, laws, religious texts; and
- explain some of the methods that cultural agents use to enforce traditional cultural mating and marriage patterns.

*Other Information:* This activity is appropriate for high school or older. It requires one class session of about 50 minutes, plus homework. Materials needed include construction paper cutouts of squares and triangles that can be stuck onto each student's forehead. Six or seven signs to represent the following groups: The media, Benjamin's family, Lisa's family, Lisa's friends, Benjamin's friends, Benjamin's religious group, Lisa's religious group (the last two can be combined if you only have six groups).

*Procedure:*

Step 1.  T (teacher) explains to students the following:
The Square Heads and Triangle Heads are two groups of people. The Square Heads have more money, power, and status than the Triangle Heads. Benjamin, a 17-year-old square head boy, has been flirting with Lisa, a 16-year-old Triangle Head girl.

Step 2.  The teacher will ask the class to form six or seven groups (random or purposefully diverse by gender, ethnicity). The groups are to represent:
- The media (TV, radio, the Web, newspapers, etc.)
- Benjamin's parents and other family members who are both square heads
- Lisa's parents, and other family members, who are triangle heads
- Lisa's friends
- Benjamin's friends
- Their religious institutions (they both belong to the same religion, but attend different services)

In your groups, your task is to figure out what you or your organization can do to "police the border"—that is, to prevent people like Benjamin and Lisa from getting together as mates. Remember, intershape relationships were declared legal in 1967, so you cannot actually throw Benjamin and Lisa in jail. (20 minutes)

Step 3. T asks groups to present their strategies to the rest of the class. (15 minutes)

Step 4. T asks students, "How did you feel while you were doing this activity?" (15 minutes)

Step 5. T asks students, "What did you learn by doing this activity?" (10 minutes)

Step 6. T summarizes the key concepts: That culture creates norms of what is an ideal mate. How is this reinforced? Through parents, peers, laws, religious texts and other cultural practices, people and institutions "guard the borders" of each "race" or ethnic group. Those different cultural agents (parents, media, religions, schools, etc.) enforce or reinforce the separation of ethnic or racial groups. These agents use a variety of methods—e.g., misinformation (the other is physically deficient, the other is less intelligent, the other has a bad character—mean, abusive, loose, etc.); invoking standards of beauty (they are ugly, they are too hairy, they smell bad, etc.); warnings of problems children will face (they won't fit in, they will look weird, they will lack a clear sense of identity, etc.); guilt (you will be deserting us, you are a sell out, etc.).

Step 7. Assessment: T asks students to write a learning reflection about this activity: What did you feel? What did you learn? How would you apply what you learned in your own life?

**Activity Idea 1: Students as Change Agents in Interracial Relationships:**

This activity engages students in a classroom inquiry project that allows students to uncover their own attitudes and beliefs about interracial dating, and to identify specific comments and misinformation they

would like to change. A detailed plan is available at the website http://
www.sjsu.edu/faculty_and_staff/faculty_detail.jsp?id = 1480.

**Activity Idea 2:** *Black Is Black Ain't*—Film and Discussion

Marlon Riggs' film, discussed in this chapter, provides a moving por-
trait of the complexity of Black identity in the U.S., including the
filmmaker's challenges in being accepted as a gay Black man. A
detailed discussion guide for use with students is available for free at
http://www.newsreel.org/guides/blackgui.htm.

# Part 4

# RESOURCES

## REFERENCES CITED

### BOOKS, ARTICLES, VIDEOS, AND CURRICULA

Adams, M., Bell, L. A., & Griffin, P. (Eds.) (1997). *Teaching for diversity and social justice: A sourcebook.* New York: Routledge.

Arce, J., Luna, D., Borjian, A., & Conrad, M. (2005). No child left behind: Who wins? Who loses? *Social Justice: A Journal of Crime, Conflict, and World Order, 32*(3), 56–71.

Arriaza, G. (2003). The schoolyard as a stage: Missing cultural clues in symbolic fighting. *Multicultural Education, 10*(3), 7–13.

Arriaza, G. (2004). Welcome to the front seat: Racial identity and Mesoamerican immigrants. *Latinos and Education Journal, 3*(4), 251–265.

Bamshad, M. J., &. Olson, S. E. (2003). Does race exist? *Scientific American, 289*(6), 78–85.

Banks, J., & Banks, C. M. (Eds.). (2007). *Multicultural education: Issues and perspectives (6th ed.).* Boston: Allyn & Bacon.

Barker, M. (1981). *The new racism.* London: Junction Books.

Benson, J. (2003). Asian Americans. In R. Scupin (Ed.), *Race and ethnicity: An anthropological focus on the United States and the world* (pp. 242–266). Upper Saddle River, NJ: Prentice Hall.

Berlak, H. (2001). Race and the achievement gap. *Rethinking Schools Online, 15*(4). Retrieved March 20, 2006, from http://www.rethinkingschools.org/archive/15_04/Race154.shtml

Berlin, B., & Kay, P. (1969). *Basic color terms: Their universality and evolution.* Berkeley: University of California Press.

Best, A. (2000). *Prom night: Youth, schools, and popular culture.* New York: Routledge.

Bigler, E. (2003). Hispanic Americans/Latinos. In R. Scupin (Ed.), *Race and ethnicity: An anthropological focus on the United States and the world* (pp. 208–241). Upper Saddle River, NJ: Prentice Hall.

Bohannon, L. (2000). Shakespeare in the bush. Reprinted in J. Spradley & D. McCurdy (Eds.), *Conformity and conflict* (10th ed., pp. 23–32). Boston: Allyn & Bacon.

Bowles, S., & Gintis, H. (1976). *Schooling in capitalist America.* New York: Basic Books.

Brison, K. (2003). The Pacific Islands. In R. Scupin (Ed.), *Race and ethnicity: An *anthropological focus on the United States and the world* (pp. 373–401). Upper Saddle River, NJ: Prentice Hall.

Brodkin, K. (1998). *When Jews became White folks and what that says about race in America.* New Brunswick, NJ: Rutgers University Press.

Brown, R. A., & Armelagos, G. J. (2001). Apportionment of racial diversity: A review. *Evolutionary Anthropology, 10,* 34–40.

Cammarota, J. (2005, December 2). *Youth participatory action research: A praxis of transformative education.* Paper presented at the American Anthropological Association, Washington, DC.

Cobern, W. W. (1995). Science education as an exercise in foreign affairs. *Science and Education, 4*(3), 287–302.

Cohen, M. (1997). Culture, rank, and IQ: The bell curve phenomenon. In J. Spradley and D. McCurdy (Eds.), *Conformity and conflict* (9th ed., pp. 252–258). New York: Longman.

Cruz, B. C., & Berson, M. J. (2001). The American melting pot? Miscegenation laws in the United States. *Organization of American Historians Magazine, 15*(4). Retrieved July 16, 2006, from http://www.oah.org/pubs/magazine/family/cruz-berson.html

Davis, A. (1981). *Women, race and class.* New York: Random House.

Denn, R. (2002a, March 15). How one school almost succeeded. *Seattle Post-Intelligencer.* Retrieved July 24, 2006, from http://seattlepi.nwsource.com/disciplinegap/61966_jameslick13.shtml

Denn, R. (2002b, March 15). Blacks are disciplined at far higher rates than other students. *Seattle Post-Intelligencer.* Retrieved July 24, 2006, from http://seattlepi.nwsource.com/disciplinegap/61940_newdiscipline12.shtml

Edwards, A. (2002, November). Bring me home a Black girl. *Essence,* 176–177.

Espiritu, Y. L. (2001). We don't sleep around like White girls do. *Signs, 26*(2), 415–440.

Estroff, S. E. (1997, March). Recognizing race: Whose categories are these, anyway? *Ethos, 25*(1), 113–116.

Fine, M., and Weis, L. (2003). *Silenced voices and extraordinary conversations.* New York: Teachers College Press.

Fine, M., Weis, L., & Powell, L. (1997). Communities of difference: A critical look at desegregated spaces created for and by youth. *Harvard Educational Review, 67*(2), 247–284.

Fish, J. M. (2003). Mixed blood. In J. P. Spradley and D. W. McCurdy (Eds.), *Conformity and conflict* (11th ed., pp. 270–280). Boston: Allyn & Bacon.

Ford, K., Sohn, W., & Lepkowski, J. (2003, May). Ethnicity or race, area characteristics, and sexual partner choice among American adolescents. *Journal of Sex Research.* Retrieved January 18, 2006, from http://www.findarticles.com/p/articles/mi_m2372/is_2_40/ai_105518223.

Fordham, S. (1996). *Blacked out: Dilemmas of race, identity, and success at Capital High School.* Chicago: University of Chicago Press.

Gardner, H. (1983). *Frames of mind: The theory of multiple intelligences.* New York: Basic Books.

González, N., Moll, L., & Amanti, C. (Eds). (2005). *Funds of knowledge: Theorizing practices in households, communities, and classrooms.* Mahwah, NJ: Lawrence Erlbaum.

Gochenour, T. (1977). The albatross. In D. Batchelder & E. G. Warner (Eds.), *Beyond experience: The experiential approach to cross-cultural education* (pp. 131–136). Brattleboro, VT: Experiment Press.

Gould, S. J. (1981). *The mismeasure of man.* New York: W. W. Norton.

Haney-Lopez, I. F. (1996). *White by law: The legal construction of race.* New York: New York University Press.

Haviland, W., Prins, H. L., Walrath, D., & McBride, B. (2005). *Cultural anthropology: The human challenge* (11th ed.). Belmont, NY: Wadsworth.

Hemmings, A. (2004). *Coming of age in U.S. high schools: Economic, kinship, religious, and political crosscurrents.* Mahwah, NJ: Lawrence Erlbaum.

Henze, R. (2001). Curricular approaches to developing positive interethnic relations. *Journal of Negro Education, 68*(4), 529–549.

Henze, R., Katz, A., Norte, E., Sather, S., & Walker, E. (1999). *Leading for diversity: Final cross-case report.* Oakland, CA: ARC Associates.

Henze, R., Katz, A., Norte, E., Sather, S., & Walker, E. (2002). *Leading for diversity: How school leaders promote positive interethnic relations.* Thousand Oaks, CA: Corwin Press.

Hernández, H. (2001). *Multicultural education: A teacher's guide to linking context, process, and content* (2nd ed.). Columbus, OH: Merrill Prentice-Hall.

Hernández, H., & Mukhopadhyay, C. C. (1985). *Integrating multicultural perspectives into teacher preparation: A Curriculum resource guide.* Chico: California State University, Chico, and Chancellor's Office.

Herrnstein, R., & Murray, C. (1994). *The bell curve: Intelligence and class structure in American life.* New York: Free Press.

Hightower, N. (2003). Memories of a prom—in color. *Teaching tolerance: Mix it up stories.* Retrieved January 17, 2006, from http://www.tolerance.org/teens/stories/index.jsp

Hirschfeld, L. (1997, March). The conceptual politics of race: Lessons for our children. *Ethos, 25*(1), 63–92.

Hyde, J., & DeLamater, J. D. (2006). *Understanding human sexuality* (9th ed.). New York: McGraw-Hill.

Jablonski, N. G., & Chaplin, G. (2005). Skin deep. In E. Angeloni (Ed.), *Annual editions, Physical anthropology, 2005–2006* (14th ed., pp. 169–172). Dubuque, IA: McGraw-Hill/Dushkin.

Jurmain, R., Kilgore L., Trevathan, W., & Nelson, H. (2003). *Introduction to physical anthropology* (9th ed.). Belmont, NY: Wadsworth/Thomas Learning.

Jurmain, R., Kilgore L., Trevathan, W., & Nelson, H. (2005). *Introduction to physical anthropology* (10th ed.). Belmont, NY: Wadsworth/Thomas Learning.

Kephart, R. (2003). Latin America and the Caribbean. In R. Scupin (Ed.), *Race and ethnicity: An anthropological focus on the United States and the world* (pp. 288–308). Upper Saddle River, NJ: Prentice Hall.

King, J., Hollins, E., & Hayman, W. (Eds.). (1997). *Preparing teachers for cultural diversity.* New York: Teachers College Press.

Kluckhohn, C. (1949). *Mirror for man: The relation of anthropology to modern life.* New York: McGraw-Hill.

Kottak, C. P. (2002). *Cultural anthropology.* Boston: McGraw-Hill.

Kottak, C. P. (2005). *Window on humanity: A concise introduction to anthropology.* New York: McGraw-Hill.

Kottak, C. P. (2006). *Physical anthropology and archaeology* (2nd ed.). New York: McGraw-Hill Higher Education.

Kramsch, C. (1998). *Language and culture.* Oxford: Oxford University Press.

Kreisberg, L. (1998). *Constructive conflicts: From escalation to resolution.* Lanham, MD: Rowman & Littlefield.

Kronenfeld, D. B. (1996). *Plastic glasses and church fathers: Semantic extension from the ethnoscience tradition.* New York: Oxford University Press.

Lakoff, G. (2004). *Don't think of an elephant: Know your values and frame the debate.* White River Junction, VT: Chelsea Green.

Lave, J., Murtuagh, M., & de la Rocha, O. (1984). The dialectic of arithmetic in grocery shopping. In B. Rogoff & J. Lave (Eds.), *Everyday cognition: Its development in social context* (pp. 67–94). Cambridge, MA: Harvard University Press.

Lee, D. (1974). Lineal and non-lineal codifications of reality. In J. Spradley and D. McCurdy (Eds.), *Conformity and conflict* (2nd ed., pp. 111–117). Boston: Little, Brown.

Lee, E. (1998). *Beyond heroes and holidays: A practical guide to K–12 anti-racist, multicultural education and staff development.* Washington, D.C.: NECA/Teaching for Change.

Lee, J., & Bean, F. D. (2004). America's changing color lines: Immigration, race/ethnicity, and multiracial identification. *Annual Review of Sociology, 30,* 221–242.

Lee, S. (1996). *Unraveling the "model minority" stereotype: Listening to Asian American youth.* New York: Teachers College Press.

Lewis, O. (1966). *La vida: A Puerto Rican family in the culture of poverty in San Juan and New York.* New York: Random House.

Lewontin, R. C. (1972). The apportionment of human diversity. In T. Dobzhansky et al. (Eds), *Evolutionary Biology* (vol. 6, pp. 381–398). New York: Plenum.

Lieberman, L. (1997). Race 1997 and 2001. A race odyssey. American Anthropological Association, General Anthropology Division. PDF file retrieved July 20, 2006, from www.aaanet.org/commitees/commissions/aec

Lieberman, L. (2003). A history of scientific racialism. In R. Scupin (Ed.), *Race and ethnicity: An anthropological focus on the United States and the world* (pp. 36–66). Upper Saddle River, NJ: Prentice Hall.

Lieberman, L., Kirk, R. C., & Corcoran, M. (2003). The decline of race in American physical anthropology. *Anthropological Review, 66,* 3–21.

Lieberman, L. and Rice, P. (1996). Races or clines? American Anthropological Association, General Anthropology division. PDF file retrieved September 8, 2006, from www.aaanet.org/committees/commissions/aec/gad_module_2.htm

Long, J. C. (2004). *Human genetic variation: The mechanisms and results of microevolution.* Based on a presentation at the 2003 annual meeting of the American Anthropological Association. For an online version of this paper, see Scholar's Website at AAA RACE Project Website, http://www.understandingrace.org.

Loving, C. (1997). From the summit of truth to its slippery slopes: Science education's journey through positivist-postmodern territory. *American Educational Research Journal, 34*(3), 421–452.

Lucey, T. (2004, summer). Commencing an educational dialogue about the economic disparities among racial groups in the United States populations. *Multicultural Education*, 27–34.

Lustig, D. (1997). Of Kwaanza, Cinco de Mayo, and whispering. *Anthropology and Education Quarterly*, *28*(4), 574–592.

Merriam-Webster's Collegiate Dictionary (11th ed). (2003). Springfield, MA: Merriam-Webster.

Miller, B. D. (2002). *Cultural anthropology* (2nd ed.). Boston: Allyn & Bacon.

Montagu, A. (1997). *Man's most dangerous myth: The fallacy of race* (6th ed.). Walnut Creek, CA: Altamira Press. (Originally published in 1942)

Moran, R. F. (2001). *Interracial intimacy: The regulation of race and romance.* Chicago, IL: University of Chicago Press.

Morgan, L. H. (1877). *Ancient society.* Chicago: C. H. Kerr.

Morgan, J. P., Jr., & Beeler, K. (1981). The albatross. In L. Thayer (Ed.), *Strategies for experiential learning, book two.* San Diego, CA: University Associates.

Moses, Y. T., & Mukhopadhyay, C. C. (1997). Using anthropology to understand and overcome cultural bias. In C. P. Kottak, J. White, R. Furlow, and P. Rice (Eds.), *The teaching of anthropology: Problems, issues, and decisions* (pp. 89–102). Mountain View, CA: Mayfield.

Mukhopadhyay, C. C. (2004a). Culture as knowledge: Do we see reality or reality filtered through culture? In P. Rice & D. McCurdy (Eds.), *Strategies in teaching anthropology* (3rd ed., pp. 160–166). Upper Saddle River, NJ: Pearson/Prentice Hall.

Mukhopadhyay, C. C. (2004b). A feminist cognitive anthropology: The case of women and mathematics. *Ethos, 32*(4), 458–492.

Mukhopadhyay, C. C. (2006). The hug. In P. Rice & D. McCurdy (Eds.), *Strategies in teaching anthropology* (4th ed., pp. 162–165). Upper Saddle River, NJ: Pearson/ Prentice Hall.

Mukhopadhyay, C. C. (forthcoming). Try not to use the word "Caucasian." In M. Pollock (Ed.), *Everyday antiracism: Concrete ways to successfully navigate the relevance of race in schools.* New York: New Press.

Mukhopadhyay, C. C., and Chua, P. (in press). Cultural racism. In J. Moore (Ed.), *Encyclopedia of race and racism.* Detroit: Macmillan Reference USA.

Mukhopadhyay, C. C., & Henze, R. (2003). How real is race? Using anthropology to make sense of human diversity. *Phi Delta Kappan, 84*(9), 669–678.

Mukhopadhyay, C. C., & Moses, Y. T. (1997). Re-establishing "race" in anthropological discourse. *American Anthropologist, 99*(3), 517–533.

Myers, S. (2000). *Racial disparities in the Minnesota Basic Standards Test scores, 1996–2000: Key findings.* Minneapolis, MN: Roy Wilkins Center for Human Relations and Social Justice.

Nam, V. (Ed). (2001). *YELL-Oh girls: Emerging voices explore culture, identity, and growing up Asian American.* New York: Quill/Harper Collins

Nanda, S. (2000). Arranging a marriage in India. In P. R. deVita (Ed.), *Stumbling toward truth: Anthropologists at work* (pp. 196–204). Long Grove, IL: Waveland Press.

Nanda, S., & Warms, R. L. (2004). *Cultural anthropology* (8th ed.). Belmont, NY: Wadsworth/Thomson Learning.

Nickolas. (2005). Interracial dating in the GLBTG world. Retrieved July 5, 2005, from Youth Resource: A project of Advocates for Youth, at http://www.youthresour ce.com/index.htm

Nieto, S. (2000). *Affirming diversity. The sociopolitical context of multicultural education* (3rd ed.). New York: Longman.

Noguera, P. (1995). Preventing and producing school violence: A critical analysis of responses to school violence. *Harvard Educational Review, 65*(2), 189–212.

NOW. (May 17, 2002). Losing ground: Global inequality. *PBS/NOW*. Retrieved July 19, 2006, from http://www.pbs.org/now/politics/income.html.

Ogbu, J. U. (1978). *Minority education and caste: The American system in cross-cultural perspective*. New York: Academic Press.

Omi, M. A., & Winant, H. (1994). *Racial formation in the United States* (2nd ed.). New York: Routledge.

Pollock, M. (2004a). *Colormute: Race talk dilemmas in an American high school.* Princeton, NJ: Princeton University Press.

Pollock, M. (2004b). Race bending: "Mixed" youth practicing strategic racialization in California. *Anthropology & Education Quarterly, 35*(1), 30–52.

Pollock, M. (Ed.). (forthcoming). *Everyday antiracism: Concrete ways to successfully navigate the relevance of race in schools.* New York: New Press.

Reiss, M. J. (1992). How should science teachers teach the relationship between science and religion? *School Science Review, 74*(267), 126–130.

Relethford, J. H. (2005). *The human species. An introduction to biological anthropology* (6th ed.). Boston: McGraw-Hill.

Riggs, M. (1995). *Black is Black ain't.* San Francisco: California Newsreel. Video.

Rogoff, B. (1990). *Apprenticeship in thinking: Cognitive development in social context.* New York: Oxford University Press.

Root, P. P. (2002). The color of love. *American Prospect, 13*(7), 54–55.

Rubin, B. C. (2003). Unpacking detracking: When progressive pedagogy meets students' social worlds. *American Educational Research Journal, 40*(2), 539–573.

Scupin, R. (Ed.). (2003). *Race and ethnicity: An anthropological focus on the United States and the world.* Upper Saddle River, NJ: Prentice Hall.

Shipman, P. (2005). We are all Africans. In E. Angeloni (Ed.), *Annual editions, physical anthropology, 2005–2006* (pp. 155–157). Dubuque, IA: McGraw-Hill/Dushkin.

Sipress, J. M. (1997). Relearning race: Teaching race as a cultural construction. *The History Teacher, 30*(2), 175–185.

Skiba, R., & Rausch, M. K. (2004). *The relationship between achievement, discipline, and race: An analysis of factors predicting ISTEP scores.* Bloomington: Indiana University, Center for Evaluation and Educational Policy.

Sleeter, C. E. (1996). *Multicultural education as social activism.* New York: SUNY Press.

Smedley, A. (1993). *Race in North America: Origin and evolution of a worldview.* Boulder, CO: Westview Press.

Spradley, J., & McCurdy, D. W. (Eds.). (2000). *Conformity and conflict: Readings in cultural anthropology* (10th ed.). Boston: Allyn & Bacon.

Stampp, K. (1961). *The peculiar institution: Slavery in the ante-bellum south.* New York: Alfred A. Knopf.

Staski, E., & Marks, J. (1992). *Evolutionary anthropology: An introduction to physical anthropology and archaeology.* Fort Worth, TX: Harcourt, Brace, & Jovanovich.

Stokes, C., & Meléndez, T. (2001). Race in 21st century America: An overview. In C. Stokes, T. Meléndez., & G. Rhodes-Reed (Eds.), *Race in 21st century America* (pp. xix–xxiv). Lansing: Michigan State University Press.

Stoler, A. (1997). On political and psychological essentialisms. *Ethos, 25*(1), 101–106.

Strauss, C., & Quinn, N. (1997). *A cognitive theory of cultural meaning.* Cambridge: Cambridge University Press.

Tatum, B. D. (1997). *Why are all the Black kids sitting together in the cafeteria? And other conversations about race.* New York: Basic Books.

Thompson, G. L. (2004). *Through ebony eyes: What teachers need to know and are afraid to ask about African American students.* San Francisco, CA: Jossey-Bass.

Tilove, J. (2003). Affirmative action finds its defenders in establishment's highest ranks. Retrieved Sept. 13, 2006 from http://www.newhousenews.com/archive/tilove061903.html

Villegas, A. M., & Lucas, T. (2002). *Educating culturally responsive teachers: A coherent approach.* Albany, NY: SUNY Press.

Waters, M. C. (2000). Multiple ethnicities and identity in the United States. In P. Spikard & W. J. Burroughs (Eds.), *We are a people* (pp. 23–43). Philadelphia, PA: Temple University Press.

Wikipedia. (2006). Miscegenation. Retrieved July 18, 2006, from http://en.wikipedia.org/wiki/Miscegenation.

Wilkinson, R. (1997). *Unhealthy societies: The afflictions of inequality.* New York: Routledge.

Williams, D. (2003). Georgia prom: Dancing against history. *Teaching tolerance: Mix it up stories.* Retrieved January 17, 2006, from http://www.tolerance.org/teens/stories/index.jsp.

Yon, D. (2000). *Elusive culture: Schooling, race, and identity in global times.* New York: SUNY Press.

Youth Together. (2002). Unpublished curriculum.

## MAJOR WEBSITES CITED IN THE BOOK

The African Burial Ground Project:
- http://www.nypl.org/research/sc/afb/shell.html

American Anthropology Association Websites:
- Anthropological Resources for Teaching Social Studies, Geography, History, and Science, Anthropology and Education Committee, AAA: http://www.aaanet.org/committees/commissions/aec/index.htm
- AAA RACE Project, Companion Site to RACE Museum Exhibit: www.understandingrace.org

Census and Related Websites
- http://www.census.gov/-data.
- www.censusfinder.com.
- http://home.att.net/~wee-monster/census.html
  http://fisher.lib.virginia.edu/collections/stats/histcensus/

ERASE Project (Expose Racism and Advance School Excellence) (See chapter 11)
- http://www.arc.org/erase/

Hampshire College, Rethinking Race Institute. Summer program and curriculum for teachers (see chapter 4):
- http://www.hampshire.edu/cms/index.php?id = 3441&PHPSESSID = 5ad9dbfc 19a6879dfaad7cfb0024d58a

Henze, Rosemary. See Teaching About Race at:
- http://www.sjsu.edu/faculty_and_staff/faculty_detail.jsp?id = 1480

Justice Matters (See chapters 10 and 11)
- http://www.justicematters.org/.

Maryland, State of. Relevant websites and teaching materials (see part 2):
- http://www.mdarchives.state.md.us/msa/stagser/s1259/123/html/
- www.let.rug.nl/usa/D/1601-1650/maryland/mta.htm (accessed September 11, 2006).

Mukhopadhyay, Carol C., See Teaching About Race at:
- http://www.sjsu.edu/faculty_and_staff/faculty_detail.jsp?id = 1472

Palomar College, Tutorials in Physical Anthropology and Cultural Anthropology, organized by Dr. Dennis O'Neil (see parts 1 and 2, especially maps in part 1)
- http://anthro.palomar.edu/tutorials/physical.htm

Race: The Power of an Illusion, companion website to the California Newsreel film, *Race: The Power of an Illusion* (cited throughout the book).
- http://www.pbs.org/race

Teaching Tolerance (classroom activities focused on addressing racism, sexism, and other "isms" in the classroom, cited in part 3):
- http://www.tolerance.org/teach

## ALIGNMENT WITH STANDARDS, MIDDLE AND HIGH SCHOOL

This table shows how this book addresses the most relevant standards created by professional educational organizations at the national level. Teachers should check with their own state standards as well, but most states draw from national standards as a guide.

## A. CONTENT STANDARDS FOR STUDENT LEARNING

| |
|---|
| Social Studies (from the National Council for the Social Studies, NCSS) |
| *Standard 1: Culture* |
| In the middle grades, students begin to explore and ask questions about the nature of culture and specific aspects of culture, such as language and beliefs, and the influence of those aspects on human behavior. As students progress through high school, they can understand and use complex cultural concepts such as adaptation, assimilation, acculturation, diffusion, and dissonance drawn from anthropology, sociology, and other disciplines to explain how culture and cultural systems function. |
| *How This Book Addresses NCSS Standard 1:* |
| Chapters 5 and 6 explain the concept of culture and how culture affects our ways of classifying everything, including human beings. Chapter 7 explains how the cultural concept of race developed in the U.S. as a stratified system by which to justify and perpetuate inequality. Chapter 8 explains how the concept of race differs cross-culturally. Chapter 9 explains how culturally imposed restrictions on mating and marriage in the U.S. have resulted in preserving some of the visible markers of race. Part 3 (all four chapters) shows how schools as microcultures function to both preserve and challenge the concept of race. |

*Standard 2: Time, Continuity, and Change*

High school students engage in more sophisticated analysis and reconstruction of the past, examining its relationship to the present and extrapolating into the future. They integrate individual stories about people, events, and situations to form a more holistic conception, in which continuity and change are linked in time and across cultures. Students also learn to draw on their knowledge of history to make informed choices and decisions in the present.

*How This Book Addresses NCSS Standard 2*: Chapters 6, 7, 8, 9, and 13 address how the concept of "race" has evolved historically in the U.S.

All chapters in parts 2 and 3 challenge students to view themselves as part of the cultural change process, making informed choices and decisions in the present that can affect the way they and others understand race.

*Standard 3: People, Places, and Environments*

During the middle school years, students relate their personal experiences to happenings in other environmental contexts. Appropriate experiences will encourage increasingly abstract thought as students use data and apply skills in analyzing human behavior in relation to its physical and cultural environment. Students in high school are able to apply geographic understanding across a broad range of fields, including the fine arts, sciences, and humanities. Geographic concepts become central to learners' comprehension of global connections as they expand their knowledge of diverse cultures, both historical and contemporary. The importance of core geographic themes to public policy is recognized and should be explored as students address issues of domestic and international significance.

*How This Book Addresses NCSS Standard 3:* Chapter 8 uses cross-cultural evidence for many continents and countries to show that classification of humans by race is not universal or inevitable, and that the U.S. model is only one of many ways that humans organize themselves.

*Standard 4: Individual Development and Identity*

In the middle grades, issues of personal identity are refocused as the individual begins to explain self in relation to others in the society and culture. At the high school level, students need to encounter multiple opportunities to examine contemporary patterns of human behavior, using methods from the behavioral sciences to apply core concepts drawn from psychology, social psychology, sociology, and anthropology as they apply to individuals, societies, and cultures.

*How This Book Addresses NCSS Standard 4:* The entire book is designed to help teachers teach students how to inquire into the meaning that race has in their own lives. Each chapter includes activities that help students examine their own individual identity in relation to the idea of race. It explores both similarities and differences among groups and individuals.

*Standard 5: Individuals, Groups, and Institutions*

Middle school learners will benefit from varied experiences through which they examine the ways in which institutions change over time, promote social conformity, and influence culture. They should be encouraged to use this understanding to suggest ways to work through institutional change for the common good. High school students must understand the paradigms and traditions that undergird social and political institutions. They should be provided opportunities to examine, use, and add to the body of knowledge related to the behavioral sciences and social theory as it relates to the ways people and groups organize themselves around common needs, beliefs, and interests.

*How This Book Addresses NCSS Standard 5:* Chapter 7 especially addresses this standard as it examines how racial inequality came to be institutionalized in the U.S., and how the changes in laws and policies in this country have produced shifting definitions of race and of racial groups. Chapter 9 addresses this standard as it examines the institution of marriage in relation to race and interracial relationships, as well as the legal recognition of children of interracial relationships.

*Standard 6: Power, Authority, and Governance*

High school students develop their abilities in the use of abstract principles. They study the various systems that have been developed over the centuries to allocate and employ power and authority in the governing process. At every level, learners should have opportunities to apply their knowledge and skills to and participate in the workings of the various levels of power, authority, and governance.

*How This Book Addresses NCSS Standard 6:* Chapters 7 and 11 specifically focus on issues of power and inequality in the construction of race.

*Standard 8: Science, Technology, and Society*

By the middle grades, students can begin to explore the complex relationships among technology, human values, and behavior. They will find that science and technology bring changes that surprise us and even challenge our beliefs, as in the case of discoveries and their applications related to our universe, the genetic basis of life, atomic physics, and others. As they move from the middle grades to high school, students will need to think more deeply about how we can manage technology so that we control it rather than the other way around. There should be opportunities to confront such issues as the consequences of using robots to produce goods, the protection of privacy in the age of computers and electronic surveillance, and the opportunities and challenges of genetic engineering, test-tube life, and medical technology with all their implications for longevity and quality of life and religious beliefs.

*How This Book Addresses NCSS Standard 8:* The entire book addresses the connections between science and the social concept of "race," showing how science was used to justify the notion of separate, unequal races, and how new scientific technologies provide data showing that races are not scientifically valid—yet the social concept of race and its consequential racism persist despite scientific evidence to the contrary!

*Standard 10: Civic Ideals and Practices*

By the middle grades, students expand their ability to analyze and evaluate the relationships between ideals and practice. They are able to see themselves taking civic roles in their communities. High school students increasingly recognize the rights and responsibilities of citizens in identifying societal needs, setting directions for public policies, and working to support both individual dignity and the common good. They learn by experience how to participate in community service and political activities and how to use democratic process to influence public policy.

*How This Book Addresses NCSS Standard 10:* Chapters 10, 11, and 12 provide models and activities to get students involved in changing various aspects of their school and community environment to be more consistent with both individual dignity and the common good in a democratic society.

---

Science (from the National Science Education Standards, NCES, 1996)

*Standard A: Science as Inquiry*

In grades 9–12, students should develop sophistication in their abilities and understanding of scientific inquiry.

*How This Book Addresses NSES Standard A:* All of the chapters in part 1 include activities that engage students in understanding scientific inquiry as it relates to race, biology, and human variation.

*Standard C: Life Science*

In grades 9–12, students' understanding of biology will expand by incorporating more abstract knowledge, such as the structure and function of DNA, and more comprehensive theories, such as evolution.

*How This Book Addresses NSES Standard C:* All of the chapters in part 1 explain why human biological variation cannot be scientifically described by traditional racial markers. Chapter 2 in particular explains that the most important kinds of human variation are not visible on the outside but occur at the genetic level. Chapter 3 shows how geography and the environment influence the genetic structures of human populations through the processes of natural selection. Chapter 4 provides the latest evidence on the "Out of Africa" theory.

*Standard G: History and Nature of Science*

The intention of the standard is to develop an understanding of the human dimensions of science, the nature of scientific knowledge, and the enterprise of science in society.

*How This Book Addresses NSES Standard G:* The entire book provides a rich example of the evolving nature of scientific knowledge, showing how science was used to justify racial classification and, more recently, how science is helping us see the fallacy of race as a valid biological construct.

---

English Language Arts (From the National Council of Teachers of English [NCTE] and the International Reading Association [IRA], 1996)

*Standard 7:* Students conduct research on issues and interests by generating ideas and questions, and by posing problems. They gather, evaluate, and synthesize data from a variety of sources (e.g., print and nonprint texts, artifacts, people) to communicate their discoveries in ways that suit their purpose and audience.

*How This Book Addresses NCTE Standard 7:* Every chapter of our book contains activities that require students to conduct research and experiments, to investigate a particular question or questions related to the concept of race, and to communicate their findings to a variety of audiences.

## B. STANDARDS FOR TEACHERS

Model Standards in Science for Beginning Teachers (from the Interstate New Teacher Assessment and Support Consortium, INTASC, 2002)

*Principle 1: Content*
The teacher of science understands the central ideas, tools of inquiry, applications, structure of science and of the science disciplines he or she teaches and can create learning activities that make these aspects of content meaningful to students.

*How This Book Addresses INTASC Principle 1:* Each chapter has a section providing educators with conceptual background, including the pathways of inquiry that have led to current knowledge. At the end of each chapter, specific activities are introduced and resources for further exploration cited.

Model Standards in Science for National Board Certification (from the National Board for Professional Teaching Standards)

*VI. Promoting Diversity, Equity, and Fairness*
Accomplished Adolescence and Young Adulthood/Science teachers ensure that all students, including those from groups that have historically not been encouraged to enter the world of science and that experience ongoing barriers, succeed in the study of science and understand the importance and relevance of science.

*How This Book Addresses Standard VI:* The entire book provides an in-depth explanation for why the U.S. continues to have unequal academic outcomes based on race. It will help teachers to understand this issue more deeply and to also involve students in studying it so that they develop the knowledge and skills to take an active role in social change.

*VIII. Making Connections in Science*

Accomplished Adolescence and Young Adulthood/Science teachers create opportunities for students to examine the human contexts of science, including its history, reciprocal relationship with technology, ties to mathematics, and impacts on society so that students make connections across the disciplines of science and into other subject areas and in their lives.

*How This Book Addresses Standard VIII:* The entire book provides a rich example of the integrative nature of scientific study. Teachers will see that to understand the concept of race requires both biological and sociocultural knowledge.

Model Standards in Social Studies for National Board Certification (from the National Board for Professional Teaching Standards)

*V. Promoting Social Understanding*

Accomplished teachers promote in their students an understanding of how the social aspects of the human condition have evolved over time, the variations in societies that occur in different physical environments and cultural settings, and the emerging trends that seem likely to shape the future.

*How This Book Addresses Standard V:* The entire book, by examining how the concept of race has evolved over time and how it varies cross culturally, presents an excellent opportunity for teachers to study a theme with tremendous implications for promoting social understanding. Teachers familiar with the book's concepts will be able to activate student learning that goes beyond superficial talk about valuing diversity.

# Comprehensive List of Teaching Activities

*Activity Plans* (AP) include fairly detailed, step-by-step procedures; *Activity Ideas* (AI) are short descriptions, sometimes referencing a website for more detailed plans; *Websites for Exploration* (WE) are sites that provide more detailed activity information or additional activity plans, or that we recommend for further student research.

## PART 1: THE FALLACY OF RACE AS BIOLOGY

| Chapter 1: Why Contemporary Races Are Not Scientifically Valid | AP | AI | WE |
|---|---|---|---|
| What is race? Defining race | | X | X |
| How many ways are there to create races? | X | | |
| Where is the dividing line for racial groups? | X | | |
| Racial traits do not co-vary | X | | |
| What racial traits shall we choose? | X | | |
| Exploring clines and other related ideas online, with illustrations | | | X |
| Chapter 2: Human Biological Variation: What We Don't See | | | |
| Sorting by blood type and race | X | | |
| Lactose intolerance and race | X | | |
| Rh Factor | X | | |
| Explore human blood in more depth | | | X |
| Explore the Human Genome Project website | | | X |
| Explore genetics and human heredity in more depth | | | X |
| Exploring my ancestry | | X | X |

| *Chapter 3: If Not Race, Then How Do We Explain Biological Similarities?* | | | |
|---|---|---|---|
| Ancestry and skin color | X | | |
| Body type and geographic ancestral location | X | | |
| Facial size, shape, and geographic ancestral location | X | | |
| Milk: Lactose intolerance and lactase persistence | X | | |
| Gene flow illustration | X | | |
| Genetic drift and gene flow illustration | | | X |
| Explore sickle cell anemia in more depth | | | X |
| Explore other population-level biological adaptations to environments | | | X |
| Explore adult milk tolerance in more depth | | | X |
| *Chapter 4: More Alike Than Different; More Different Than Alike* | | | |
| Human biological variation: More alike than different | X | | X |
| Race and DNA: Who am I more alike? | X | | X |
| Sorting into races | X | | X |
| The story of Desiree's baby | X | X | X |
| Explore our African ancestor: Eve | | X | X |
| Exploring my ancestry | | X | X |
| Explore additional resources for teachers at Hampshire College | | | X |

## PART 2: CULTURE CREATES RACE

| *Chapter 5: Culture Shapes How We Experience Reality* | *AP* | *AI* | *WE* |
|---|---|---|---|
| Culture as a symbolic system: Culture shapes how we see the world | X | | X |
| Exploring the concept of culture using school culture | | X | X |
| Explore additional teaching ideas | | | X |
| *Chapter 6: Culture and Classification: Race Is Culturally Real* | | | |
| Color terms | X | | |
| Classifying relatives | X | | X |
| Classifying in other cultures: A cultural IQ test! | X | | X |
| Examine old IQ tests | | X | X |
| Examine IQ tests from non-mainstream U.S. cultures | | X | X |

| | | | |
|---|---|---|---|
| Students create an IQ test for their peer group or generation | | X | |
| Analyze a current IQ test for cultural bias | | X | |
| **Chapter 7: Race and Inequality: Race As a Social Invention to Achieve Certain Goals** | | | |
| Census activity | X | | |
| Starpower: Experiencing a stratified society | | X | X |
| Ethnic diversity in the U.S. | | X | |
| Relevant social categories on public documents | | X | |
| Build on activities in other chapters, especially Mating Choice and Exploring My Ancestry | | X | X |
| Jamestown: Planting the seeds of tobacco and the ideology of Race | | | X |
| Just an environment or a just environment? Racial segregation and its impacts | | | X |
| The growth of the suburbs and the racial wealth gap | | | X |
| The impact of racial inequality: The African Burial Ground Project | | | X |
| **Chapter 8: Cross Cultural Overview of Race** | | | |
| U.S. racial categories vs. categories in other cultures using public documents, census, interviews | | X | |
| Research how history and local circumstances shape racial classification | | X | |
| **Chapter 9: If Race Doesn't Exist, What Are We Seeing? Sex, Mating, and Race** | | | |
| Mating activity | X | | |
| Film and discussion: Guess who's coming to dinner | | X | |
| The ethnic me (or who did my ancestors marry?) | | X | |
| Explore antimiscegenation laws | | X | X |

## PART 3: RACE AND HOT BUTTON ISSUES IN SCHOOLS

| Chapter 10: Assemblies, Clubs, Slurs, and Racial Labels | AP | AI | WE |
|---|---|---|---|
| Investigating events and clubs on campus | X | | |
| Collecting and analyzing data on racial slurs and racial labels | | X | X |
| Facing the N-word | | | X |

| Chapter 11: The Academic Achievement Gap and Equity | | | |
|---|---|---|---|
| Unequal resources | X | | |
| Chairs | | X | X |
| The growth of the suburbs and the racial wealth gap (see Ch. 7) | | | X |
| Resources for educators to foster equity and address the achievement gap | | | X |
| **Chapter 12: Racial and Racialized Conflicts** | | | |
| Understanding racial conflict | X | | |
| **Chapter 13: Interracial Flirting and Dating in School** | | | |
| Creating and enforcing racial "purity" | X | | |
| Students as change agents in interracial relationships | | X | X |
| Film and discussion: Black is black ain't | | X | X |

# List of Illustrations with Locations

W = Web-based, T = Table, F = Figure

| Description | Location in Text | Web Source, if any |
|---|---|---|
| W1.1. Some unusual variable physical traits | p. 20 | Mukhopadhyay, http://www.sjsu.edu/faculty_and_staff/faculty_detail.jsp?id = 1472 |
| W1.2. Fingerprints: Loops, arches, whorls | p. 9 | http://www.pbs.org/race/000_About/002_02_a-godeeper.htm |
| W1.3. Examples of clines for skin color; for Australian Aborigine yellow-brown hair; nonclinal distribution of red hair in Britain | p. 12 | http://anthro.palomar.edu/vary/vary_1.htm |
| W1.4. Variations in facial characteristics; illustration of non-overlapping traits | p. 14 | http://www.pbs.org/race/002_SortingPeople/002_01-sort.htm |
| W1.5. Geographic distribution of nose shape, head shape, skin color | p. 14 | www.pbs.org/race/004_HumanDiversity/004_01-explore.htm |
| Table 1.1. Sample chart showing that many physical traits do not co-vary | p. 19 | |
| Table 2.1. Sample matrix of blood type by race | p. 37 | |
| W2.1. Maps showing geographical distribution of A, B, and O blood types in different regions of the world | p. 33 | http://anthro.palomar.edu/vary/vary 3.htm |
| W2.2. Frequency of milk (lactose) intolerance in some different regions of the world | p. 34 | http://anthro.palomar.edu/adapt/adapt_5.htm |

# Index

# About the Authors

**Carol Chapnick Mukhopadhyay** began her career as a junior high school teacher in South Central Los Angeles, immersed in the educational "wing" of the Civil Rights Movement, and later returned to graduate school for a Ph.D. in anthropology. She has 40 years of experience teaching, consulting, and doing research on issues of cultural diversity and education related to race, ethnicity, and gender, in both the United States and India. Her publications address scholarly and general audiences. She is a key advisor for the American Anthropological Association's public information project, RACE, and a professor in the Anthropology Department at San José State University, San José, California.

**Rosemary Henze** brings to this project a background in education, anthropology, and linguistics. She began her career as an ESL teacher, and later obtained her doctorate in education with a minor in anthropology. She worked with K–12 schools for 14 years as a consultant, researcher, and curriculum designer in the areas of bilingual, multicultural, and antiracist education, and has done research on education in Greece, Alaska, and Hawai'i. Her most recent book, *Leading for Diversity,* focused on how school leaders promote positive interethnic relations in 21 schools across the U.S. She is currently a professor in the Department of Linguistics and Language Development at San José State University.

**Yolanda Moses** is an anthropologist and university administrator at University of California, Riverside who brings over 25 years of research, writing, and teaching on race and ethnicity from fieldwork in the United States, the Caribbean, South Africa, and Brazil. She has held national leadership roles as president of the American Anthropological Association, the City College of New York/CUNY, and the American Association of Higher Education. She has been a driving force behind the American Anthropological Association's recent initiatives on race and currently chairs its National Advisory Board for the AAA public information project, RACE.

"This splendid and much-needed resource makes it possible for students (and educators!) to interrogate their own myths and misconceptions about race. Drawing from diverse fields—anthropology, history, biology, genetics, sociology, even literature—the rich readings and exercises help students adroitly manage a counter-intuitive two-step: Race is not biological. But that doesn't mean it's not real. Race, or more precisely, racism, resides not in our bodies but in our history, our social structures and our cultural beliefs, helping shape life outcomes and opportunities."

—Larry Adelman
California Newsreel, executive producer, *RACE: The Power of an Illusion*

"This book takes seriously the power that teachers can wield in effectuating social change. By clearly laying out the biological fallacies of race and racial classifications, the authors lay the foundation for educators to dismantle historically constituted inequities based on race. The book communicates complex biological material within a framework that is both accessible and compelling. Teachers and teacher educators will find this book to be a repository of information that can constantly be tapped."

—Norma González
professor, Department of Language, Reading and Culture, University of Arizona

"Mukhopadhyay, Henze and Moses's book stands to be one of the most important written about the illusory idea and enduring salience of race. Why so important? It is not only the first book to assemble an expansive series of teaching exercises about various aspects of race and racism, it also does so by brilliantly contextualizing race with exercises that lead to a deeper appreciation of ideology, power and human variation. *How Real is Race? A Sourcebook on Race, Culture, and Biology*, ought to be available in all school systems and to all teachers."

—Dr. Alan H. Goodman
president, American Anthropological Association and professor of Biological Anthropology and Natural Science, Hampshire College

"Finally, Mukhopadhyay, Henze, and Moses have created an easy to read, level-headed, and definitive book on race which explains the issues involved in a manner that undergraduates preparing for teaching and other social fields can read. The strength of this book is that it combines information from biology and cultural studies to create a synthesized and balanced view of race, which demonstrates how this topic can at once be a chimera and a large and heavy elephant, depending on one's perspective. Pre-service teachers need both to deal with and to diffuse this ghostly elephant, and will greatly benefit from reading this book. In addition, the book provides useful activities appropriate to multicultural education, social foundations, and even community college or high school courses, which can help professors to manage this potentially explosive topic in a balanced way."

—Lorie Hammond
associate professor of teacher education, California State University at Sacramento

"The authors have done teachers a great service by providing a framework for addressing this sensitive but important topic, along with activities that help students investigate the things that divide and unite us."

—Sandy Miller
science teacher, Morrill Middle School, San Jose, CA

"Drawing upon a wealth of classic and cutting-edge anthropological research, *How Real Is Race?* provides a clear guide for educators seeking to navigate through the contentious issues surrounding the concept of race and its sociocultural meaning. The breadth of topics examined in this sourcebook—from race as biological fiction to race as a social and culture reality—is truly amazing. Solidifying its uniqueness is the authors' attentiveness to how race plays out in school settings. Overall, they highlight how students can develop critical thinking skills by interrogating human variation and understanding the connections, and disconnections, between race, culture, and biology."

—Dr. Michael Omi
associate professor, Ethnic Studies, Department of Sociology, University of California, Berkeley

"This book is an excellent beginning to fulfill the challenges that race, culture, and biology present in U.S. society. It certainly goes a long way in filling the void in social science standards and curriculum in terms of teaching youth about our society as well as how to cope with the problems of race in our society."

—Dorothy Allen
co-chair, Ethnic Studies department, James Logan High School, Union City, CA

"An important book for teachers, administrators and community members—it should be on the shelves of all school and district libraries. Many might think the 'race issue' is no longer an issue—I often heard that amongst students and pre-service teachers alike—but it is so inherent and part of U.S. institutions and culture, that people do not notice it—as the authors state, 'the fish is the last to discover water.' This book gives an inside look at the issue of race and the role it plays in education and in our schools from an anthropological perspective. It affords us the opportunity to look more critically and deeply at the status quo and what we consider to be 'normal.' It would be an opportune time for schools that are undergoing any kind of reform or change to read this book and see how these concepts play a role in the current model, and how they might be considered when coming up with a new model of school. I highly recommend this book!"

—Siv Kristin Spain
Gear Up Literacy and Math teacher, former social studies teacher,
Bellingham School District, Bellingham, WA

"This is a book about race that teachers across the country have been waiting for and the timing couldn't be better. The increasing racial and ethnic diversity of U.S. students coupled with the likelihood that teachers are geographically, socially and culturally isolated from the students they teach, makes this an indispensable book for teachers everywhere. Though reams of pages have been written on the themes explored in this sourcebook—the biology, culture, psychology and schooling of racial categories, stratification and conflict—no book has yet combined these multiple perspectives with teaching and learning activities for classroom use in secondary and post-secondary settings. Through this book, students and teachers will unlearn what U.S. culture has taught them about race as a sorting mechanism, at the same time that they will learn how to use scientific, historical, and anthropological data to understand what makes race such an enduring, but not inevitable category of difference."

—Wendy Luttrell
Aronson Associate Professor, Harvard Graduate School of Education

"Finally, a book that succeeds in creating a coherent approach to the topic of race—how it matters and doesn't matter. Based on the most current transdisciplinary information and research from biology, anthropology, history, psychology, and sociology, the authors succeed in framing the issues of race in ways relevant to everyday questions and assumptions. The text includes a wonderful chapter on "hot-button" issues in schools such as the use of racial slurs, racial incidents, achievement gaps and how to engage them. As a professor, researcher, and practitioner, I look forward to using the resources and the approach to facilitate conversations in a variety of educational settings, though they would be equally useful in community settings as well."

—Daryl G. Smith,
professor, Education and Psychology, Claremont Graduate University

"No subject is more central to education in the United States than race. Without understanding race and racism, young people cannot make sense of past and present political actions, economic differences, or movement of people in their communities and nation. Without knowledge of how race has shaped mainstream academic knowledge, today's students may never realize that the ways in which they are taught today to divide the world actually developed from the racist ideology of European explorers and colonists who used what they perceived as "racial" differences to set themselves apart from Africans, Asians, and other indigenous peoples of color and therefore justified slavery and colonialism. Race is the keystone in moving beyond imperial worldviews toward multicultural and global perspectives.

*How Real Is Race?* takes on race and its permutations in American education. This volume not only challenges the usual misperceptions and misuse of the term race, it digs into the deep structure of society and schooling to bring to light the many effects of race and racism in schools. Unlike most of the multicultural books out there for preservice and practicing teachers (and there are many good ones), *How Real Is Race?* sets itself apart by its in depth examination of the scientific meaning of race. The first four chapters truly educate teachers about race and science and will be powerful tools in counteracting many misperceptions and misinformation that are rarely challenged by the media or mandated curricula. The last half of the book applies these ideas to teaching and learning with activities and resources. *How Real Is Race?* is an exciting new resource for anti-racist multicultural education."

—Merry M. Merryfield
professor, Social Studies and Global Education, The Ohio State University